W9-DAO-446

Praise for Robert Fitts's *Wally Yonamine: The Man Who Changed Japanese Baseball*

"Extensively researched, well-written, and endlessly informative and fascinating, this book makes an excellent addition to anyone's baseball library and is absolutely required reading for anyone interested in Japanese-American baseball relations."
—Michael Street, *Baseball Daily Digest*

"Serves as a great primer on the general historical evolution of Japanese baseball, seen through the career of Wally Yonamine."
—Eric B. Salo, *NINE*

"2005 *Sporting News*-SABR award winner Fitts deserves high marks for bringing forth this title sure to grasp pro football and baseball enthusiasts alike."
—Southern New England Chapter Society for American Baseball Research

"This is a must-read and a must-add to the bookshelf for those with an interest in the history of Japanese baseball, and a worthwhile read for baseball fans looking to broaden their knowledge of this great game that has spread around the globe."
—Pat Lagreid, Baseballbookreview.com

"For over fifty years, Wally Yonamine has been an important bridge between Japanese and American baseball. He brought a new, exciting style of play to Japan and taught us the finer points of the game. I am glad that Americans can finally learn about Wally's contributions through this outstanding biography."
—Hideki Matsui, NY Yankees outfielder

"A great read about a Japanese baseball player who has been too long overlooked."
—L. A. Heapy, *CHOICE*

"Wally Yonamine is one of the most important figures in the long, rich history of baseball in Japan. His life story, from the rustic schoolyards of prewar Maui to modern-day state-of-the-art Tokyo stadiums, is filled with drama and color. Author Rob Fitts has done us all this favor with his richly detailed, thoroughly researched, and heartfelt work."
—Robert Whiting, author of *The Samurai Way of Baseball*

"This book is much more than a smart biography of Wally Yonamine, the first American to play professional baseball in Japan; it is also a fascinating account of the game and culture of the Japanese national pastime."
—George Gmelch, author of *Baseball without Borders: The International Pastime*

"I got to know Wally in 1977 while he was still managing the Dragons, but wish I had seen him play twenty-five years earlier. Reading this biography is the next best thing. [Robert] Fitts leaves no stories untold about Yonamine's life in this excellent book."
—Wayne Graczyk, *Japan Times*

Praise for Robert Fitts's *Banzai Babe Ruth: Baseball, Espionage, and Assassination during the 1934 Tour of Japan*, winner of the 2013 Seymour Medal

"In this book, Fitts strikes a perfect balance, weaving baseball history with American diplomatic efforts and Japanese cultural and political development into a striking tapestry."
—Kenneth R. Fenster, *NINE*

"Deserves a spot in any baseball (or Japan) lover's library."
—Robert Whiting, *Wall Street Journal*

"How did two nations that shared the values of the same national pastime go from baseballs to bullets? Historian Rob Fitts tells a dark tale of baseball caught between democracy and fascism in prewar Japan. *Banzai Babe Ruth* is a sayonara home run!"
—John Thorn, official historian for Major League Baseball

"Fitts, a master at depicting all of the key elements in prewar Japanese social and political life, gives the reader valuable insights into the influential moderates trying to hold the line against the army, as well as the American ballplayers taking a victory lap in front of adoring foreign fans. This book is a powerful snapshot of men from two contrasting cultures attempting to stop a slide into aggression."
—*Publishers Weekly*

"This dramatic story, equal parts baseball and history, should appeal to anyone interested in Japanese cultural and political history and the sports-politics nexus."
—*Library Journal*

"The history lessons in *Banzai Babe Ruth* go well beyond merely chronicling the games and the players. This is a well-researched, fascinatingly told tale of two super powers whose shared passion for baseball wasn't enough to maintain the peace, though it did help to restore it in the years following World War II."
—James Bailey, *Baseball America*

"*Banzai Babe Ruth* reads like a multi-stranded mystery novel. . . . Fitts has an eye for the quirky details that make historical writing vivid."
—Michael R. Stevens, *Books & Culture*

"Far more than just a sports story. . . . No one could have told this incredible story better than Robert K. Fitts."
—*ForeWord Reviews*

"Fitts is excellent at capturing occasional bouts of dissension among the American players, describing the respectable quality of play by their Japanese opponents, and especially at capturing the ominous atmosphere that surrounded the tour. Fans will love the stats and player photos, too!"
—Tom Lavoie, *Shelf Awareness*

"Rob Fitts masterfully incorporates the forty-plus Japanese actors and American counterparts, detailing their various baseball, business, political, and military concerns and motives."
—Southern New England Chapter Society for American Baseball Research

MASHI

MASHI

The Unfulfilled Baseball Dreams of Masanori

Murakami, the First Japanese Major Leaguer

ROBERT K. FITTS

UNIVERSITY OF NEBRASKA PRESS | LINCOLN AND LONDON

© 2014 by Robert K. Fitts

"Sukiyaki," written by Hachidai Nakamura and Rokusuke Ei © 1962 EMI Music Publishing Japan LTD. All rights administered by Sony/ATV Music Publishing LLC., 8 Music Square West, Nashville TN 37203. All rights reserved. Used by permission.

All rights reserved
Manufactured in the United States of America

Library of Congress Cataloging-in-Publication Data

Fitts, Robert K., 1965–
Mashi: the unfulfilled baseball dreams of Masanori Murakami, the first Japanese Major Leaguer / Robert K. Fitts.
pages   cm
Includes bibliographical references and index.
ISBN 978-0-8032-5521-0 (cloth: alk. paper)
ISBN 978-0-8032-6981-1 (epub)
ISBN 978-0-8032-6982-8 (mobi)
ISBN 978-0-8032-6983-5 (pdf)
1. Murakami, Masanori, 1944– 2. Baseball players—Japan—Biography. 3. San Francisco Giants (Baseball team) I. Title.
GV865.M782F58 2015
796.357092—dc23
[B]
2014038468

Set in Garamond Premier by Renni Johnson.
Designed by N. Putens.

For Ben and Simon,

May your dreams be fulfilled

I look up while I walk
Counting the stars with teary eyes
Remembering those summer days
But tonight I am all alone
Happiness lies beyond the clouds
Happiness lies above the sky
I look up while I walk
So the tears won't fall
Though the tears well up as I walk
For I am alone tonight
ROKUSUKE EI
"SUKIYAKI" (*UE O MUITE*)

There was a grand stage before me
And I was ready to take it
But I could not actually go on
So many regrets   ,
MASANORI MURAKAMI, 2012

CONTENTS

Acknowledgments   *ix*

CHAPTER 1   *1*

CHAPTER 2   *8*

CHAPTER 3   *19*

CHAPTER 4   *28*

CHAPTER 5   *35*

CHAPTER 6   *43*

CHAPTER 7   *54*

CHAPTER 8   *66*

CHAPTER 9   *78*

CHAPTER 10   *88*

CHAPTER 11   *97*

CHAPTER 12   *109*

CHAPTER 13   *113*

CHAPTER 14   *125*

CHAPTER 15   *136*

CHAPTER 16   *147*

CHAPTER 17   *156*

CHAPTER 18   *170*

Afterword   *177*

Appendix   *189*

Note on Sources   *197*

Notes   *199*

Bibliography   *211*

Index   *215*

ACKNOWLEDGMENTS

This book would not have been possible without the enthusiastic cooperation of Masanori Murakami. Mashi made himself available for countless hours of interviews and follow-up questions, shared his personal scrapbooks and photo albums, and provided introductions to his friends. I am incredibly thankful for his support and willingness to participate in my project.

Keiko Nishi provided invaluable support as my research assistant, translator, and interpreter. After the initial interviews with Murakami in July 2012, Keiko handled all the correspondence and follow-up questions with Mashi. I could not have written this book without her help. Thank you so very much.

I also want to give a special thanks to Wayne Graczyk. Wayne approached Murakami on my behalf and convinced him to work with me on this project. The book would never have gotten off the ground without Wayne's help.

Numerous people helped me by sharing their knowledge and/or research. I especially want to thank my "Go-To Guys"—five men whom I have bothered many times in the past year with annoyingly specific and unusual questions. They always came through. Yoichi Nagata and Bob Whiting, two of the foremost experts on Japanese baseball, were always there to provide timely detailed answers to my many inquiries. Rob Garratt and Steve Treder helped out on the history of the San Francisco Giants, and Masanori "Max" Ninomiya provided detailed and thoughtful responses to questions on Japanese culture and social behavior.

Special thanks also go out to Juli Osaka Tachibana and Walter Osaka for sharing stories about Masanori's time with their family and answering general questions about the Japanese American community of San Francisco in 1965.

Among the many others who helped me are the following: Marty Appel, Gary Ashwill, Dave Baldwin, Adam Berenbak, Clifford Blau, Ron Briley, Merritt Clifton, Joel Franks, Izumi Ishii, Bill Kelly, Emi Kikuchi, Marty Kuehnert, Yoichi Kurihara, Andy McCue, Mitchell Nathanson, Kerry Yo Nakagawa, Rob Neyer, Ralph Pearce, Allan H. "Bud" Selig, Donald Slinkard, Jim Small, Bill Staples, Taka Tanaka, Hideki "Rick" Tsuruoka, Dave Vincent, Richard Walker, and Myrna Watkins. My sincere apologies to those who lent a hand but whom I have forgotten to include in this list.

I would like to thank Carlton Hanta, Ken Henderson, Tom Meehan, Yoshiko Murakami, Walter Osaka, Gaylord Perry, Joe Stanka, Juli Osaka Tachibana, and Taisuke Watanabe for making themselves available to be interviewed.

The staffs of the libraries at the National Baseball Hall of Fame in Cooperstown and the Japan Baseball Hall of Fame in Tokyo were, as always, extremely helpful. I especially would like to thank Tim Wiles for searching through the archives for uncatalogued material on the Murakami contract dispute.

Becky Biniek of the San Francisco Giants helped me contact Murakami's former teammates, and Suzanna Mitchell, also from the Giants, provided photographs for the book.

This is my third book with the wonderful people at the University of Nebraska Press. They are a great group who make the publishing process a pleasure. A big thanks to Sports Editor Rob Taylor, who has helped me through the entire process, and Courtney Ochsner, who is always there to answer my many questions. I would also like to thank my project editor, Joeth Zucco; copy editor Bojana Ristich; and cover designer Nathan Putens.

A special shout-out goes to Bob Lapides, a good friend and Masanori Murakami's number one fan. Bob's fascination with Murakami's career led to my interest in Mashi's story.

Most of all, I would like to thank my family, Sarah, Ben, and Simon, for their support.

MASHI

CHAPTER 1

Masanori Murakami saw his father for the first time a few days after his fourth birthday. Cowering behind his mother's legs, he peeked through the living room's sliding paper doors. His grandparents sat on the tatami floor beside a scary-looking man. He was slight, with a narrow face accentuated by hardship, his expression severe despite the joyous occasion. Even at first glance, you knew that he rarely laughed. Instead, anger boiled just below the surface. Masanori shrank back behind his mother.

World War II had been over for two and a half years, but Kiyoshi Murakami was only now returning. Drafted by the Japanese Imperial Army in late 1943, Murakami left behind his pregnant wife Tomiko and two daughters to fight the Soviets in Manchuria. An accident while building fortifications at the front sent him to the hospital. The injury probably saved his life but left him with a lifetime of guilt. As he convalesced, his regiment rushed to defend the Philippines from American invasion. Doctors gave Murakami a choice: stay in the hospital to recover or join his comrades. He chose to remain. In the ensuing battle the regiment was decimated. Murakami recovered from the wound but not from the guilt of surviving while his braver brothers in arms died.

At the end of the war, over a half million Japanese soldiers, including those stationed in Manchuria, surrendered to Soviet forces. Kiyoshi Murakami and his countrymen were transported to forty-nine labor camps within the Soviet Union and forced to work on large-scale construction projects. During his three-year imprisonment, Murakami was moved from camp to camp. Conditions were harsh, with malnutrition, disease, and physical abuse common.

The Russian winters were nearly unbearable—almost 10 percent of the prisoners died during the first winter of captivity (1945–46). Kiyoshi used to joke, "When I peed, I had to break it with a hammer because it would freeze." Unlike the other Allies, who released most of their prisoners of war in 1946, the Soviets detained the captives for several years. In 1948, Kiyoshi and 175,000 of his countrymen were returned to Japan.[1]

The hardships of war and the prison camps, as well as the guilt of not joining his regiment in the Philippines, altered Murakami's personality. He returned home a quiet, sullen man with a quick, violent temper. Today he would probably be diagnosed with post-traumatic stress disorder. He would lash out at family members and punish young Masanori with his fists or swift kicks for even the slightest offenses. The boy soon grew to fear his father.

Kiyoshi Murakami returned to a country in ruins. Allied bombing had destroyed sixty-seven Japanese cities, killed approximately a half million civilians, and left 5 million homeless. Many urban areas became vast plains of flattened, burned rubble. Survivors, dressed in rags, built lean-to dwellings from scrap to protect their families from the elements. Basic infrastructure, such as electricity, telephones, railways, sewers, and municipal water, no longer existed in most cities. Starvation raced through the devastated cities as most of the food and medical supplies had been consumed or destroyed during the final months of the war.

Under the Allied Occupation, Japan began to rebuild in 1946 and 1947, but poor harvests and inadequate transportation kept food and building materials scarce in urban areas. Black markets sprang up across Japan and soon became a mainstay of the economy. Even in 1949, former middle-class urbanites would take third-class trains to the countryside to trade family treasures to farmers for food.[2]

Luckily for the Murakamis, their hometown of Otsuki was too small to be a significant target of Allied bombing. Located in the mountains fifty miles west of Tokyo, Otsuki contained under twenty thousand people in 1945 and escaped harm until August 8, 1945. An atomic bomb had obliterated Hiroshima two days earlier, and Nagasaki would be bombed a day later. The war would be over in a week. Still a squadron of bombers, probably finding no significant targets left in the urban areas to the east, dropped their payloads on the quiet town center. The Murakamis' home, located in the village of Saruhashi, about a mile and a half east of the town center, was undamaged.

Despite the deprivation in Japan's urban areas, the Murakamis lived comfortably. Masanori's paternal grandfather was the town's postmaster—a prestigious position at the time—while his maternal grandfather had graduated from Keio University and was a wealthy businessman producing soy sauce and sake. His mother's family were local landlords and had been samurai before the class was officially disbanded in the 1870s. As a child, Masanori would play with his cousins at his grandfather's house, decorated with ancient armor and swords. When the adults were not watching, the boys would grab the weapons and pretend to be samurai warriors.

Masanori's home was a large, two-story farmhouse built in the traditional style during the early 1940s. Ornate clay tiles covered the arched roof, and the floors were covered with tatami. Like most Japanese families of the time, the Murakami household was multigenerational, with Masanori's paternal grandparents and aunts also living in the home. The family grew rice, daikon radish, potatoes, and vegetables in the fields surrounding the house. They also produced silk and employed two silk weavers, as well as seasonal farmer laborers. As a boy, Masanori helped with farm chores—weeding, carrying tools and supplies, doing whatever needed to be done. The produce from the farm allowed the family to avoid the food shortages common throughout Japan.

Masanori's childhood was similar to that of many Japanese country boys in the early 1950s. After school he gathered with the neighborhood gang, climbed nearby mountains, and played various forms of tag and ball. The boys particularly enjoyed gambling games such as marbles, *menko*, and *Kana kuji u chi*. Marbles, of course, are known throughout Western culture, but *menko* and *Kana kuji u chi* are traditional Japanese games. *Menko* were similar to American trading cards or pogs. They were round or rectangular pieces of cardboard with an image on one side (the reverse side could be blank or contain writing or patterns). The pictures often showed popular actors, baseball players, sumo wrestlers, or historical figures. One could judge a celebrity's popularity by the number of *menko* he or she adorned. *Menko* were tossed much as mid-century American boys flipped their baseball cards. The exact rules of the game varied, but generally boys tried to capture opponents' *menko* by flipping or covering them with their own toss.

Kana kuji u chi was similar. The boys tossed five-inch nails, attempting to land them upright in the earth. A successful toss entitled the player to keep all of the horizontal nails (unsuccessful tosses) on the playing field. One could only defeat an upright nail by knocking it over with another successfully tossed nail. Masanori often emerged victorious and soon acquired extensive collections of all these boyhood treasures.

When not playing with friends or doing farm chores, Masanori cared for his two dozen pigeons or worked at carpentry, once building a large birdhouse for his flock. When hammering, Masanori favored his left hand. He had learned to use chopsticks and write right-handed by mimicking others, but he found that when he needed power, his left hand responded better. He also found it more comfortable to throw left-handed.

In those days before a true world economy, Masanori's life was vastly different from that of most American boys. At breakfast he sat on the tatami floor and dined on a small table raised about a foot off the ground. A typical American breakfast of cereal, pancakes, or bacon and eggs was rare in rural Japan. Even fresh cow's milk was a luxury that Masanori rarely tasted. Instead breakfast would usually consist of rice, an egg, miso soup, and pickles. Other meals and treats were also traditional Japanese fare, although he had a fondness for manufactured caramels and would often scrounge the neighborhood for recyclables to earn candy money. Of course Masanori slept on a futon laid on the floor each night rather than on a bed.

Most Japanese boys were avid baseball fans. Introduced by American teachers in the early 1870s, the game spread quickly, with thousands watching collegiate games by the first decade of the twentieth century. Japanese university teams traveled to the United States to improve their skills, and American professional and amateur squads visited the Land of the Rising Sun almost every year from 1906 to 1935. After Babe Ruth, Lou Gehrig, and the All-Americans crossed the Pacific in 1934, the Japanese created the Nippon Professional Baseball League (NPB). The league flourished and continued until August 1944, when Allied bombing made it too dangerous to hold games. Realizing the importance of baseball to Japanese morale, the Allied Occupation forces restarted professional baseball only months after the war. On November 23, 1945, the NPB held the first of four all-star games played that fall, and the league restarted its full schedule in the spring of 1946. Despite the country's poor economy, the league's popularity spread and the stars became Japan's newest heroes.

Yet young Masanori had no interest in the sport. His father disliked baseball, so the family did not listen to games on the radio, nor did they follow the league in the newspapers. The Murakamis did not own a television, but Masanori would occasionally watch shows at a neighbor's home. They rarely, if ever, watched baseball. Even years later as Masanori considered signing a professional contract, he could not name all of the teams in the NPB.

In elementary school Masanori began playing softball and immediately fell in love with the sport. He had no equipment, but a neighbor gave him an old cracked bat that he repaired with nails and rubber tape. He began to practice. As Masanori was large for his age and naturally athletic, he soon became the neighborhood's top player. His career, however, was nearly cut short.

Kiyoshi Murakami had little tolerance for his son's passion. He did not object to the softball playing when Masanori was just in elementary school, but that changed when Masanori graduated. Kiyoshi wanted Masanori to become a doctor. He had seen the carnage of war and the difference a good doctor could make in the world. When Masanori enrolled in middle school, Kiyoshi forbade him from joining the baseball team. Instead he sent his son to cram school and persuaded him to sign up for the judo club.

At first, Masanori obeyed. He soon discovered, however, that he hated judo. His father had no objections to his abandoning the sport as long as he continued to concentrate on his studies. Masanori still longed to play baseball but dared not defy his father. He would spend his lunch hour with the ballplayers as they met in a classroom to discuss the game. As he sat in the bleachers and watched his friends play, the frustration grew.

In his second year of middle school, Masanori could no longer just watch. Without telling his parents, he joined the team in September 1958 and began skipping cram school. His mother soon realized the deceit, but to Masanori's surprise she kept the secret to herself.

In October 1958 Masanori was at practice when he noticed a man trudging across the diamond toward the school. His heart sank as he recognized his father. Once the bills for cram school had stopped coming in the mail, Kiyoshi had figured out that his son was playing ball on the sly. Masanori knew that he was caught and would probably be beaten when he returned home. Had he ventured near the school, he would have heard his father screaming at the coach. At one point, the coach even feared that Kiyoshi would throw a punch.

After practice, Masanori slunk home. His father sat formally on the living room floor between his two uncles. They ordered Masanori to sit. The boy fell to his knees, bowed apologetically, and kept his eyes on the tatami mats. This will be bad, he thought.

Obviously fuming, his father began, "I went to the school today and spoke to your coach." Masanori waited for the explosion, but it did not come. Instead Kiyoshi explained that the coach told him that his son was a talented ballplayer and had promised to mentor the boy both on the diamond and in his studies. If he could keep his grades strong, he would be allowed to play baseball. Masanori blinked with surprise. He realized later that after his father had returned from the school, his grandfather had called his other sons to calm Kiyoshi and convince him to accept the coach's offer.

At the top middle school baseball programs across Japan, hundreds of boys tried out for a spot on the team. Coaches designed grueling practices and encouraged hazing to discourage all but the most serious players. After the first month, teams would be left with a few dozen baseball fanatics. But Saruhashi Middle School was no baseball powerhouse. The team contained only a dozen players, and they had never won even a local championship. Training consisted of running up and down the local mountain but never became too strenuous as the coach feared that boys might quit. Occasionally seniors needed to beg younger players to remain on the team. But now with Masanori on the mound, the team began to improve and even qualified for the regional championship tournament. The team's inexperience would unfortunately prove costly.

The tournament's opening ceremonies began at 8:00 a.m., but Saruhashi was not scheduled to play until 4:00 p.m. The team dutifully attended the pageant and sat in the bleachers watching the morning games. By mid-afternoon the boys were dehydrated from the hot sun. Masanori and his listless teammates took the field at four, only to be routed by an experienced team whose starters had arrived at the ballpark just prior to the game. Despite the loss, Hosei II High School, a baseball powerhouse in Kawasaki, had noticed Murakami.

Left-handed pitchers, like Murakami, are valued throughout the world, as only 10 percent of the population are natural southpaws. In Japan, however, the percentage is even lower. With the importance of stroke order in the writing of kanji, most Japanese lefties born in the mid-twentieth century were converted by their parents into righties through early training. An early twenty-first-century study, for example, found that less than 1 percent of Japanese write with their left hands.[3] A school like Hosei II could easily find a spot for an effective left-handed hurler like Murakami.

Masanori had expected to enter the local high school after graduating from Surihashi Middle, but in January 1960 Hitoshi Tamaru, the coach of Hosei II, invited him to visit the campus and work out with the team. Located just southwest of Tokyo and north of Yokohama, Kawasaki is the ninth largest city in Japan. The three cities form a continuous urban landscape, dominated by factories, ports, transportation routes, and small, densely packed homes. During the 1960s and 1970s, the air quality of Kawasaki became infamous, leading to widespread environmental and health problems.

Murakami took the train to Kawasaki, spent the day touring the school, and then attended baseball practice. Under Tamaru's scrutiny, he ran, played catch, and then threw 20–30 pitches from the mound. After a two-hour train ride, he returned home late that evening to find a message waiting for him. Tamaru had telephoned to offer Masanori a scholarship that included the dormitory fee if he could pass the entrance exam.

At first, Kiyoshi objected to his son's focusing on baseball. He still hoped that Masanori would become a doctor. It was difficult, however, to argue with a scholarship to a major Tokyo-area high school. With Masanori's grandfather advocating for accepting the offer, Kiyoshi agreed with one condition. "If you want to be a ballplayer," he told his son "you will have to be the best in Japan."[4]

CHAPTER 2

On March 25, 1960, Masanori and his parents hauled his baggage to Otsuki Station and boarded the train for Kawasaki. Hosei II's academic year would start April 1, but the ballplayers were required to come a week early to begin training.

On the first day of practice between 150 and 200 boys showed up, hoping to make the team. The next few weeks were spent weeding out those who were not serious. During this time the rookies rarely touched a ball or bat. Most of the practices were spent standing in rank on the foul lines, cheering for the upperclassmen as they ran through drills. The boys did not cheer in an individualistic or spontaneous manner like American boys but instead as a regimented group. Upperclassmen supervised as the freshman chanted team slogans in unison and yelled with all their might. Boys who did not yell loudly enough were punished, often with a cuff to the head.

Practices would end with "the Derby." In this drill three upperclassmen would sprint around the perimeter of the field as all of the rookies followed. When the upperclassmen completed a lap, they would rest as three new seniors took their turn. The rookies, however, would continue sprinting behind the new group of runners until all of the upperclassmen had finished. By the end of the first week, just a hundred freshmen remained. Soon the remaining first-years were allowed to practice. Most lacked the baseball skills needed to play for a top team like Hosei II and were cut. A dozen or so, including Murakami, made the team.

The most cherished quality in a Japanese high school ballplayer was not ability but spirit or heart. The first week of practice was designed to test the boys' mettle and weed out the weak-spirited.[1] This emphasis on spirit—a term that goes far beyond the American concept of hustle—is the most important difference between Japanese and American baseball. Baseball came to Japan in the 1870s, a time of great cultural change and unrest. Less than twenty years before, Japan had existed in near isolation, with only limited contacts with the Western world. That changed when Commodore Matthew Perry sailed his famous Black Ships into Tokyo Harbor in 1853 and demanded that the country open itself to foreign trade. Awed by the Western technology and military power, Japan's leaders vowed to modernize. Over the next few decades Japan changed its form of government, social structure, economy, and educational system. Western styles and fads swept through the nation as wealthy Japanese discarded many age-old traditions and customs. Not surprisingly, some Japanese feared that the country was losing its native culture. This led to the concept of *wakon yosai* (meaning Japanese spirit, Western technology), the philosophy that Japan could import Western technology, institutions, and even ideas but would imbue them with Japanese spirit. This philosophy may be illustrated best in baseball.

The distinctive approach that would come to characterize Japanese baseball developed in the early 1890s at Japan's elite First Higher School, often called Ichiko. Following the concept of *wakon yosai,* the Ichiko players approached baseball as a martial art. "Sports came from the West," a team member later explained. "In Ichiko baseball, we were playing sports but we were also putting the spirit of Japan into it.... *Yakyu* is a way to express the samurai spirit."[2]

Using an idealized image of samurai behavior—commonly known as Bushido after the publication of Inazo Nitobe's book *Bushido: The Soul of Japan* in 1899—the Ichiko players viewed themselves as modern samurai battling on the baseball diamond. They modeled their practices after how they believed a traditional warrior would prepare for battle.[3] An integral part of this training was preparing the spirit as well as the body. "The spirit of bushi[do] is required in every aspect of training," wrote one Ichiko player.[4]

Believing that a strong spirit could overcome physical shortcomings and lead to victory on the field, Ichiko players put in long hours of punishing practice to improve not only their skills, but also their mental endurance. Pitchers would fire hundreds of pitches each practice, and batters would take a thousand practice swings. Tsunetaru Moriyama, Ichiko's great left-hander, practiced his fastball against the clubhouse's brick wall, eventually boring a hole in the façade. The school left the gap "for later generations to view with amazement."[5] The lefty would also practice his control by trying to extinguish a candle's flame with the breeze from his pitches.[6] After workouts the pitchers would hang from the branches of the cherry trees surrounding the playing field to straighten their arms, crooked from throwing too many curve balls.[7]

The extreme approach worked, and Ichiko soon became Japan's top baseball team and even defeated American adult teams in widely publicized games held in 1896. Ichiko's dominance faded in the early twentieth century, but its philosophy was kept alive by Waseda University coach Suishu Tobita, who created a winning program built on a brand of baseball that surpassed even Ichiko's rigor.

Tobita explained in one of his many tracts on baseball theory, "A manager has to love his players, but on the practice field he must treat them as cruelly as possible, even though he may be crying about it inside. That is the key to winning baseball. If the players do not try so hard as to vomit blood in practice, then they cannot hope to win games. . . . The purpose of training is not health but the forging of the soul. To hit like a shooting star, to catch a ball beyond one's capabilities . . . such beautiful plays are not the result of technique but . . . are made possible by a strong spiritual power."[8]

Calling his practices *shi no renshu* (death training), Tobita worked his players past their limits of endurance to improve their spirit. Players would field ground balls "until they were half dead, motionless, and froth was coming out of their mouths."[9] Few teams adopted all of Tobita's methods, but his general philosophy soon became the pervasive approach in Japan and still survives in a watered-down form today.

At Hosei II, the coaches' methods were a far cry from Tobita's death training. The program was not known for either harsh discipline or fanatical training methods, but it was still harsher than most, if not all, American high school programs. The drills were designed to push Murakami and his teammates to exhaustion. Yet they were never allowed to drink during practice. In the summer months as the Tokyo humidity became oppressive and players became dehydrated, the boys would devise ways to get water. As a pitcher, Masanori found it relatively easy to sneak a drink. After throwing, pitchers were allowed to change their undershirts in the clubhouse. Once inside, it was easy to take a sip from the faucet when nobody was looking. Position players had it more difficult. Outfielders waited for a long drive during batting practice to clear the school's fence and fall into an adjacent yard. They would then climb the fence, retrieve the ball, and knock on the neighbor's door to apologize for intruding on the property. While apologizing, they would beg for a mouthful of water. Infielders would take advantage of foul balls landing in the adjacent rice paddy. The water in the paddy was often foul, but the boys would sip it anyway or dip a small towel in it and then suck on the damp cloth when nobody was watching.

The players were also responsible for maintaining the field and equipment. They spent hours grooming the dirt infield and manicuring the outfield grass. As practice balls deteriorated and their strings loosened, first- and second-year players would take the damaged balls back to the dormitory and restitch them before the next practice. If the stitching was done incorrectly, the player would have to rip out the thread and do it over.

Masanori and his teammates attended Hosei II primarily to play ball. They slept in the team dormitory; attended endless baseball meetings in the evenings; and endured long, difficult practices. Classes were of secondary importance.

The ballplayers woke up early and met at the park to exercise before breakfast. By the time school started, Masanori was so tired that he often fell asleep during class. Underclassmen were required to be on the baseball field five minutes after school let out. To accomplish this Herculean task, the boys would pack up their books and notebooks five minutes before the last class finished, dash to the clubhouse the moment school ended, change into their uniforms, and rush to the fields.

Before stepping onto the all-dirt diamond, each player followed a ritual practiced throughout Japanese baseball. He would bow toward the pitcher's mound and ask the field's permission to play by saying, "*Onegai shimasu*" (Please, may I). Like so much in Japanese baseball, the practice originated from the nineteenth-century Ichiko players who wished to show the same respect to the diamond that samurai gave to their dojos. Similarly at the end of practice the boys would thank the field with another bow and an "*Arigato gozaimasu*" (Thank you very much).

Life for a rookie Japanese high school ballplayer was difficult. At the time Japanese baseball teams, and even much of Japanese society, followed a rigid social hierarchy. The younger players (known as *kohei*) were subordinate to their elders (known as *sempai*) in every way. *Kohei* were responsible for doing a multitude of menial tasks for their *sempai* in return for the elders' guidance.

Like all first-years, Masanori shared a dormitory room with a senior. The underclassmen were responsible for laying out the futons each night and putting away the bedding in the morning. They were required to clean the room, the bathroom, and even their roommates' clothes. Boarding the ballplayers together had also originated with the Ichiko teams, who isolated their players from the rest of the students to strengthen team bonds and instill the "samurai" values of frugality and Spartan discipline. An Ichiko player wrote, "The dormitory . . . is a place for practicing self-discipline, the spirit of our baseball club. Both the club and the dormitory should collaborate to train the player's mind to achieve self-discipline as an objective."[10]

On nearly every Japanese high school baseball team, including Hosei II, brutal hazing was common. "Freshman year on the baseball team was for learning that the individual always subordinated himself to the team," recalls Japanese home run king Sadaharu Oh.[11] If a rookie made a mistake, the seniors usually punished the entire group of first-years. A mental mistake on the diamond often resulted in a long lecture by the team captain, with the rookies being forced to squat with their heels in the air for the entire session. Players who lost their balance were hit in the back of the thighs with a bat. When feeling sadistic, seniors would place bats behind the squatting freshmen's knees. The rookies needed to squeeze their legs to hold the bat in place, as a dropped bat would lead to a beating. Once a senior ordered Murakami to sing. When Masanori refused, the upperclassman forced him to sit on his knees by the dormitory entrance for an hour. A common dinnertime ritual was known as "Rawhide." If an upperclassman sang the theme from the television show *Rawhide*, rookies had to do sit-ups on the dining room table until the song finished.

After enduring the abuse, few of the rookies would actually play in meaningful games. Hosei II had a strong team. Led by future Yomiuri Giants all-star Isao Shibata, upperclassmen held down nearly every position, and rookies sat on the bench and watched. During Murakami's rookie season, the team qualified for the 1960 National High School Baseball Championship.

The National High School Baseball Championship (played in the summer) and the National High School Baseball Invitational Tournament (played in the spring) are both held at Koshien Stadium in Nishinomiya, between the cities of Osaka and Kobe. The tournaments, usually just referred to as Summer Koshien and Spring Koshien, are Japan's most popular sporting events—followed far more closely than the Japan Series or Grand Sumo tournaments.

Founded in the early twentieth century (the Summer Koshien in 1915 and the Spring Koshien in 1924), the tournaments are steeped in ritual. They begin with elaborate opening ceremonies in which teams march on the field in military style with arms swinging in unison and high-stepping gaits. At the start and end of each game, teams line either side of home plate and bow. To qualify for Summer Koshien, a team must win one of the forty-nine regional championships held across Japan each summer. A spot at Spring Koshien is by invitation only and is based on a team's record of the previous fall season. The teams battle in a single elimination format. The do-or-die atmosphere pushes the boys to their limits. It is not unusual for pitchers to hurl complete games on several consecutive days and runners to make irrational head-first slides into first base to show their fighting spirit. Many boys come home seriously injured, as sitting out a tournament game is inconceivable. Upon elimination, players, fans, and even managers often weep inconsolably as the boys gather up a handful of the "sacred" infield dirt to keep as a souvenir. Most participants, even those boys who go on to play professionally, view their Koshien experience as the highlight of their lives.

Although he would spend the tournament on the bench, the 1960 Summer Koshien tournament would change Masanori's life. In the third round, Hosei II faced Waseda High, the feeder school to Waseda University that had produced Sadaharu Oh just two years earlier. After an 8–0 victory, Murakami and his teammates went to Osaka Station to catch a train back to Kawasaki. With time to kill before their departure, Masanori and a friend headed for a restaurant. As they ate, a middle-aged man approached and, recognizing their school uniforms, congratulated them on the victory. He introduced himself as Eikichi Hoshino and, following Japanese ritual, presented them with his business card. He explained that he had recently moved from Tokyo to Osaka, so he was at the game cheering for Waseda, but nonetheless he would like to buy the boys coffee. After the coffee, the three walked to the train platforms before Hoshino hurried off to meet his daughter Yoshiko, who was arriving from Tokyo. A short time later, as the boys were about to board their train, Hoshino returned to introduce his daughter to the boys. A pretty girl just six months younger than Masanori, Yoshiko attended a private school in Tokyo. They soon parted, and Murakami gave the encounter little thought except to add Eikichi Hoshino to his New Year's card list—a typical action by a polite Japanese.

In the fall of 1960 and spring of 1961 Murakami became Hosei II's second pitcher behind ace Isao Shibata. The team won the National High School Baseball Invitational Tournament (Spring Koshien) in early April 1961. Shibata pitched three complete games at the championship tournament, but with a 10–1 lead in the semi-final, coach Hidehiro Otani allowed Masanori to finish the game for Shibata. Murakami pitched a shutout inning and looked ready to take over as the team's ace after Shibata graduated. Fate, however, would be against him. The inning would be his only appearance in the storied tournament.

As the 1961 summer tournament approached, Murakami hoped to help Hosei II to another championship. To qualify for Koshien, the team first had to win the Kanagawa Prefectural Tournament. Directly after the opening ceremonies, the ball field was empty, so Hosei II decided to practice. Masanori threw his usual hundred pitches on the sidelines and was about to head to the clubhouse when he was told to take the mound and pitch batting practice. Already tired, he hesitated but did as he was told. As the third batter stepped up to the plate, Murakami grooved a pitch down the middle. It came back at him in a flash. With no time to move, it slammed into his left elbow, breaking the bone. Masanori would miss the summer tournament. Shibata led the team to the semi-finals at Koshien before losing 4–2 to the eventual champion, Nami of Osaka.

In September 1961, Hosei II began the fall season. Following convention, third-year players, including Isao Shibata, did not play after the Summer Koshien tournament, even though they would not graduate until March. This tradition allowed the club more time to hone the squad that would be eligible to play in the Spring Koshien tournament. Shibata and his classmates, however, continued to practice with the team, as several needed to stay in shape for professional careers.

It was now Murakami's turn to lead Hosei II to Koshien, but he remained on the sidelines, recovering from the injury. Frustrated, Masanori kept in shape by running while waiting for his chance. In October Murakami felt well enough to begin throwing. He worked hard, built back his arm strength, and soon reigned as the team's ace. But his recovery was too late for the team to gain an invitation to the Spring Koshien tournament of 1962. Murakami and his teammates would have to focus on the summer tournament.

The spring began well. Masanori's arm was fully healed and Hosei II had a winning team. In June they played in the Kawasaki City Tournament, advancing easily through the early rounds behind Murakami's fastball and strong hitting. Masanori shined in the semi-final, pitching a two-hitter and striking out 18, but as he walked back to the dormitory after the game, his stomach began to cramp. Five or six sharp pains shot through his intestines before he doubled over and slumped to the street. A doctor examined him that afternoon and gave him an injection and some medicine. If you want to continue playing baseball, the doctor warned, do not tell anybody about this.

For the next ten days, however, baseball was out of the question. Plagued with chronic diarrhea, Masanori could barely eat. When he recovered, he had lost weight and felt feeble. He was too weak to practice with the team, so he went alone to the school's soccer field, where he ran and did calisthenics to build back his strength.

Even without Masanori, Hosei II won the Kawasaki City Championship and readied for the prefectural tournament. Murakami began to recover and took the mound again for the start of the tournament in mid-July. The games started well for Hosei II, with a 10–0 rout of a team from the small town of Odawara and two subsequent victories. Yet Masanori still felt weak from the illness. When he took the mound against Keio High School in the semi-final, he knew that he was not at top form. An hour later, his dreams of returning to Koshien were shattered. Masanori's high school career ended with a 5–1 loss.[12]

For Murakami the loss was more than just a disappointment. He carried a sense of responsibility for the team's success and guilt for its losses. Instilled with a team mentality, Masanori felt personally responsible for Hosei II's not reaching Koshien for the first time in five years—a burden he still carries fifty years later.

With the end of his baseball season, Masanori focused on college. As Hosei II was associated with Hosei University, Murakami figured that he would attend the university and pitch for its baseball team. After graduating from college, he expected to enter the business world as one of the ubiquitous Japanese salary men. If that did not work out, he would return to Otsuki and take his father's place as the town's postmaster. Playing professional baseball never entered his mind.

As Masanori thought about his future, his high school teammate Yasushi Yamamoto asked him if he would like to join Yamamoto's father for dinner. Yasushi's father, Kazuto Tsuruoka, was among the most famous men in Japanese baseball.[13] He had attended Hosei University before signing professionally with the Nankai Hawks in 1939. As a rookie, Tsuruoka led the league in home runs but following the season was drafted by the Imperial Army. He spent the next five years defending the Japanese homeland, eventually becoming an officer in charge of anti-aircraft artillery. He returned to professional baseball in 1946 as the player-manager of the Nankai franchise (known for that season only as the Kinki Great Ring) and captured the Most Valuable Player Award and pennant. Tsuruoka played for six more seasons, winning the 1948 and 1951 MVP awards and leading Nankai to three pennants before retiring as a player to concentrate on managing. By the time he left baseball in 1968, he had managed the Hawks for twenty-three consecutive seasons, leading them to eleven pennants and 1,807 wins. Although Murakami had heard of his friend's father, he knew few of these details as he still did not follow professional baseball. But with the promise of a steak dinner at a fine restaurant, Masanori was happy to meet the baseball icon.

Over dinner they spoke about baseball in general, and Masanori told Tsuruoka of his plans to play college ball. The manager did not try to dissuade Murakami but as they parted for the evening asked that he think about turning pro. Masanori decided not to respond other than to thank Tsuruoka again for the steak. On the train back to Kawasaki he told Yamamoto that even a steak dinner would not induce him to give up college.

During the summer vacation in August, however, representatives from the Taiyo Whales, Daimai Orions, and Kintestu Buffaloes contacted Murakami about signing a professional contract. In August, Kazuto Tsuruoka visited the Murakami household in Otsuki and met with Masanori's parents. The Murakamis listened politely to the manager's enthusiastic invitation for Masanori to join the Hawks but remained uncommitted. All of the teams emphasized the money Murakami would make by turning pro, but Tsuruoka offered something else. As he was about to leave he said, "Well listen, Murakami-kun, if you sign up with the Nankai Hawks, we would seriously consider letting you go to train in America."

The idea intrigued Murakami—not because he was a fan of Major League Baseball or had strong feelings for the United States but because he was curious about the country where his favorite television show, *Rawhide*, took place. Traveling to the United States at the time was prohibitively expensive for most Japanese. It was so far away that it seemed more like a dream than a real place to young Masanori.

"Really?" Murakami asked, "You would really be willing to let me go?"

"Yes, maybe," countered Tsuruoka.

The opportunity to go to America made Murakami rethink his post-graduation plans. When he returned to school in September, he met with his old coach, Hitoshi Tamaru, who was now coaching at Hosei University. If Murakami decided to attend Hosei the following year, he would become one of Tamaru's top pitchers, but nonetheless his old coach advised him to accept Tsuruoka's offer. "If you pitch in college and hurt your arm," Tamaru explained, "you will probably not get another chance to become a pro. Take this opportunity now."

Masanori, however, was still not excited about entering professional baseball. He loved playing ball but was unsure if he wanted to spend his life focusing on a sport. Somewhat reluctantly, Murakami accepted Tsuruoka's offer.

On September 29, 1962, Masanori, his parents, and three uncles boarded an early express train and headed toward Osaka. Murakami was tall and broad for his age. He would soon reach six feet and weigh 180 pounds when the average Japanese seventeen-year-old at the time was just five-foot-four.[14] But other than his size, he must have looked like most other high school seniors, with his shaved head and high-collared black wool military-style school uniform.

On a perfect Japanese fall day Masanori watched the countryside flash by—the industrial ports of Kawasaki and Yokohama, Mt. Fuji, seaside villages, rice fields, the city of Nagoya. The young man was not nervous. He had lived away from home throughout high school, so he was comfortable with moving to a new city. Instead he wondered about Osaka—what it would be like to live there and what Osaka Stadium, the Hawks' home field, looked like.

At Osaka Station, Yoshio Tominaga, Nankai's head scout, met the Murakamis. After checking into their *ryokan* (traditional Japanese inn), they went straight to Osaka Stadium. The stadium, located in the center of town, was a four/five-storied classic fan-shaped ball park built in 1950. Steep grandstands bordered the all-dirt infield, while more gently pitched bleachers surrounded the grass outfield. Advertisements in Japanese adorned the low outfield fence and the façade behind the seating. It was a cozy ballpark, 380 feet to dead center, just 300 feet down the lines, and seating nearly thirty-two thousand.

Tominaga ushered the Murakamis into the team offices behind home plate, where Tsuruoka and other Nankai officials waited.

After the usual pleasantries and introductions, at 3:30 Masanori signed the contract. He would receive a $30,000 signing bonus. Once he had committed to the Hawks, the uneasiness about becoming a professional disappeared. But even now he was not ecstatic, the way many young men in his position would be. Instead he felt a sense of responsibility to his new team and vowed to work like a professional to help the team and improve his skills. There was no formal press conference after the signing, but the Hawks announced the contract and spoke to the media. Then Tominaga took the family to dinner.

The next afternoon Masanori accompanied the Hawks on the team bus to a doubleheader at Fujidera Stadium in southern Osaka. "I had signed the contract so I was part of the team, but there I was on the team bus, shaven-headed and wearing a school uniform, and on both sides of me were old-looking guys. I didn't really feel that I had become a professional baseball player."

When they reached the stadium, the players went to the locker room, and Masanori sat in the stands with the team officials. It was only the second professional game he had ever seen, and it would be memorable. In the ninth inning of the second game, the last inning of the season, Nankai's fireplug catcher, Katsuya Nomura, hit a line-drive home run to break the single-season home run record for the Pacific League. Two years later Nomura would top his own record of 44 by blasting 52.

Earlier that day the major sports papers had announced Murakami's signing. The Hawks' general manager, Makoto Tachibana, told *Hochi Sports*, "We have been looking for a strong lefty pitcher for the last few years and Murakami is perfect. He cuts a good figure, and I hope he will become a pillar on our team. I expect him to pitch often starting next season." When asked his thoughts, Masanori proclaimed, "A couple of teams contacted me, but I decided to play for Nankai because Mr. Tsuruoka pursued me so aggressively, and I think I can reach my full potential under him. I am confident I will do well as a pro. I will try to improve my fastball first and would like to become a great pitcher like [Masaichi] Kaneda." Tsuruoka added, "I watched him pitch at the pre-Koshien tournament this year, and his pitches were quite fast. I am not certain if we can use him right away. I will need to watch him in practice. But he has not overused his arm in high school, so he will have a long career as a pitcher. He is our future."[15]

CHAPTER 3

On the last day of January 1963, Murakami boarded a train for Kure, a small city nineteen miles southeast of Hiroshima. Although he was still a high school student and would not graduate until mid-March, Masanori was excused from classes. Instead of studying, he would be attending spring training with the Nankai Hawks.

Japanese spring training camps have become infamous among Americans for their rigor. Foreigners playing in Japan, known as *gaijin*, complain that they are worse than Marine boot camp. "Camp is going to be hell. Pure hell," Yomiuri Giants outfielder Reggie Smith told his new teammate Warren Cromartie when he arrived in Japan.[1] Even the mildest camps are far more challenging than the most difficult American spring training programs, while the harshest hark back to practices of the Ichiko teams of the 1890s.

Many teams begin spring training in mid-January by making a pilgrimage to a Zen temple or local shrine to ready their spirits for the new season. The players then embark on six weeks of savage conditioning and drills before they begin practice games in early March. In recent years Japanese managers have focused more on developing baseball skills and building stamina during these spring camps, but in the 1960s many teams still emphasized the development of fighting spirit through brutal drills.

The Yomiuri Giants, in particular, were known to embrace many aspects of Ichiko's and Suishu Tobita's philosophies of spirit/samurai baseball. The Giants became Japan's first lasting professional team, created in December 1934 from the remnants of the All-Nippon team brought together to play Babe Ruth and the All-Americans during their famous tour earlier that fall. After touring North America in 1935 and the spring of 1936 to sharpen their skills, the Giants returned to Japan to challenge six newly formed professional teams in a series of tournaments held in July. To nearly everyone's surprise, the heavily favored Giants compiled losing records at all three tournaments, including an 8–1 drubbing at the hands of their future rivals, the Hanshin Tigers of Osaka.

Appalled at his team's play, manager Sadayoshi Fujimoto created a practice camp near the Morinji Shrine in Tatebayashi to ready the Giants for the fall tournaments. A former Waseda University player under Tobita, Fujimoto explained, "The purpose of this camp is not to improve our fielding or our hitting but to hone our fighting spirit."[2] For the next nine days the players were pushed to their physical and mental limits. Practice began at 7:00 a.m. and, despite temperatures above 90 degrees Fahrenheit, lasted all day. Players were run through the Thousand Ball Drill, where coaches would hit balls alternately to their left and right until a thousand were fielded cleanly. The drill could take hours, and many vomited by the side of the field. The camp, call the Vomit Practice, revitalized the Giants, who went 18 and 9 during the fall tournaments. With the Giants' success, other teams copied the camp.

In 1963 the Giants, now managed by Tetsuharu Kawakami, who had played for Fujimoto's Giants, continued to practice spirit/samurai baseball. Kawakami, known as the God of Batting when he was a player, ruled over the Giants with an iron fist. Developing a system known as *kanri yakyu* (control baseball), Kawakami was a strict disciplinarian who demanded complete sacrifice for the team. "Lone wolves are the cancer of the team," he once proclaimed.[3] He maintained his authority through a combination of fines, scoldings, binds of obligation, and even public humiliation. He once removed a rebellious starting pitcher with 2 outs in the fifth inning and a 10–0 lead just to prove his authority. He was also a throwback to the early days of Japanese baseball, when managers approach the game as a martial art.

The Giants' training camp was highly regimented, with a rigid and demanding schedule reminiscent of the Vomit Practice. Kawakami reinstituted the thousand-ball fungo drill, emphasized intense conditioning, and made batters take hundreds of swings each day. Echoing Suishu Tobita, Kawakami explained that these activities were designed to produce better athletes by strengthening their spirit. "An ordinary person practices until he gets tired.

An ordinary professional ballplayer practices until he collapses. A true professional player is able to reach a higher level, a state of being outside himself, and keep going."[4]

The Hawks' training camp was mild compared to the Giants' regimen. Although Nankai's spring training practices were regimented and long, manager Kazuto Tsuruoka did not institute the grueling spirit-building exercises common in Japanese high schools and among Kawakami's Giants. Instead Tsuruoka used psychology to motivate his players. He realized that the same approach did not work on every player—some he would praise, some cajole, some scold, some befriend. He often motivated players with his famous saying, "There's money to be made on the field," meaning hard work would be rewarded financially. Joe Stanka, an American who pitched for the Hawks from 1960 to 1965, wrote in his autobiography, "Tsuruoka had a seasoned understanding of human nature that defied the confines of culture and a way of imposing his will without waving any red flags or creating lasting resentment. He had a gruffness about him that indicated he meant business, but when he did chastise, he never broke a player's spirit, allowing dignity to be retained."[5]

During the first couple of weeks of the Hawks' camp, the players rarely touched a bat or ball. Instead coaches put them through conditioning drills. Tsuruoka favored running and often started practice with jogging laps around the field. One player remembered going around and around, each time convinced that it had to be the last lap, until he nearly dropped with exhaustion. They would then move to stretching and calisthenics. Neither American nor Japanese baseball players lifted weights at the time, so they built core strength by jumping rope, doing endless sit-ups, and even chopping wood. "We had one drill," Murakami recalls, "where half the team would line up on the left-field foul line and the other half on the right-field foul line. The coaches would then hit a fly ball to center field, and we would have to sprint, catch it, and then continue running to the other side and get in line there." The conditioning practices lasted all day and ended with a run up a steep hill. One of Tsuruoka's favorite drills called for players to sprint up the hill while carrying a teammate piggyback style. As a rookie, Masanori knew better than to smile, but it must have been difficult to keep a straight face watching 162-pound pitcher Mutsuo Minagawa struggling to carry six-foot-five, 211-pound Joe Stanka up the hill as the American's long legs dragged on the ground.[6]

Once in prime condition, the players would begin to sharpen their skills during long days of regimented drills held six days a week. A typical day would start early with a light run and stretching, followed by playing catch and then pepper. Once the players were warmed up, they would break into groups. Position players would take hundreds of swings each day and spend hours fielding balls. Murakami and the other pitchers would work on their fielding and pick-off moves, as well as their pitching technique. They would then pitch batting practice, build core strength with endless sit-ups and back exercises, and finish with sprints. After a dinner break, the team would reconvene for strategy meetings or further practice.

Managers and coaches demanded that pitchers develop pinpoint control. Few Japanese pitchers reared back and attempted to throw the ball past batters. Instead they tried to finesse the edges of the strike zone. Counts often ran full as they coaxed batters to swing at bad pitches with an array of breaking balls. To acquire the desired control, pitchers threw a hundred or more balls each practice, believing that only through repetition could they truly master the art of pitching. At times the Hawks would have special days set aside for pitcher training, where the hurlers would throw more than two hundred times. During the season pitchers were also expected to throw every day. It was, and still is, common to see pitchers who had been removed from a game go straight to the bullpen and throw until they reached their daily quota of pitches.

Hawks' pitchers also worked on their control by throwing at targets. Coaches planted two bamboo poles in the earth, about five feet apart. They then ran two rubberized strings two feet apart between the poles. The lower string was roughly a foot off the ground. Vertical strings, tied between the two horizontal ones, divided the zone into three parts. With Tsuruoka and dozens of spectators looking on and catcher Katsuya Nomura set up behind the strings, pitchers practiced throwing into the various zones, up and down and from side to side.

Throughout the practices the team's five coaches swarmed around prospects, offering constant and sometimes contradictory instructions. The role of the coach in Major League professional baseball in the United States and in Japanese baseball is fundamentally different. In the United States a coach offers advice and pointers to help a player find the style that will bring him success. In Japan a coach's role is to mold a player into the franchise's model.

Players are taught identical batting stances and ways to hit, throw, and pitch. It is not unusual in a Japanese big league game to see a succession of hitters with indistinguishable batting stances. A coach's instruction is also the law. It may not be rejected. Carlton Hanta, a Hawaiian-born Japanese American who played and coached in Japan from 1958 to 1972, noted that many promising careers were ruined by coaches who insisted that players change their mechanics to suit the franchise's ideal.

The Hawks had a strong team. Since the creation of the Pacific League in 1950, Tsuruoka had led Nankai to six pennants. In the other seasons they had finished second. They were runners-up in 1962, and would miss the pennant by one game in 1963. Tsuruoka controlled all aspects of the team—from the field strategy to where to house the players. But unlike many Japanese managers—and especially Kawakami of the Giants—Tsuruoka was not a harsh disciplinarian. Players followed him out of respect and loyalty. He was nicknamed "Oyabun," a term literally meaning "boss" or "family head" but commonly used to denote a powerful head of a Yakuza gang—equivalent to a Mafia godfather. Tsuruoka became a father figure to many of the younger players. He was famous for helping his players with their personal lives and offering sage advice. For example, when Carlton Hanta came to the Hawks in 1958, nobody on the team spoke English. The team soon found a stadium usherette who had attended a Japanese Catholic school and spoke English. The two fell in love, but before they could marry, Hanta needed a go-between, a *nakōdo*, to approach her family and arrange the marriage. He turned to Tsuruoka. With such a famous and respected *nakōdo*, the marriage was quickly organized.[7]

Tsuruoka had especially strong relations with his American players. Unlike many Japanese managers who tried to force foreigners into a Japanese mold, Tsuruoka not only gave his *gaijin* players latitude, but also used them to teach his native players American-style baseball. He understood that the key to his foreign players' productivity was a happy home life. He would look after the American families, making sure that the transition to Japan went smoothly. Occasionally he would take out the American wives to fine tempura dinners, treating them as honored guests, knowing their happiness would directly affect his ball club.

Under Tsuruoka's leadership the Hawks were a relaxed, fun-loving bunch of young men. There were no team curfews, and Tsuruoka himself would often stay out late drinking with his coaches and friends. But once he reached the ballpark and put on his uniform, Tsuruoka was all business. He rarely cracked a smile, focusing completely on the game. He made no written notes and did not consult statistics but seemed to remember every player's tendencies. "He was one of the smartest managers—bar none," Carlton Hanta remembers. "When I was a defensive coach for him, he'd be sitting in the dugout picking his nose, and all of a sudden he would say, 'Carl, move the third baseman to his left.' And by God, the ball would be hit right there. He would do that all the time. He knew those things without a computer. His mind was a computer!"[8]

Catcher Katsuya Nomura led the Hawks' offense. Built like a fireplug (five-foot-nine and 187 pounds), Nomura was the premiere power hitter of the Pacific League. He would win nine home run crowns (including eight straight from 1961 to 1968), seven RBI titles, the 1965 triple crown, and five Most Valuable Player Awards. He presently has the second most home runs, hits, and RBIs in Japanese history and is the all-time leader in games played and at bats. Nomura was not the league's best defensive catcher, but most Americans playing in Japan in the 1960s considered him the smartest. He had a deep understanding of the game and would later become one of the country's top managers.

Hitting behind Nomura was former Yankee farmhand Kent Hadley. Hadley began his career in Japan by hitting a home run in his first at bat. He would play six years for the Hawks, pounding out 131 home runs. Yoshinori Hirose, a future member of the Japan Baseball Hall of Fame, led off the lineup. One of the fastest men in the history of Japanese ball, Hirose stole 596 bases, was a superb center fielder, and hit for average with moderate power. Carlton Hanta remembered Hirose scoring from first on a single to right field as the outfielder casually tossed the ball back to the infield.

But Nankai's true strength lay in its outstanding pitching. Japanese teams in the early 1960s did not follow set rotations as their Major League counterparts did. Instead they used their starters much as Major League managers had done in the prewar era. Most teams had one or two aces whom the manager used as often as possible. "Once they got an ace pitcher, that guy would just throw and throw and throw," remembers Glenn Mickens, who pitched in Japan from 1959 to 1963. "The other guys on the staff were just fillers." "Managers would hang with [their aces] a long time, thinking that they could lose with them and not lose face," added Hankyu Braves outfielder Gordie Wind-horn. "If they brought some rookie in there and he lost the ball game, that would make them look bad."[9]

These aces pitched a disproportional number of innings. For example, in 1962 the Hanshin Tigers' two aces, Masaaki Koyama and Minoru Murayama, each threw over 350 innings and completed 59 percent of the club's 1,221⅔ innings. That year the top two pitchers for each of the twelve Japanese teams threw an average of 46 percent of their teams' entire innings. Not all teams, however, relied so heavily on two aces. The Hawks and several other teams used true four- or five-man rotations. Tsuruoka had learned the hard way not to rely on a single pitcher.

Nankai's ace was Tadashi Sugiura, a slight (five-foot-nine and 156 pounds), bespectacled underhand pitcher. In 1957 Sugiura and teammate Shigeo Nagashima had led Rikkio University to the Tokyo Big Six championship. After graduation Nagashima signed with the Yomiuri Giants and became Japan's most popular player, while Sugiura went to the Hawks to become, for a short time, the most dominant pitcher in Japan. "He threw three-quarters underhand, so he wasn't a complete submarine pitcher," recalls Mickens. "He could turn the ball over and make it sink from the letters down to your knees. The ball would just explode! Then he could turn his wrist and make the ball explode up because he was coming from down underneath."[10] Following the prevailing wisdom, Tsuruoka used his new ace often. As a rookie in 1958, Sugiura led the Hawks with 299 innings pitched. The following season, he went 38–4 with a 1.41 ERA and pitched 371⅓ innings. His most remarkable feat, however, came in the 1959 Japan Series, where he won all four games in a sweep of the Yomiuri Giants while pitching 32 of the 37 possible innings.

In his first four years of professional ball Sugiura racked up 116 wins against 36 losses, but he also logged in 1,244⅔ innings. "He would pitch nine innings, and the next day if they had a small lead, he was back there again . . . out of the bullpen," recalls Mickens. "You would just be sitting there in awe. If it was my arm, it would be hanging on the ground! . . . As the ace of the pitch-ing staff, he was never going to say that he couldn't pitch. It was an honor to be the ace."[11]

In 1961 Sugiura's arm began to tire, and he was no longer as effective. His ERA rose three-fourths of a run, although he still won 20 games. The fol-lowing season (1962) arm injuries again plagued Sugiura, and he was limited to just 172⅔ innings. His record fell to 14–15, and his ERA of 3.07 was just below the league average. Probably realizing that overuse had compromised his ace, Tsuruoka began using a four- or five-man rotation in 1961. His ace still logged the most innings, but his top two pitchers would pitch in only 36 percent of the team's total innings in 1962—the lowest percentage for any pair of aces in the Japanese leagues.

Mutsuo Minagawa, another submarine hurler with pinpoint control, was the team's second ace. He had won 19 games for the Hawks in 1962 and would eventually be inducted into the Japan Baseball Hall of Fame. His piggyback partner, Joe Stanka, a power pitcher, had pitched with the 1959 Chicago White Sox before coming to Japan the following year. Stanka's fastball and his penchant for the brush-back pitch made him both feared and highly effective. Rounding out the rotation were two young phenomenons, Kiyohiro Miura and Chikara Morinaka. Miura had won 17 games the previous season, and Morinaka would win 17 in 1963. Both would be future all-stars.

As a high schooler who had only pitched one inning at Koshien and had never won a major championship, Murakami should have been awed by his new teammates. But with the cockiness inherent in eighteen-year-old boys, Masanori felt himself their equal. Listed as five-foot-eleven and 179 pounds, he was the largest Japanese on the team's roster and physically one of the strongest. He was throwing well in practice and now that he had committed to turning professional was determined to make his mark on the game.

In early March Murakami heard that Sugiura, rookie pitcher Toshihiro Hayashi, and coach Kazuo Kageyama were leaving camp to join the Detroit Tigers for spring training camp in Lakeland, Florida.[12] "I thought that the Hawks might have forgotten their promise to send me to the United States since they sent these other players—I never had anything in writing. So I decided to concentrate on making the Hawks' rotation. During practice Tsuruoka-san would encourage me, saying things like, 'Are you getting with the program? Do your best and come up to *ichi-gun*.'" (Japanese minor league teams are known as *ni-gun* [literally second troop], while the top "major league" teams are called *ichi-gun* [first troop]).

The March 4, 1963, issue of *Baseball Magazine* reported that Murakami was a one-in-a-million find for Nankai. The team had high expectations for the young lefty but was still surprised by the speed of his fastball and the array of his other pitches. Tsuruoka told the magazine reporter, "The fast ball coming from his tall body is outstanding. I think he is great. I will use him a lot in the exhibition games."[13]

True to his word, Tsuruoka used Murakami regularly in the preseason. On March 2, in the team's first exhibition game, Murakami pitched a scoreless ninth against the Hiroshima Carp, impressing reporters with his velocity. The following day he threw another scoreless inning against Hiroshima—walking a batter and striking out another. Masanori felt confident that he would make the big league club.[14]

But fate intervened.

"One day it was snowing really hard," Murakami remembers. "I pitched in the game for about forty minutes. My fastballs and curveballs were pretty good, but the pitching coach came up to me and said, 'Hey, raise your arm a little higher when you throw the ball.' I followed his directions, and he complimented me on how well I did. It was really cold and snowing hard. A few pitches later, I heard this strange sound—a click from my elbow—and it began to hurt."

Despite the injury, Murakami continued to throw in practice and pitch in exhibition games. But the sore elbow limited his effectiveness. On March 12 against the Yomiuri Giants, for example, Masanori lasted just 2⅓ innings as he gave up 3 hits and walked 5.[15] Tsuruoka's initial enthusiasm for his rookie southpaw began to wane. When camp broke, he assigned Murakami to the minor league team to recuperate and regain his form.

CHAPTER 4

Unlike North American professional baseball, which contains hundreds of minor league teams organized into various tiers, each Japanese professional club has just one affiliated minor league team, known as the farm club or *ni-gun*. These teams are divided into two leagues based on the parent club's location. The Eastern League is centered on Tokyo and in 1962 included the farm teams of the Yomiuri Giants, Kokutetsu Swallows, Taiyo Whales, Toei Flyers, and Daimai Orions. The Western League, centered on the Osaka or Kansai area, consisted of farm teams of the Nankai Hawks, Hanshin Tigers, Hankyu Braves, Chunichi Dragons, Nishitetsu Lions, Kintetsu Buffaloes, and Hiroshima Carp. Most Japanese minor leaguers are young men straight out of high school. The veteran minor leaguer waiting for his chance to make the big league squad does not exist in Japan. Older players either ride the bench on the top club or are encouraged to find another career.

The Nankai Hawks had a dormitory for minor league players located in the Minami section of downtown Osaka, walking distance from the city's "pleasure quarters," which were "crowded with theaters, picture-halls, restaurants, cabarets, etc."[1] Plush with their first paychecks, many young players succumbed to the area's numerous temptations—ruining their careers by overindulging with drink and women. As Masanori was still a minor (the legal age of majority in Japan was twenty-one) and by his own admission rather naïve, Tsuruoka decided to board Murakami in his own home.

Masanori and fellow rookie Toshihiro Hayashi spent the season living on the second floor of Tsuruoka's house. For the year the boys were all but adopted. They shared meals with the Tsuruoka family, did chores, and obeyed household rules. Although Tsuruoka himself would often be on road trips with the *ichi-gun*, he and his wife Kazuko kept close tabs on the boys, keeping them away from liquor and women, as well as cautioning them on avoiding the *yakuza*, the organized criminals who often tried to influence the outcomes of sporting events.

"I was just an eighteen-year-old boy, knowing nothing about the world," Murakami remembers. "Except when I was at the ball field, I probably did many strange things. For example, to go to Osaka Stadium or the minor league facility at Nakamozu from Manager Tsuruoka's house, we took the Nankai train (owned by the same company that ran the Hawks). In the beginning Hayashi and I were always with the manager, so we just greeted the station staff and strolled through the entrance. Mr. Tsuruoka was so famous that everyone knew him and he passed through the gates freely, and Hayashi-kun and I just followed. I assumed that all Nankai players had a free pass to take a train. Later Hayashi and I went alone and continued to just walk through the gates. A few days later the station staff came to Mrs. Tsuruoka to complain, 'They take a train without buying a ticket.' We were scolded, and I'm still embarrassed by that."

The minor league season was monotonous—each practice day seemed to follow the same schedule. Practice at the farm team's training facility in Nakamozu began at 10:00 a.m. The players would stretch, run, and do calisthenics in unison. They would then play catch and move into agility games such as pepper. Fielding practice filled the rest of the morning. At midday they would break for a light lunch, usually rice balls consumed on the practice field. In the afternoon the team took batting practice, and pitchers would refine their craft—often throwing over a hundred pitches each day to develop their control.

Practice ended at 3:00 p.m. with running. The players then hit the communal bathtub in the clubhouse and changed into street clothes. If the Nankai Hawks *ichi-gun* was playing at home, the minor leaguers would take the train from Nakamozu to Osaka Stadium in the Naniwa section of the city. They would find unoccupied seats or stand in the aisles and study the action to learn the finer points of the game.

When the *ichi-gun* was on the road, the minor leaguers often had the nights off. Players would socialize, play pachinko, or enjoy the nightlife. "I had plenty of free time because I was mainly practicing at the farm in

Nakamozu," recalls Murakami. "I don't know why, but I didn't feel like playing pachinko, so I spent time chatting at a café or watching movies. Now I look back, I had such a great life."

The farm clubs played a forty-eight-game season, with most games held in the afternoons. As the majority of the Western League teams were in the Kansai area, the teams usually took buses to the opposing ball clubs and returned the same day. Occasionally, however, they would have to travel to Hiroshima, Fukuoka, or Nagoya. The *ni-gun* took the regularly scheduled express trains with reserved seats. The trains were comfortable but slow as the famous Shinkansen (Bullet Train) was still a few years in the future.

Minor league games were often dull. The purpose of the farm team was to train and instruct prospects, not to turn a profit or even to win. When Carlton Hanta became a Hawks farm team coach in 1966, Tsuruoka told him, "I don't care what the team's record is. Your responsibility is to develop players for the big league squad."[2] As a result, few people came to watch. Games were usually played in front of several hundred fans—five hundred was a large crowd.

As the 1963 minor league season began, Masanori's elbow continued to hurt. Simple tasks, such as washing his face or grasping objects, became painful. Sometimes it was no more than a dull ache. Other times the sharp stabbing pain seemed unbearable. At first, he tried the folk remedy of soaking the elbow alternatively in hot and cold water. The pain, however, continued. Finally, he went to the hospital and received injections—probably of cortisone, which was beginning to be widely used as an anti-inflammatory. A single injection allowed Murakami to pitch without pain for four to six days. By the end of the season he was taking two injections each week and pitching pain-free.

The Hawks sidelined Murakami for the first six weeks of the season, but with the injections he was ready to play in mid-May. His first start came on May 19 in Fukuoka against the Lions' farm team. It was not a particularly strong club. Although the team would finish the season in fourth place with a winning record, two games behind the Hawks, the team batting average would be just .244 for the season—the second lowest in the league. They were also free swingers, leading the league in strikeouts.

In his first official professional game Murakami threw sharp breaking curveballs to the inside corner of the plate and a fastball that, according to *Hochi Sports*, "is not seen in the Western League." The Lions' batters could barely get their bats on the ball. By the eighth inning Masanori had struck out 16 and had allowed just 2 hits. At times, however, he was unable to find the strike zone. At one point he loaded the bases with consecutive walks and then forced in a run with another free pass. Since this was his first game back, Murakami tired in the eighth and gave up consecutive home runs but managed to get out of the inning with his lead intact.[3]

As Murakami sat on the bench after the eighth inning, the official scorer came over to whisper that he was just two strikeouts shy of the league record. Murakami got the first two batters in the ninth, one by strikeout, and had two strikes on the third when the batter hit a foul pop near the first base stands. He yelled, "Don't catch it!" But the first baseman either ignored him or didn't hear and snagged the pop-up to end the game.

"I was a little annoyed," Murakami recalls, "as I thought I would certainly strike out the batter if I threw a curve ball. When I went back to the bench, the manager asked me if I would have set a record if I had struck out another batter. 'Yes,' I answered, and he scolded me for not telling him. But if I had told him, I'm sure that he would have scolded me by saying, 'Just throw your pitches and don't think about it!'"

After the game Hawks coach Susumi Yuki told reporters, "We know that he has ability to pitch for the top team. All we have to do is to make him learn how to sequence pitches." When asked about his performance, Masanori told the press nonchalantly, "It was nothing special. I became tired easily because I hadn't practiced enough. I will throw faster once I play more."[4]

Murakami pitched two more games in May, winning one and losing another, with a stellar 2.25 ERA. After he had pitched in just three games, his 26 strikeouts were the second highest in the Western League. On June 1 Nankai decided that he was ready for the top club. Tsuruoka told the press that he had been waiting for a long time to see Murakami pitch in the Japanese Major Leagues.[5]

Whatever elation Murakami may have felt with the promotion was quickly crushed. In his first pregame practice, nineteen-year-old Masanori was ordered to warm up with a group of older players. During the exercise he made an innocuous comment. "Shut up, rookie!" a veteran player snapped. After that he kept to himself and kept his mouth closed unless spoken to first.

Tsuruoka wasted no time acclimating Murakami to the Pacific League. On his first evening with the club the manager had Murakami pitch the top of the ninth, with the Hawks holding an 8–0 lead over the Daimai Orions. With the game in hand and no real pressure, it was the perfect opportunity for Murakami to debut. It was his first time pitching in a big stadium, and at first the bright floodlights blinded Masanori, but he settled down and faced Takeo Daigo, the Orions' burly catcher. Daigo, not known for his power and with a career .324 slugging percentage, nonetheless pounded Murakami's offering to deep left field. Luckily for Masanori, the ball stayed in the park—caught for a loud out.

After striking out the next batter, he then gave up a walk and a single to Kihachi Enomoto, one of the top hitters in Japan. Up next was the fearsome Kazuhiro Yamauchi. The sixteen-time all-star and future member of the Japan Baseball Hall of Fame could hit for power and average against both Japanese and Major League pitching. In 216 at bats against visiting Major League teams, Yamauchi would hit .301, the highest average ever by a Japanese with 100 or more at bats. On the mound Masanori was nervous and admitted after the game that "[I] was sweating a lot" when Yamauchi came to the plate. But soon he could give a sigh of relief as the star hitter popped out to catcher Katsuya Nomura to end the game.

Murakami's debut did not impress Tsuruoka or Nomura, as both noted that he did not throw particularly hard. "Murakami's pitches were not as fast as when I watched him on the farm club," the manager told the press after the game. "I was happy to be on the bench for the first time, but I became nervous," Murakami explained. "I was frightened by the long fly to left field by the first hitter, Daigo-san. I was truly relieved when I got Yamauchi-san to pop out to the catcher."[6]

After pitching on his first day with the club, Murakami sat on the bench for the next ten days. During practice he was relegated to the typical duties of a rookie—pitching batting practice and retrieving stray balls after drills. Afterward the rookies would wash the socks and undershirts of the more senior players. When the Hawks traveled by train, Murakami was responsible for carrying a case of one hundred balls, a fungo bat, and Tsuruoka's overnight bag, as well as his own clothes, uniform, and equipment.

On June 10 Tsuruoka gave Masanori another opportunity. The Hawks were already behind in the fourth inning against the Kintetsu Buffaloes when Hawks starter Eiichiro Takahashi allowed the first two batters to reach base; Tsuruoka decided to bring in Murakami to face the light-hitting left-handed

Shigeo Hasegawa. Hasegawa, who would hit just .171 that season, battled Masanori and after eight pitches drew a walk to load the bases. Tsuruoka has seen enough of his young pitcher. He brought in Mutsuo Minagawa to finish the inning and the next day demoted Murakami to the farm club.

Murakami would spend all but the tail end of the 1963 season in the minors. The team finished in third place with a 26–19–3 record, a few games behind the champion Tigers farm club, but as Carlton Hanta pointed out, winning was not the objective. Masanori emerged as the Hawks' top prospect, leading the team in every major pitching category. He won 7 games while losing 3 in 81⅔ innings. His 68 strikeouts were the third highest in the Western League, and his 1.87 ERA was fifth.

In October Tsuruoka once again promoted Masanori to the *ichi-gun*. He would pitch just one inning. Already losing 9–4 against the Toei Flyers on October 10, Tsuruoka brought him in at the top of the ninth. He retired the side, striking out a batter, but not before surrendering a one-run homer. Murakami's 1963 *ichi-gun* totals were unimpressive—a 4.50 ERA in 2 innings with 2 strikeouts, 2 walks, and 2 hits allowed.

Earlier in the season Masanori had telephoned Eikichi Hoshino, the man who had bought him coffee in 1960 during his only trip to Koshien. With his busy practice schedule, Masanori was unable to meet with Hoshino during the season, but they promised to keep in touch. Japanese professional players practice throughout the year with only short breaks in October, December, and the beginning of January. After the regular season ends, the players attend a fall training camp that lasts through most of October and November. In 1963 the Hawks finished in second place and had a week off before fall camp, while the Yomiuri Giants faced the Nishitetsu Lions in the Japan Series. Instead of returning home to Otsuki, Masanori decided to stay in Osaka and do some sightseeing. He had never been to Nara, the splendid capital of Japan from 710 to 784. Now a small town twenty-six miles to the southeast of Osaka, Nara contains some of Japan's most famous temples and shrines. He decided to ask Hoshino to give him a tour of the historic city.

Hoshino was busy, but his daughter Yoshiko had just returned from school and would be happy to take him. Masanori had not seen Yoshiko since their brief meeting on the train platform three years before. She gave him the grand tour. They visited Nara Park and saw the herds of deer that beg food from visitors; the famous five-story pagoda at Kofukuji Temple; the Daibutsuden, which contains a twelve-hundred-year-old, fifty-three-foot bronze statue of Buddha; and other highlights. But Masanori was not much of a conversationalist. The Japan Series had begun, and he had brought a small transistor radio and an earplug with him. He barely listened to Yoshiko as he concentrated on the play-by-play. Yoshiko kept her temper, as expected of a proper young lady, but was not pleased. What a boring young man, she thought. After they returned home for dinner with her father, they made no effort to see more of each other.

Murakami trained hard during the fall camp, but his elbow still ached. During the winter break before spring camp he went with his uncle to a hot spring near Nagano in Yamanashi Prefecture that was renowned for healing burns and nerve damage. Famous for its macaque monkeys who bathe in hot springs during snow storms and the site of the 1998 Winter Olympics, Nagano's winters are cold. For two weeks Masanori followed a regimen to cure his elbow. Four times a day he would run a mile through the snow-covered countryside before plunging into an ice-cold mineral spring and then soaking in a steaming hot spring. By the end of the trip the pain had disappeared.

With a healthy elbow Murakami pitched well during his second spring training. He felt that he should make the *ichi-gun* roster, but the competition was stiff. Nankai had a plethora of pitchers. The starters from 1962—Sugiura, Minagawa, Stanka, Miura, and Morinaka—were all in top form, and others, such as Masanori's 1963 housemate, Toshihiro Hayashi, were also throwing well.

On February 20, 1964, Masanori was lounging in the *ryokan* that housed the team during spring training when he was told that the manager wanted to speak to him. Exhibition games would start soon, and Murakami must have been apprehensive about the meeting. Would Tsuruoka be telling him that he would make the big club or spend another year on the farm team? He entered the manager's room and sat down. As usual Tsuruoka got straight to the point: "Hey, Murakami, it's been decided that you are going to the States."

CHAPTER 5

Masanori stood on the mound, took a deep breath, and stared toward home plate. A chilly gust of wind whipped at his jacket and bent the long, unmanicured infield grass. Two levels of steep grandstands rose beyond the batter's box. Behind him a large scoreboard, advertising dual-filter Tareyton cigarettes and Coca-Cola, towered high above the center-field fence. A single level of bleachers stood beyond the left-field fence. Today the seats were empty.

Masanori went into his windup, his charcoal gray sports jacket tugging under his armpits as he raised his hands above his head, his bright red tie dangling awkwardly from his neck. He threw an imaginary pitch over the plate as flash bulbs popped.

Candlestick Park! He imagined the stadium full of cheering fans as he faced down a Major League hitter. Then Masanori smiled. It was a wonderful picture but just a fantasy. No Japanese had ever played in the Major Leagues. Most experts agreed that Japanese baseball in the 1960s was equivalent to AA or maybe AAA baseball in the States and that only a handful of players were talented enough to possibly play in the big leagues. These players, such as Masaichi Kaneda, Shigeo Nagashima, and his Hawks teammate Tadashi Sugiura, were superstars in Japan not nineteen-year-old Japanese minor leaguers like himself. Still, it was fun to imagine.

Around the mound stood a few members of the San Francisco Giants front office; Kiyoshi Fujie, one of Nankai's coaches who could speak a little English; Cappy Harada, the liaison between the Hawks and the Giants; and two of Masanori's teammates, Hiroshi Takahashi and Tatsuhiko Tanaka.

Like Murakami, Takahashi and Tanaka were young prospects who the Hawks felt needed more seasoning. Takahashi, who was celebrating his eighteenth birthday that very day, had been a star catcher with Miyazaki Commercial High School. His .340 batting average had led Miyazaki to the 1963 Koshien summer tournament, but the team lost in the second round despite Takahashi going 4-for-4. With his laid-back personality he would adapt easily to American baseball and return to make the Nankai Hawks *ichi-gun* in 1965. He would remain in the Japanese professional leagues for eighteen seasons, mostly as a backup catcher and utility player. On September 29, 1971, however, he would make NPB history by becoming the first to play all nine positions in a single game. Tanaka was also eighteen years old and, like Takahashi, had starred in the 1963 Summer Koshien tournament. Playing third base and batting cleanup, Tanaka had helped Choshi Commercial High School reached the quarterfinals as he hit .438 with a home run. Unfortunately poor eyesight would end his career after just two years on the Hawks' farm team.[1]

After Tsuruoka had informed the trio that they would be going to the United States, the young men returned to Osaka to procure passports and visas and prepare for the trip. On March 7 the three travelers and Coach Kiyoshi Fujie took the train to Tokyo and spent the night at a *ryokan* near the Meiji Shrine at Harujuku. The next morning they dressed in business suits, piled their baggage into a taxi, and drove to Haneda Airport.

At the terminal a crowd of friends and family waited to say goodbye. Masanori's parents had procured a bus and brought down many of his relatives from Otsuki to wish him bon voyage. A group of high school friends also came to wish him well. After many bows (Japanese rarely hug), the passengers left the terminal and boarded the plane on the tarmac. Looking out of the small window, Masanori could see his family and friends crowded by the terminal windows, straining to see him. "I realized that they couldn't see me through the small airplane window, so I had an idea. I asked to borrow a flashlight from the stewardess, and using it, I wrote out my name in kanji on the window glass." His signal was spotted, and his well-wishers waived their final goodbyes as the plane taxied to the runway.

On the airplane Masanori finally had the opportunity to speak with Cappy Harada, the man responsible for—and later blamed for—Murakami's sojourn into American baseball.

Tsuneo "Cappy" Harada is ubiquitous in the first decade of postwar Japanese American baseball relations. If you examine a photograph of an important baseball event, he is likely to be in the background. Cappy's involvement with Japanese baseball started when he was just fourteen years old and the Yomiuri Giants visited his hometown of Santa Maria, California, during their 1936 tour of the United States. As a Nisei, Cappy grew up bilingual, so when the local white team needed a translator for the game with the visiting Japanese, they enlisted Harada. He conversed with the Giants and spoke with the team's traveling manager, Sotaro Suzuki, for some time.

Harada had played high school baseball and hoped to turn pro, but World War II intervened. With his bilingual background he was assigned to military intelligence. During the invasion of New Guinea he was working as a scout with the famed Navajo Code Talkers when their plane crashed behind the Japanese lines, leaving Harada injured and immobile. The Navajo tended his wounds for seventeen days until rescued by an Australian patrol. Cappy was reassigned to General Douglas MacArthur's staff and was shot during the invasion of the Philippines. Then, as he lay in a hospital bed recovering, a Japanese plane strafed the building, wounding him in the head. Somehow Cappy survived and recovered to rejoin MacArthur's staff during the Allied Occupation of Japan.

Harada became the aide-de-camp of General William F. Marquat, head of the Economic and Scientific Section General Headquarters for the Supreme Allied Powers. With his interest in baseball, Marquat put Harada in charge of restarting Japanese sports to help boost morale. Cappy began by clearing out the ballparks, which were being used by the occupational forces as motor pools. He helped restart both the high school and professional leagues, renewing his acquaintance with Sotaro Suzuki. In 1949 Harada worked with Frank "Lefty" O'Doul to bring the San Francisco Seals to Japan. During the tour's opening ceremonies Harada arranged for the American and Japanese flags to be raised in unison and both national anthems played for the first time since the war. The action moved many Japanese to tears and helped the Seals' tour become, in General Douglas MacArthur's words, "the greatest piece of diplomacy ever."[2]

In the early 1950s Harada retired from the military but stayed in Japan as an adviser to the Yomiuri Giants and a promoter. Critics complained that Cappy was best at promoting Cappy. Harada did have a predilection for self-aggrandizement and was often loose with the truth, but he also accomplished extraordinary things. He had a hand in bringing Wally Yonamine, the first American to play in Japan after World War II, to the Yomiuri Giants in 1951. He helped organize the 1951 MLB tour of Japan and escorted Joe DiMaggio and Marilyn Monroe during their 1954 Japanese honeymoon.

During the spring of 1953 Harada brought the Yomiuri Giants to his hometown of Santa Maria for spring training. Lefty O'Doul arranged games with Pacific Coast League clubs and the New York Giants, who held their spring camp in Phoenix, Arizona. It was during these exhibition games that Harada met Giants owner Horace Stoneham and developed a business relationship that would ultimately bring Murakami to San Francisco.

In the fall of 1954 Harada again took the Yomiuri Giants on the road, this time to Australia and South America. During these trips Harada acted as the traveling secretary, organizing games, hotel arrangements, and meals, and taking care of the personnel, but he styled himself as the general manager of the Yomiuri Giants. When the American press mistakenly began referring to Harada as the Yomiuri Giants' manager, Cappy made no effort to correct it. Even fifty years later Harada's obituary lists him as managing the Giants to four straight championships in the early 1950s.[3]

To repay Stoneham and the New York Giants for their hospitality during the 1953 spring training, the Yomiuri Giants invited their New York namesakes to Tokyo that fall. Harada once again acted as the intermediary between the two teams. The continued acquaintance with Stoneham led to a job offer, and in the late 1950s Cappy came to San Francisco to work for the Giants as a scout. By this time, however, Harada had upset baseball commissioner Ford Frick. His offenses are unknown, but in 1956 Frick had warned Dodger owner Walter O'Malley not to rely on Harada during Brooklyn's fall tour of Japan as he was "an unsavory character."[4]

While with the Giants, Harada continued as an intermediary between Japanese and American baseball. He helped with logistics for visiting teams and procured American players for Japanese teams. In late 1959 he had arranged a contract for Joe Stanka with the Nankai Hawks and three years later helped the Hawks obtain Kent Hadley. When the Hawks wanted to place Murakami with an American team, they once again turned to Cappy Harada.

Nankai retained Harada as an official adviser with the authority to negotiate contracts on the ball club's behalf and even sign agreements. His compensation for these services is unknown. Cappy immediately contacted Horace Stone-ham and began negotiations with the San Francisco Giants to train Murakami, Takahashi, and Tanaka for the 1964 season. The three would become the first players from the Japanese professional leagues to play in Organized Baseball. Stoneham was pleased to oblige, as "it would help Japanese American relations, and it was also good publicity for the Giants."[5] But Harada was still associated with the Giants and may have been on their payroll as a scout, a conflict of interest that would soon create an international incident.

The final contract between the Hawks and Giants was just over one typed page and was about as one-sided as possible. It contained eight points:

First, Nankai agreed to release the three players and allow them to sign standard player contracts with the Fresno Giants for the 1964 season at a salary of $400 per month.

Second, the Hawks would pay round-trip air fare for all three players.

Third, Nankai would pay the portion of the $400 salary that the San Francisco Giants would normally pay a farm club for holding one of its players. Furthermore, the Hawks would pay the employer's social security tax and the workmen's compensation premiums on the three players.

Fourth, the Giants "have the right to purchase the contracts and full right to the baseball playing services of the players . . . for a consideration of $10,000 per contract at the close of the [1964] baseball season."

Fifth, any players whose contracts were not purchased by the Giants would be given their unconditional release at the end of the 1964 season, but the Hawks could not transfer the released players to another team for one year without first offering the contract to the Giants.

Sixth, the Giants would pay the players' room and board, as well as provide uniforms.

Seventh, the Giants would furnish transportation for the players during the season.

Eighth, if the Giants concluded that any of the players were "too inexperienced or lacking the necessary ability to play professional baseball," they could be released and returned to the Hawks. On the other hand, if any of the players "shall become homesick or be unable to adjust themselves to living and playing in the Unites States and shall request to be sent home, they will be released unconditionally and returned to Japan."[6]

In January 1964 Harada met with the Hawks' managing director, Tsug-ihiro Iwase, and chief scout, Yoshio Tominaga, at his Tokyo apartment to examine the terms of the agreement. Harada later told reporters, "Iwase and Tominaga said they would consult the head officials of the Hawks' club in Osaka. They later informed me that the agreement was quite satisfactory."[7] Iwase, however, returned the contract to Harada unsigned. When Cappy asked why, Iwase reportedly replied that the president's signature was not necessary as Harada was acting as their agent and could sign the contract on the team's behalf.[8] Cappy, therefore, signed the agreement and returned it to the Giants.

The Giants sent along the standard release form used for agreements with winter ball teams in the Caribbean. Harada gave the document to Iwase, who returned it by messenger a short time later. The one-page document had two sections with blanks to be filled out for specific transactions. The first half, written in both English and Spanish, was to be completed by the club. It read, "To Player *Masanori Murakami*, you are hereby notified that you have been unconditionally released from all contractual obligation to this club. *Osaka Baseball Club, Japan (Pacific League)*," and it was signed by Tsugihiro Iwase, Managing Director. The second section, completed by the player, stated, "I hereby acknowledge receipt of unconditional release from the *Osaka Hawks Baseball Club*, and I understand that I am no longer under obligation to play for said club in any future Winter League season. I fur-ther understand that if I sign a contract for Summer League service with a National Association club that I may play Winter League baseball only if such club, or its assignee, consents." Without being able to read the docu-ment, Murakami had signed.[9]

Although all of the necessary documents had been completed and signed in January, the teams waited until February 22 to announce that the three players would train in the States. In retrospect it is obvious that the Hawks and Giants already had different interpretations of the agreement. Nan-kai viewed the agreement as an opportunity to have their prospects trained by American coaches so that the young players could return to Japan and lead the Hawks to future championships. The Nankai management did not expect the Giants to be interested in retaining the players and viewed the signed agreement as a mere formality for making the season abroad possible.

In a letter to Horace Stoneham, Tsugihiro Iwase wrote:

We would like to take this occasion of extending our sincere thanks for your invitation to our players who are to play and study advanced baseball.

It is needless to say that we are inferior to your baseball which has far advanced in skill, manner and knowledge as a professional baseball, but you may understand that baseball in Japan is the most popular next to that in the U.S.A. Here in Japan, people are most interested in baseball among many other sports, but we regret to say that the players are not well trained in skill and manner, and that there are more room for them to be trained.

In this connection, we have kept in mind the players' study plan in the U.S.A. for which you kindly offered us kindest cooperation and invitation to put into effect. As a matter of fact, it is most delighted and honorable to have our players join you, whom you are kindly requested to train well and strictly in every point.

We hope that this project will be contributing to cement close relationship between your club and ours, and further friendship between the United States of America and Japan through the medium of baseball.[10]

The San Francisco Giants, however, saw it not only as an opportunity to increase cooperation between American and Japanese baseball, but also as a chance to open the market for Japanese talent. The *Sporting News* wrote, "No one, either within the structure of the Giants or in Japan, expects any of the three to immediately shake up the 'big club' and play as regulars in the National League. But it represents the first step toward what the Giants feel is an inevitability—a Japanese on the varsity."[11]

Jack Schwartz, the administrative secretary of the Giants' farm system, told reporters, "It's a great benefit to Japanese baseball because they'll get a year of development in our farm system. And if one of them should be a Willie Mays or Mickey Mantle we'll certainly put him right on our roster."[12] For San Francisco the articles of the agreement with Nankai were binding, not just formalities.

The press on both sides of the Pacific, excited by the novelty of Japanese playing in American baseball, reported on the historic agreement. The *New York Times* printed a photograph of the three young players and ran a short

Associated Press article announcing, "The first three native Japanese baseball players ever signed by a United States major league club will play in the farm system of the San Francisco Giants this year. . . . Many United States major leaguers have gone to Japan to play, but this is the first time that the talent has flowed the other way."[13] The *Sporting News*, reprinting a longer story on the three players originally published in the *San Francisco Chronicle*, also noted that although many Japanese baseball teams had toured the United States or sent players to spring training camps, "this marks the first time Japan has sent any of its sons into Organized Baseball."[14]

Although Murakami, Tanaka, and Takahashi were the first players from Japanese baseball to sign with Organized Baseball, they were technically not the first Japanese nationals to make the jump. Prior to 1924 Japanese law dictated that any children of Japanese parents, regardless of where they were born, were subjects of the Japanese Empire. Under this criterion Andy Yamashiro, Kenso Nushida, and Jimmy Horio, all Japanese Americans with immigrant parents and all of whom had played in the minor leagues prior to World War II, had preceded the three Nankai Hawks prospects.[15]

As the Pam Am flight began its descent into San Francisco, nineteen-year-old Masanori Murakami knew little about the details of the agreement, nor did he care. He had only been told that he would train in the United States for a few months with the Giants' minor leaguers and then come home. "I looked out the window, down at the city," Murakami remembers, "and was so impressed with how beautiful the city was. It was like a dream."

CHAPTER 6

Just as preseason camp in Japan shocked American players, the Giants' spring training surprised Masanori. "The daily workouts in American spring training camps are too short," he told reporter Walt Averill. "The two to three hour working stint in the first days of spring training seemed like child's play to these rookies," Averill reported. "Grinning broadly, they pointed out through an interpreter, [Kiyoshi] Fujie, traveling secretary for the Nankai Hawks of Japan's Pacific League, that they are accustomed to practicing five or six hours and then playing a regulation game."[1]

The Japanese entourage of Murakami, Tanaka, Takahashi, Cappy Harada, and Fujie arrived in Phoenix, Arizona, by Western Airlines on March 12, after spending a few days sightseeing in San Francisco and Los Angeles. During the descent Masanori stared out the window at the vast desert. This was the country of *Rawhide*—what he had yearned to see. In Phoenix the group stopped at a souvenir shop, purchased white cowboy hats, and posed for photographs before paying their respects to Giants owner Horace Stoneham at his Arizona home. That evening they drove south for about an hour to the Giants' spring training facility, Francisco Casa Grande.

Under any circumstances the complex was extravagant, but after the Hawks' Spartan facilities at Kure, Francisco Casa Grande must have seemed astonishing to the young Japanese. Built just two years earlier in the middle of the desert, the complex was designed by Stoneham to be a self-contained baseball center during spring training and a resort open to the public for the remainder of the year. It contained a 450-person-capacity motor inn with a nine-story luxury tower topped by a roof shaped like a baseball cap, a bat-shaped pool, a ball-shaped hot tub, and an eighteen-hole championship golf course. Amenities included the Hall of Fame Cocktail Lounge and skytop penthouses. According to the 1965 Giants' yearbook, Francisco Casa Grande was "a desert showplace! With all the deluxe trappings, spacious lobbies and public rooms, and food and beverages to satisfy the most discriminating." Furthermore, it was all air-conditioned, and visitors could arrive on a private airstrip.[2]

The baseball facility consisted of a three-thousand-seat ballpark, usually reserved for Minor League exhibitions (the Major League Giants played at the brand new Phoenix Municipal Stadium), and four practice fields. In the center of the fields stood the crow's nest, a round observation platform with a roof providing escape from the desert sun. From the nest Giants officials could watch prospects at all levels of the organization.

The Giants' Minor League dormitories were cleaner and more modern than the Hawks' facilities, but they posed an unusual problem for the Japanese players accustomed to sleeping on the floor—bunk beds. Masanori quickly claimed one of the two lower beds and Takahashi grabbed the other, while Tanaka was relegated to a top bunk. This new experience became fraught with danger, as twice during the first few weeks Tanaka rolled over in his sleep and fell from his perch with a loud thunk, causing the others to spring from their beds. Luckily he was unhurt.

On their first morning the Japanese toured the complex before boarding a private jet (owned by a Giants' stockholder) and flying back to Phoenix to watch San Francisco's big league club take on the Cleveland Indians. For the three young Japanese it was their first Major League game, and the differences between American and Japanese baseball were eye-opening. Everything seemed bigger, faster, stronger. The stadium itself was huge—345 feet down the lines and 410 feet to dead center. Most Japanese stadiums at the time ran only 300 feet down the lines and 360 feet to center field. The trio were really surprised when Willie McCovey blasted a homer well over the outfield wall into the lot behind the stadium. "McCovey hit ball harder than Nomura," Murakami exclaimed to reporters in broken English. He was equally amazed by the Giants' ace, Juan Marichal, warming up on the sidelines. But what impressed the three the most was the hustle. Even in a spring training game the players ran out every ground ball or pop fly at full speed. In Japan, especially during exhibition games but even during the regular season, players were apt to trot to first on sure outs. The young newcomers realized that baseball was played at a different level here.[3]

Although spring training for the Giants' AAA and AA affiliates would not officially start until Monday, March 16, on March 14 the Japanese were told to suit up and report to the practice fields at 1:00 p.m. The fields were already spotted with players who had reported early and Latino walk-ons trying to gain a professional contract.

Masanori had barely finished warming up when two older men approached. The first was about six feet tall and lean, with short-cropped gray hair. Dressed in casual street clothes, even at sixty years old he looked fit enough to take the field. He introduced himself as Carl Hubbell, the director of the Giants' farm system. With little knowledge of Major League baseball at the time, Murakami did not know that Hubbell had been the ace of New York Giants teams of the 1930s and perhaps the greatest screwball pitcher in the history of the game. The second man, also close to six feet but with the solid build of a former catcher, wore the uniform of the Tacoma Giants. A bespectacled man of forty-two, he was Charlie Fox, the rookie manager of the Giants AAA team.

The two told Masanori to take the mound and put him through a full workout, noting his form and different pitches. Fox immediately picked up a problem and showed the young pitcher how to hide the ball in his glove as he went into his delivery so that batters would not see which type of pitch was coming.

Although Murakami had trained with the Hawks for a month and was in shape, he had not touched a baseball since leaving Japan. He lacked full command of his pitches and was disappointed with his performance. Hubbell, however, was pleased, telling reporters, "This boy has a real good, loose arm. He throws everything our pitchers throw—fastball, curve, slider and change-up. His fastball has a hop on it and his curve spins."[4]

After only about an hour on the playing field, the Japanese were told that practice was over and they had the rest of the day off. Confused by the short workout, they returned to their dormitory and later went to visit the famous Casa Grande fifteenth-century Native American ruins.

To Masanori's surprise, in his first days at Casa Grande, the most prevalent language wasn't English but Spanish. Initially the Japanese contingent shared the Minor League hotel with the large group of Latino walk-on players. Many were Mexican, but there were also Venezuelans, Puerto Ricans, and Dominicans (among others). In Japanese baseball there were no walk-on players at training camp. Each player was already under contract.

"It was unbelievable for us who only knew the world of Japanese baseball," Murakami remembers. "Some of the guys only had the clothes they were wearing. They didn't have any money. The Giants would let these players stay at the hotel, feed them three times a day, give them a few dollars, and watch them play until the main players arrived. These guys were trying desperately to make a rookie or A team. Some of them played so poorly that I wondered how they could even consider coming, but they didn't care. They were just desperate. Those low-level players were told to leave at once. Some were allowed to stay for a week; others would last for two. A few were able to sign professional contracts with the Giants, but their salaries were very low. The Hispanic guys were very friendly and easy to talk to, so I became very close to some on the day we met. They were always joking around. They taught me some Spanish, like 'good morning,' 'how are you,' and things like that. And they told me the basic swear words. I would say things like *Que pasa?* to the American players, and some actually thought that I could speak Spanish! But when I would go to the practice fields in the morning, some of my new friends would be gone, and by the next morning some more would have left. After seeing the situation, I realized how fortunate we Japanese were."

On March 16 the players from the AAA Tacoma and AA Springfield clubs reported to camp, and Hubbell assigned the three Japanese to train with Tacoma. One of the first things that Masanori noted was how many African American and Latino players were on the squad. Since signing Hank Thompson in 1949, the Giants, along with the Dodgers, had been at the forefront of integration. In 1951 Thompson, Willie Mays, and Monte Irvin formed the first all-black outfield, and in 1956 the Giants signed Ozzie Virgil as the Major Leagues' first Dominican player. In 1963 and 1964 the Giants would routinely field five or six non-white players in their starting lineup. In contrast, black players were rare in Japan. After Jimmy Bonna played seven games in the 1936 inaugural season of Japanese pro ball, only seven African Americans played in Japan from 1937 to 1964. Most of these signings were short-lived and concentrated, as John Brittain, Jimmy Newberry, Rufus Gaines, Alvin Spearman, and Larry Raines all played for the Hankyu Braves in 1952–1955, and Larry Doby and Don Newcombe played on the Chunichi Dragons in 1962.[5] The lone Latino player in Japan prior to 1964 was Cuban Chico Barbon, who joined the Braves in 1955 and still works for the organization.

Practice started at 10:00 a.m. and was light, consisting mostly of stretching, playing catch, and easy running. On the first day about fifteen pitchers took turns throwing batting practice for about fifteen minutes each. Masanori was not asked to pitch, so he shagged balls in the outfield. "The team [effort] was unexpectedly leisurely," he wrote in his diary that night. The three Japanese continued to practice with Tacoma for the next eight days. Most workouts consisted of little more than throwing, batting practice, and light running. They lasted just a few hours before players retired to the pool or golf course. Used to throwing a hundred pitches every day in Japan, Masanori asked if he could throw more, but his appeal fell on deaf ears as the coach told him to rest his arm. He would get to pitch his first real game on March 24 against the Cleveland Indians B team. On March 20, Murakami had a chance to warm up in an inter-squad game, pitching 2 innings. He did well, not allowing a hit and striking out 4 of the 6 batters he faced.[6] For the next three days the players barely practiced. They did some light running and played exhibition games, but Murakami did not get to pitch. Bored and edgy from the inaction, Masanori decided to increase his workout with calisthenics, including jumps from a squatting position. A coach quickly stopped him, telling him that the exercise was not good for his knees. A little frustrated, he wrote in his diary, "It seems that they don't practice as hard as Japanese players do in camp." He told a reporter, "In Japan, we run and get in shape for two weeks before we even play any ball. Here, they've had us playing games since our arrival and we've been doing a lot of sitting around."[7]

Later Murakami realized that the American players were using the first weeks of camp to get back in shape after four months off. They were gradually easing into the routine to prevent injuries. Under the more rigorous Japanese system with year-round practice and only a few weeks off in late December and January, Masanori and his countrymen stayed in constant playing shape, with little need to rebuild their bodies each spring.

It rarely rained in the desert surrounding Casa Grande, but when Masanori awoke on March 24, the day he was supposed to pitch, rain drummed against the windows. The shower was short-lived, but it left the field unplayable and forced the Giants to cancel the game. Before giving them the day off,

Charlie Fox called the three Japanese players to his office. The following day the three were to report to the Fresno Class A team for practice. They were being demoted. He had an ability to win 20 games, Fox told Murakami, if he could master throwing all of his pitches—fastballs, curves, and change-ups—from the same position. "I was disappointed," Murakami recalls. "I already had a sharp breaking ball, and most single A-level players were not at that level yet, but I told myself to do my best even in the lower-ranked team."

The Giants' front office had always felt that Fresno was the ideal team for the young Japanese visitors. Fresno was in the single A California League. The roster was filled with young prospects, and the emphasis was on instruction and building experience through league play. The level of competition would be high enough for the Japanese to experience American baseball and improve their skills but not so high that they would take playing time away from the Giants' primary prospects. Fresno and other cities in the California League also had large Japanese communities, providing a sympathetic fan base for the only Japanese in organized ball and a support network should the young boys feel homesick. Indeed members of the Japanese American community had already offered the Fresno Giants' business manager, Tom McGurn, their assistance in housing the players.[8]

Bill Werle managed Fresno. Like Murakami, Werle had been a left-handed pitcher during his playing days with the San Francisco Seals (1943–1948), Pittsburg Pirates (1949–1952), St. Louis Cardinals (1952), and Boston Red Sox (1953–1954). More important for the Japanese players, Werle had played under Lefty O'Doul, who had helped organize the 1934 All-American tour of Japan and had helped create Japanese professional baseball. O'Doul was enamored with Japan and felt that the mutual love for baseball would better Japanese American international relations. In 1949, when O'Doul brought his Seals on their goodwill tour of the Land of the Rising Sun, Werle came along, even though his contract now belonged to the Pirates. The future manager of Fresno enjoyed Japan greatly and returned two years later, when O'Doul and Joe DiMaggio toured with a team of all-stars. During his two trips Werle studied the culture and even learned a little Japanese. The Giants were confident that Werle could make the boys feel comfortable.

That evening Cappy Harada stopped by to talk to Masanori about the assignment. He explained that it was usual for young players to spend a year in single A ball before moving up the Minor League ladder. "If that is the case," Murakami responded, "I would like to stay in the U.S. for two years" and asked Harada to contact Tsuruoka to ask if this was possible.

On Wednesday, March 25, Murakami, Takahashi, and Tanaka joined the Fresno Giants for practice. Prior to their arrival Werle had held a team meeting. He told his young players to treat their new foreign teammates with respect and warned them to never use the term "Jap." After a light workout Masanori drove to Phoenix for the evening with his new teammates, ate Chinese food, shopped, and went to the dog races. It was his first experience "hanging out" with American teammates; he loved it, but it became an expensive night as he dropped $50.

Masanori would finally get his chance to pitch against an opposing team on Friday, March 27, so Thursday was spent in preparation. He ran, played catch, practiced fielding, and at long last threw hard. After he had not pitched at full speed for some time, his arm felt stiff and his shoulder began to hurt. He decided to ignore the pain and finish the workout.

For the second consecutive night a group from the team went into Phoenix for the evening. Murakami went along but this time decided to watch his money carefully. He had brought the equivalent of $400 with him from Japan, expecting to receive his salary from the Giants at the end of March. He had spent money freely so far. Everything seemed so new and interesting, and he wanted to try different foods and experience American culture. Now most of the $400 was gone.

The next day Fresno faced Springfield, the Giants' affiliate from the AA Eastern League. Masanori came in the seventh inning and finished out the game. No box score for the game has been located, but Murakami wrote in his diary, "I couldn't pitch as I wanted because of the shoulder pain, [but] I felt very good when I got a strikeout with a change-up. I have been working on this pitch while in the United States."

That afternoon Cappy Harada and Kiyoshi Fujie came to say goodbye to the three Japanese players. Harada would return to his travel agency in California, and Fujie needed to return to the Nankai Hawks in Japan. The two had acted as the players' interpreters and had helped ease their acculturation into American spring training. But from here on out Masanori and his two young countrymen would be alone to fend for themselves.

Without their interpreters the trio were forced to interact more with their new American teammates. Armed with his ever-present Japanese-English dictionary, Masanori joined the Americans as they hitchhiked to town to shop or eat out. Soon he was eating regularly with some of his teammates and playing pool with them in the evenings. Murakami found most of them friendly, helpful, and fun. There was an easygoing openness about Americans he found refreshing and enjoyable. They did their best to communicate, show him how to do things the American way, and teach him English.

Bill Werle told Tom Meehan of the *Fresno Bee Republican* that Masanori "gets along with the boys real well. In fact, all three [Japanese] have been real good boys to work with. They have been accepted 100 per cent by the players. They joke around and manage a smile when the joke is on them." Meehan's article continued: "The Japanese players have picked up a few English base-ball terms, some of which cannot be printed. They always bring a roar from the other players when the Japanese utter the phrases. When Murakami worked in relief this week, he struck out the first two batters on seven pitches and had two strikes on the third. The batter ripped the next pitch for a single. Two English cuss words escaped from catcher Takahashi which brought more laughter from the Giants than a three-ring circus. The game was delayed until the Fresno play-ers regained their composure and Murakami then struck out his third batter."[9]

Following this first outing, Masanori practiced lightly and rested his arm over Easter weekend, but his shoulder continued to throb. After the elbow injury the previous season, he was now quite worried. He had no idea why it hurt and was unable to explain his concerns to Werle. If the shoulder did not heal soon, it might jeopardize his season in the United States. Being sent home would be unbearable. He went to the trainer for a massage but, used to the professional masseurs in Japan, found the treatment unsatisfactory. Nev-ertheless, the rubdown loosened the joint, and he pitched three solid innings against Springfield on Tuesday, March 31, surrendering three hits and no runs.

It was the final day of March, but the paychecks for the Japanese players still had not arrived. Now that Fujie and Harada had left, they were unable to communicate the problem to the Giants' management. The three decided to pool their resources and conserve their money until payday. Despite being short, Masanori needed a haircut. He hitched a ride into town and found a barber. With broken English and a lot of hand gestures, he managed to com-municate but ended up with an unevenly cropped head.

The shoulder pain continued for the remainder of spring training. Masa-nori became convinced that it derived from the lack of hard training and decided to throw hard every day to loosen the joint and build arm strength. Werle, however, disagreed and ordered Murakami to rest between games.

Masanori pitched well in the exhibition games, often dominating single A and double A opponents with his curve. He continued to work on his change-up. The pitch was improving, but he still had much to learn. After Masanori gave up a two-run home run against El Paso, Giants slugger Orlando Cepeda, who was watching the game, took him aside to explain that a change-up was less affective once a pitcher had two strikes on a batter. A week later, after a batter singled on a change-up with two outs, Werle realized that Muraka-mi's change-up was too slow. After the game, he explained, "If your fastball is thrown at 100 percent, you are throwing your change-up at 50 percent, so the batter has time to be ready. Your change-up needs to be three-quarters of your fastball's speed."

Werle started by using Masanori for two- or three-inning stints, but as the preseason progressed, instead of allowing him to start games, Werle began using him just in the ninth inning in the role now known as the closer, although the term did not become common until the 1980s. As Murakami had been a starter in Japan, he viewed this new role as a demotion. Just before the end of the training camp, Murakami confronted his manager to ask why he was not allowed to start. Werle explained that he needed relievers with good control.

"But," Masanori countered, "I was told in Japan that I don't have good control, and I prefer to be a starter."

"You have very good control, so you're best suited for relief," was the terse reply. A little confused and unhappy Murakami acquiesced.

The idea of a relief specialist was unheard of in Japan and even a relatively recent development in American baseball. In the early days of the Major Leagues and in Japanese baseball during the early 1960s, a starting pitcher was expected to finish his games. In 1905, for example, Major League start-ing pitchers completed more than 80 percent of their games. Pitchers who were knocked out and unable to finish a game were usually relieved by other starters. The percentage of complete games in the Major Leagues gradually declined, making relievers more common by the 1930s. At first relievers were primarily used in mop-up roles and were pitchers who could not make the starting rotation.[10]

That began to change in the 1920s, when Washington Senators manager Bucky Harris began using his top reliever, Firpo Marberry, to protect leads in close games rather than just finish games already lost. Marberry became Major League Baseball's first true star reliever. Over the next few decades not all managers adopted Harris's innovation, but enough did to produce a series of star relievers such as the Yankees' Joe Page and the Phillies' Jim Konstanty. Unlike today mid-century managers did not wait until the ninth inning to deploy their top relievers but instead used them in any key situation. It was not unusual for a relief ace to enter in the sixth inning and to finish the game. For example, in his 1950 MVP season, Konstanty threw 152 innings in 74 games, averaging over 2 innings per appearance. Twice, in the heat of the pennant race, he pitched 9 or more innings in one game—all in relief.

At the time, teams had just one or perhaps two reliable relievers. The relief corps, as we now know it, was nonexistent. That began to change in the 1950s, when Yankee manager Casey Stengel started platooning his position players.[11] Most batters have more trouble hitting pitchers who throw from the same side as they bat—thus left-handed hitters generally have more difficulty hitting a left-handed pitcher than a righty. For some batters that difficulty is acute. Stengel tried to overcome this tendency by stacking his lineups with right-handed batters when they faced a left-handed pitcher and vice versa. To accomplish this, his Yankee teams had two players, a lefty and a righty, for some positions; the starting player would be determined by the opposing pitcher.

To combat these platooned lineups, opposing managers needed both left-handed and right-handed quality relief pitchers. By the early 1960s nearly all Major League teams had a bullpen stocked with lefty and righty pitchers who specialized in relieving. These pitchers, however, were used differently than today. They were expected to pitch for an inning or two rather than a batter or two. The modern specialized bullpen would not emerge until the late 1980s. Japan would not adopt relief aces in the mold of Marberry, Page, and Konstanty until the mid-1970s.

Werle told the press, "Murakami has all the assets to become a Major League relief pitcher if he continues to develop. He has great control, ice in his veins, brains between his ears, and he's a low-ball pitcher."[12] Murakami did display extraordinary control during the exhibition games. In 15 innings pitched, Masanori gave up just 8 hits for 5 runs (all scored on 2 home runs), struck out 14 batters, and walked nobody. "This boy's control is amazing," Werle bragged to reporter Walt Averill while they watched Murakami strike out 2 batters in succession on 6 pitches and then force the next to pop out. "He hasn't issued a walk all spring. He's probably the only pitcher on my staff who can be depended on to throw the ball where the catcher wants it."[13]

A week before the end of camp the Giants made their final roster cuts. Tanaka and Takahashi would be sent to Twins Falls, Idaho, in the Rookie League, while Murakami would stay with Fresno. "It was hard to break up the Japanese boys but Takahashi and Tanaka need more experience," explained San Francisco's Minor League traveling secretary Jack Schwarz. "They've shown up well in the field but they've done very little with the bat," Werle added. "We know Japanese players don't have great power, but we did expect these kids to hit better."[14] Werle seemed to expect bigger things from Murakami. "I'm real happy to have Murakami. He has been amazing. He still is young and if he is not bothered by night baseball and the crowds, he has the makings of going a long way."[15] As the Rookie League did not begin until June 20, all three Japanese would begin the season in Fresno.

Spring training for the Minor Leaguers ended on Friday, April 17, with a mixed-squad game with the Springfield AA Giants. Masanori finished camp with a flourish, striking out 5 of the 6 batters he faced. That evening the Fresno Giants sang "California Here I Come" as they packed their bags. Although most players only knew the song's first two lines, they taught them to the Japanese so that they could join the harmony. This, Murakami must have thought, was sure different from the Japanese leagues![16]

CHAPTER 7

Masanori's first days in Fresno were challenging. They had boarded the team bus in Casa Grande at 6:00 a.m., and an hour later the bus blew a tire in the middle of the desert. The team disembarked and waited for two hours as the driver fixed the wheel. Several hours later a second tire went. After twenty hours, they limped into Fresno at 2:00 a.m. The team put the Japanese and other rookies into a nearby hotel for the first few days but made it clear that they were expected to find and pay for their own housing. That posed a problem.

Murakami and his countrymen were nearly out of money. They had only a few dollars left among them from the cash they had brought from Japan, and the Giants still had not paid them. For the past week or so they had been pooling their money and sharing meals. Cappy Harada had made arrangements for a local Nisei to meet the ballplayers and help them get settled, but the man never materialized.

After a few days the boys found a branch of the Bank of Tokyo in Fresno's Japantown. They explained who they were and received a small cash loan and a promise to help them find a place to live. A day or two later bank employees brought the boys to Japantown to look at a house for rent. The exterior was made of brick, but it was small and run down. Uneasily they went inside. They looked at each other in disbelief. There was just one room with a dirt floor and a single small window. It was no more than a shed. The boys walked out.

As they stood confused on the sidewalk outside the slum, a young Japanese American approached them. "What are you doing here?" he demanded in English. The bank employees explained. "You don't have a place to live, do you? Why don't you live with us? I'll call my mother," he said. On the way to a telephone the man explained that he was Howard Saiki, and he had recognized the ballplayers from their photographs in the newspaper. His parents owned a large house with an orange grove and even a swimming pool. They also spoke Japanese. A few minutes later it was all arranged. Saiki's mother had told him to bring the boys straight over. They could stay for free.

The Saikis were among the older Japanese American families in Fresno. In many ways their life was typical of most Japanese Americans living in California. Howard's grandfather, Rokuro Okusa, had left the town of Hagi in Yamaguchi Prefecture on the southern tip of Japan's main island of Honshu in 1898 to find a better life in the United States. Rokuro was among the earlier Japanese to settle in California. Prior to his arrival fewer than eighteen thousand of his countrymen had immigrated to mainland United States. Another eighteen thousand would immigrate in the next three years, followed by thirty-five thousand more before the 1907 Gentlemen's Agreement between Japan and the United States barred Japanese laborers from entering the country. The vast majority of these early immigrants were single men, hoping to make quick fortunes before returning to Japan. Their dreams of swift financial success, however, were hampered by strong anti-Japanese sentiment among white Americans. Most Japanese immigrants found themselves relegated to menial labor; many found work on the railroads or as agricultural laborers.

Rokuro's life was different. He settled in Fresno, married Yoneko Saito, and started a business selling bicycles. They were two of the six hundred Japanese living in Fresno County at the time. In 1904, however, Rokuro's infant died, followed shortly by his wife. Rokuro returned to Japan in 1909, married Mime Saiki, and took her last name to carry on the family line. The couple came back to Fresno in August 1909.

Rokuro continued to sell bicycles while Mime, who had graduated from Koto Shihan Gakko, a school in Tokyo that trained women to be high school teachers, taught at the local Japanese school. In the mid-1910s the couple settled at 1558 North Ninth Street, where they raised vegetables and grapes and ran a poultry farm. California's 1913 Alien Land Law, however, prohibited the Saikis and all other "aliens ineligible for citizenship" from owning the property or leasing it for more than three years. Like many Japanese immigrants,

Rokuro probably circumvented the law by having their American-born daughter Setsu purchase the property.

Rokuro and Mime had six children before they died together in an automobile accident on September 16, 1940. Upon their death Kiyoto, their twenty-seven-year-old son and third child, inherited the property.

Kiyoto ran a business identifying the gender of chickens. Most hatcheries raise only females and destroy male chicks just after birth. To conserve feed and space the hatcheries must determine a chick's gender within a few days of birth. "Chicken sexing" was a highly skilled trade that originated in China and was perfected in Japan. In 1935 Kiyoto traveled to Nagoya to attend the International Chicken Sexing School. When he returned to Fresno, his business flourished, and he became one of the most sought-after chicken sexers in the industry.

Within a year of Kiyoto's inheriting the farm, World War II began, and the U.S. government incarcerated Japanese Americans living on the West Coast. Kiyoto and his new bride, Fumiko Nishioki, moved to Minnesota for the war's duration, thus escaping the detention camps. While most Japanese Americans lost their homes and businesses during their absence, German friends of the Saikis cared for the house and readied it for their return in 1946. Twenty years later Kiyoto and Fumiko still lived at 1558 North Ninth Street. They had four children—two sons, Howard and Gregory, and two daughters, Jereann and Janis.[1] With the three young ballplayers the house became crowded.

In 1964 Kiyoto still ran his chicken sexing business and had interests in several other small enterprises. He generally left the home at 4:00 a.m. and was in bed by the early evening. The Japanese ballplayers rarely saw him except on holidays. Instead Fumiko Saiki took care of them. She did their laundry, cooked their meals, and drove them around town. "They were so kind," recalls Murakami. "Thanks to Mr. and Mrs. Saiki, our lives in Fresno became extremely comfortable. My real American life started when I began living in their house."

The Fresno Giants met at John Euless Park for their first practice on their home field on April 19. Since he was expecting a grand venue, the ballpark disappointed Murakami. "It was a dirty stadium. There were so few lights that I wondered if it was possible to play a night game. There were only four small lights. The outfield fence was a dirty wood wall. When a deep fly ball was hit and I looked back at the fence, I couldn't even see the ball." Built in 1941 as Fresno State College Park, the playing field was larger than most Japanese fields, measuring 407 feet to dead center and 335 feet down the lines. It could hold 3,500, fans but the Fresno Giants rarely drew more than 1,000 on a good night.

At the end of practice Bill Werle emerged from a storage room with four cardboard boxes and addressed the team. Murakami could only pick up a word or two here and there, and he glanced at Tanaka and Takahashi dumbfounded when the other players rushed to the boxes and began rifling through them. Players pulled out pants and jerseys, occasionally swapping garments with each other. Realizing that they were picking out their game uniforms, the Japanese walked over to find the boxes nearly empty. Masanori reached into a box and discovered a lone home uniform left at the bottom, number 6. Luckily it fit. A single jersey also remained in the away uniform box, but it was number 8. He showed the different numbers to Werle, who shrugged. It would be okay to have different numbers for home games and away games, he finally said.

On April 21 the Fresno Giants opened the 1964 season at home. A record crowd of 2,575 watched staff ace Pedro Reinoso pitch a complete game, a 5–1 win over the Salinas Mets. Reinoso, a Dominican left-hander, would lead the California League with 18 wins and post a 2.88 ERA. He would be stellar again in 1965 but would never make it to the Majors. Yet Fresno's true strength lay in its hitting. Outfielder Ollie Brown, who would have a thirteen-year Major League career, would pound 40 home runs to lead the circuit and hit .329. Bobby Taylor, another outfielder who would play briefly for the 1970 San Francisco Giants and later three seasons in Japan, would lead the league with a .364 batting average. A solid cast of career Minor Leaguers backed up these stars.

Murakami watched from the bullpen for the entire three-game series against Salinas. He warmed up several times but was not sharp. Used to throwing hard every day, he had not faced a live batter for five days and had lost his edge. The American belief that pitchers should rest their arms still confounded him.

After dropping a 2–1 game to Salinas on April 23, the ballplayers boarded the team bus for the six-hour drive to Santa Barbara. It was Murakami's first road trip in the States, and the distances between cities amazed him. The main

Japanese island of Honshu contains 88,996 square miles, making it 56 percent the size of California, but ball clubs rarely drove between cities. With one of the most efficient rail networks in the world, Japanese could cover hundreds of miles quickly and comfortably. Having to endure six hours in a cramped bus seat and then play a ballgame at the end of the trip seemed ludicrous.

That evening the Giants met their rivals—the Santa Barbara Dodgers at Laguna Park. Fresno lost control of the game early as the Dodgers tallied 5 runs off starter Bobby Jones in the first three innings. Werle brought in Murakami to start the fifth inning, probably thinking that with nothing at stake it would be a good time for the young Japanese to make his professional debut. Masanori dazzled. He breezed through the Santa Barbara lineup for 5 no-hit shutout innings as Fresno battled back to take the lead. Using what the umpire called "a Major League curve ball," Murakami struck out 9 batters en route to his first win. "When the game was finished and everyone came to me and shook my hand, I was very happy. Even though it was a single A game, I thought it was worth coming to the U.S." Murakami had accomplished what no other native Japanese had ever done: he had won a game in Organized Baseball.

A week later, in front of just 433 hometown fans, Fresno was clinging to a 4–3 lead over the Baltimore Orioles' affiliate, the Stockton Ports, in the seventh inning, when the visitors loaded the bases with just one out. With the game on the line Werle signaled for Murakami to come on in relief to face left-hander Ferdinard Reed. Fresno brought the infield in hoping to cut off the tying run at home when Reed hit a soft line drive down the line. Third baseman Bob Powell dove, spearing the ball at the last moment to save at least a run. According to the *Fresno Bee Republican*, "Murakami then did something which is not seen in American baseball. He walked off the mound and halfway to third base and thanked Powell for making the catch. Then Murakami took over. He struck out long ball hitting Larry Smith to end the threat [and was] given a standing ovation by the fans. However, the best was yet to come [as] Murakami, with a sneaky fast ball, a Major League curve and uncanny control, struck out the side in the eighth." In the ninth Masanori retired the first two batters before he gave up his first hit in 8⅓ professional innings—a double. With the tying run on second, "the tension mounted as Murakami faced Michael Gordon, who had collected two doubles and a single in three trips. Murakami never faltered as he struck out the slugging third baseman to end the game [and then] was mobbed by his teammates."[2]

Although he could not hold a conversation in English, the adventuresome Murakami became popular in the clubhouse. He readily joined groups going out for meals or other excursions. Unable to read menus, Masanori often pointed to another diner's plate and said, "Same" or ordered a standard item like a hot dog or hamburger. Hot dogs, cheap and unavailable in Japan, had become one of his favorite meals. He brought his bilingual dictionary everywhere, pointing to the English translation of Japanese phrases to help him communicate. Some teammates helped him learn the language by patiently repeating words until he mastered them. Others took advantage of the situation—like the prankster who taught him the "correct phrase" with which to greet his host-mom.

When he arrived home, Masanori greeted Fumiko Saiki with his new phrase—consisting mostly of vulgarities. She gasped in surprise and ran to find her husband. Kiyoto Saiki strode over, obviously upset. "Why did you say that?!" he demanded in Japanese. Confused, the young man explained. Saiki curtly explained that he was never to use those words again and that if he used them in public, he could be arrested.

Most of Masanori's teammates had difficulty saying his name. Instead of pronouncing his last name Mura-kami, they often said My-raka-mi. The less linguistically talented could only manage something uncomfortably close to macaroni, no matter how many times he repeated the correct pronunciation. They had just as much trouble with his first name. Masa-nori became Masumu-ri. For some reason, he noted, Americans had trouble saying "masa." His teammates soon settled on Mashi or sometimes Massy. It was easy for them to say and close enough to his name to make Masanori comfortable. Even today Murakami usually signs English letters and autographs "Mashi."

To attract Fresno's Nikkei population to the ballpark and to honor their popular reliever, the Giants decided to hold Japanese American Baseball Night at Euless Park on May 6—not coincidentally Murakami's twentieth birthday. In the second game of a doubleheader Murakami would be given the start, and Tanaka and Takahashi, although not technically on the Fresno roster, would also be in the starting lineup. Ceremonies before the game would include the presentation of gifts to the players from the Japanese American community and speeches from Consul General Tsutoru Wada of San Francisco and Giants owner Horace Stoneham. Proceeds from the game would be donated to the Fresno Japanese Athletic Club's Sansei Baseball Team for 15–20 year olds.

The night before the special day the Nikkei community threw a party for the players at the Fresno Buddhist Church Annex. About a hundred guests came to meet manager Bill Werle and his three Japanese players and listen to speeches by community leaders. The next morning Fumiko Saiki baked Masanori a large birthday cake and hosted a party in his honor. The weather, however, would ruin the big day. Snow had already postponed three of the four games at Reno earlier in the week, and the previous night's game at Euless Park had been rained out. With the forecast reading "scattered showers and possible thunderstorms," the Giants decided to postpone Japanese American Baseball Night and the second game of the double header. Nonetheless, before the remaining game, fans celebrated Masanori's birthday with a standing ovation. "When I got to the stadium, I was told to address the crowd," Murakami remembers. "I was shy, but I said a few words while everyone applauded. An old American couple, who came to the stadium often but whose names I never knew, gave me a homemade cake. I was really impressed by the warmth of Americans."

Not all Americans, however, were so hospitable. The horrors of World War II and the distrust of Japanese remained fresh in some minds—and one of these belonged to a teammate. Several days after Masanori's birthday the team traveled to Bakersfield. As they warmed up for the game on May 9, a few of the players were horsing around and began teasing Murakami. Masanori often joked with his teammates and was known for his good sense of humor, but this time one player became nasty and made racial slurs.[3] At first Masanori tried to ignore him, but the comments were relentless and increasingly sarcastic and offensive.

"Shut up!" Murakami yelled, but this only encouraged the bully. With the game about to begin, the players trudged onto the field, formed a line, and removed their caps for the national anthem. Murakami remained on the bench. "I just blew my top. I decided that I wasn't going to respect the national anthem of the man who said these things to me. So I didn't line up for the anthem but sat on the bench with my back to the ball field. Now that I think back on it, I wonder how I could have made such a bold protest. But I was so angered by that one American's abuse about my being Japanese."

Once the game started, the player approached Murakami and demanded to know why he had turned his back. Masanori ignored him and remained silent. "Other teammates seemed to understand how much the abuse hurt me, and they came over to flatter me, but I kept showing my back and remained silent. We won the game 15–11. There were a lot of hits, and it was a long game. But for me, remaining silent, it was a long, long game. After that incident no one made sarcastic racist comments to me."

During his time at Fresno Murakami had only one other unpleasant incident. He now feels that he wasn't targeted for being Japanese but that the pranksters believed that a "passive Japanese" would not challenge them.

"We traveled by bus. Sometimes the trips took two hours, sometimes as much as eight. I brought an 8mm camera to shoot the landscape through the bus window, so I always sat in the front seat. On one of the longer trips, probably to Reno, I fell asleep. I woke up when something hit my head. I turned around and looked behind me, but everyone was just sitting there, pretending nothing had happened. I settled into my seat again to go back to sleep when something hit my head again. Somebody was throwing crumpled pieces of paper at me. I turned around again. and everybody still pretended that nothing had happened. 'Stop it!' I yelled. But they wouldn't. After about the fourth time, I stood up and grabbed a large wrench that was under the driver's seat. I was so angry. I knew pretty much who was throwing the paper at me, but I went to each and every one of the twenty teammates on that bus, stared at them, and shouted, 'Is it you? Is it you?' My eyes must have been on fire because of the anger and my right hand, which was holding the wrench, must have been shaking. All of them said, 'No, it wasn't me.' It seemed that they were blown away by my spirit—standing up to them with a wrench in my hand. I knew I had won.

"On that day I decided to continue that attitude in the U.S. It was not that I would act big. I would try to get along with other people. But if someone messed around with me because I was Japanese, I would stand up and face it."

In early May Murakami settled comfortably into his role as the team's top reliever as the Giants pulled off 10 straight victories. He gained his second win on May 7 as he came on against the San Jose Bees in the top of the ninth with 1 out, a runner on first, and the score deadlocked at 3–3. Masanori then retired the next two batters, and in the bottom of the inning reached base on an error that set up a game-winning single by Bobby Taylor. Five days later he closed out the Giants' 7–4 win over the Modesto Colts. After he struck out 5 Colts to preserve another Giants win on May 14, sportswriters outside of Fresno took notice. "Masanori Murakami, a curve ball specialist from Japan, is aiming to become the first from his country to play in the American Major Leagues," claimed a May 15 Associated Press article. A day later, in an article headlined "Japanese Import Yields One Hit in First 8⅓ Innings," the *Sporting News*, known as the Bible of Baseball, quoted umpire Bob Sievers: "He's got a major league curve right now and he threads the needle with his fast ball. I think this boy has definite potential as a big leaguer."[4]

On May 19 Fresno was ready to host the second Japanese American Baseball Night, and this time it went off without a hitch. As in the postponed event, Murakami would start the second game of a scheduled double header, and the break between the games would be filled with ceremonies honoring the three Japanese players.

By the time the Giants defeated the Reno Silver Sox 7–5 in the opening game, 1,593 fans had arrived for Japanese American Baseball Night—three to four times the usual weeknight attendance. Special guests included Lord Abbott Kosho Otani, head of the Japanese Buddhist sect Jodo Shinshu Hongwanji-ha and cousin to the emperor of Japan; Wallace Henderson, Fresno's mayor; and numerous dignitaries from the city's Japanese American community and government. Neither Horace Stoneham nor Consul General Tsutoru Wada could be present, but they sent congratulatory telegrams that were read before the crowd. The *San Francisco Examiner* sent sportswriter Will Connolly to cover the event. In his colorful description, full of stereotypes and "oriental" imagery absent in the *Fresno Bee Republican*'s articles, Connolly noted that "the ceremony was ornamented by Marie Nakai, a doll in a pinkish kimono, she being 'Miss Bussei' of central California, and distributor of plaques from the local Issei-Nisei community to the three players from afar. At home plate, nobody in the stands whistled at her. It was that kind of a disciplined crowd. But they ogled."[5]

Murakami took the mound to start the second game. So far he had been nearly unhittable in California League play. In 15 innings he had surrendered only 4 hits and 3 walks. Nobody had scored off him, and he had struck out 24—almost half of the batters he had faced. Reno was not a strong team. It languished in last place with a 7–19 record, but Masanori couldn't help thinking, "There was no way I was going to lose this game, but it was my first game as a starter, and if I was hit hard and lost, I would be too embarrassed to walk on the street."

That bit of self-doubt manifested itself soon after the national anthem ended. Reno leadoff batter Sam Bryne jumped on Murakami's first pitch, lining it sharply to center but right into Bobby Taylor's glove. The next batter, Gary Clemens, rifled a single to left and scored one out later on a hard-hit double into the gap by Larry Nichols—the first run given up by Murakami. Obviously nervous before and now rattled, Masanori then walked Bienvenido Herrera and threw a wild pitch by catcher Larry Smoot to advance the runners to second and third. Somehow he regained control and struck out Larry Fidalgo to end the threat.[6]

The butterflies were gone, and Murakami then settled down to pitch masterfully for the next 5 innings, striking out 11. Werle noted that his young pitcher was throwing harder than he had during his previous games. Meanwhile, the Giants picked up a couple of runs to lead the game 2–1 as Reno led off the top of the seventh—the last inning in the second game of California League doubleheaders.[7] It was about 11:00 p.m.—a late hour, the *San Francisco Examiner* noted, for the many Japanese American farmworkers in attendance who routinely started their days at 4:00 a.m.—and a cold wind began blowing across the field, but few, if any, of the fans left. "I stood on the mound in the seventh inning and was confident that I would finish and win the game," Murakami remembers. "I already had 14 strikeouts and couldn't even imagine losing the game. I may have been overconfident, or maybe I was tired from throwing seven innings in my first game as a starter, but I made an error and gave up a single and the score was tied. I was quite disappointed."

Murakami was due to lead off the bottom of the seventh. To give him a chance for the win on his special night Werle let him bat. Masanori was adept with the bat but this time grounded out. A walk to second baseman Don Pope and a strikeout by left fielder Tom Snyder reduced Fresno to its final out with a runner on first. The league's top batter, Bobby Taylor, came to the plate and lined the ball cleanly into left field. Pope ran past second, looking to reach third, when to everybody's surprise Bill Werle, coaching at third base, waved him home. Pope put on a burst of speed as left fielder Gary Clemens hit the cutoff man with a perfect throw. The relay came home in plenty of time. Catcher Larry Fidalgo planted himself in front of the plate and applied the tag as Pope attempted a desperate slide. He was clearly out. "SAFE!" yelled umpire Jim Corrington.

The call brought the crowd to its feet in celebration and the entire Reno team to home plate in protest. However tainted, Murakami had his win on Japanese American Baseball Night. "It was a typical humorous yet idyllic Fresno scene," Murakami mused.

That same week Murakami's parents wrote him about a Japanese newspaper article that stated he would be returning to Japan at the end of May or in early June. This was news to Masanori. When a letter from Cappy Harada also arrived, Murakami opened it thoughtfully, guessing that it was his instructions for returning home. Instead it was just a note saying that Cappy was in the hospital and would write Murakami when he recovered. There was nothing about returning to the Hawks.

Masanori hoped that the newspaper article was in error. The Hawks had always been vague on how long he would train with the Giants, but he had assumed that it would be for several months. "If there is any way to stay here, I want to," he thought. He did not know the details of the contract between the Giants and Hawks but knew he had to abide by them. Resigned, he went shopping for *omiyagi*—gifts for friends and superiors that polite Japanese are required to purchase during their travels. He found cuff links and neckties for Hawks manager Tsuruoka and the top coaches. "I was prepared to leave, but I probably didn't look happy."

To clear up the confusion Fumiko Saiki went with Masanori to speak to Bill Werle. With Saiki translating, Werle told Murakami, "Mashi, you are not allowed to go home. You have to play in the U.S. for a year. There is your signature on the contract."

"He said it so clearly and confidently that I was even more puzzled," Murakami recalls. "I wondered when and how my stay had been extended for a full year. But as long as I could play in Fresno, that was good. Nankai hadn't said anything to me formally about returning, and Harada-san was hospitalized. So all I could do was to let things happen."

After starting him on Japanese American Night, Werle put Murakami back in the bullpen, explaining to reporters, "His control is incredible. That's why I put him in tight spots in late innings. With the bases loaded, he isn't liable to walk a run in or choke up. His low curve makes the batsmen tap grounders for double plays."[8] Over the next two weeks Masanori continued to baffle hitters, picking up his fourth and fifth wins as Fresno increased its lead in the California League to 5½ games. By May 7 he had a 5–0 record and a 0.53 ERA in 34 innings. He had also struck out 54 batters and had allowed only 20 batters to reach base for an incredible WHIP (walks plus hits divided by innings pitched) of 0.59. It was then that things began to go wrong.

CHAPTER 8

The difficulties began in early June, soon after Takahashi and Tanaka left for Twin Falls, Idaho, to play for the Magic Valley Cowboys of the Pioneer League. The two had impressed Bill Werle with their fielding, but even the three months of practicing in the American Minors had failed to improve their hitting. "When they do hit," Werle told the media, "they slice to right field. They don't get around fast enough on the low-down pitching in this country. In Japan, the pitching is slower. They tease the batter with soft curves and what we would call change-ups." Consequently Will Connolly of the *San Francisco Examiner* told his readers, "A big, strong thrower . . . whizzes the ball past . . . before [either one] can get the wood off his shoulder."[1] The players fared a little better in the Pioneer League. The shortstop, Tanaka, played in 55 of the Cowboys' 65 games and hit .267 with 6 home runs in 172 at bats. The catcher, Takahashi, on the other hand, played in just 24 games, hitting .250 with no home runs in 76 at bats.

After enduring eight straight losses, only 180 fans showed up at Sam Lynn Park on June 8 to watch their hometown Bakersfield Bears play Fresno. These stalwarts had little to cheer about as the Giants built a 3–1 lead going into the bottom of the seventh. Fresno starter Dan Rivas had pitched well until allowing the first two batters to reach base in the seventh. With the winning run at the plate, Werle called in Murakami once again to preserve the victory. But this time things went awry. According to the *Bakersfield Californian*, Elmo Lam greeted "the temperamental lad from the Orient" with "a crackling double off the left-field boards" to score a run. Murakami then hit first baseman Gene Stone with a "painful fastball" to load the bases. A double by Larry Baughman, an intentional walk, and an infield ground out scored three more runs. An inning later the Bears' winning pitcher, Don Hammitt, "was mobbed by his happy mates" as Murakami trudged to the clubhouse with his first loss.[2]

Pitchers sometimes have poor outings. Murakami was not pleased by his performance, but he knew that a bad game was nothing to fret over. The next day the team drove north to Salinas to play the second-place Mets. The California League played a split-season format. The team with the best record in the first half of the season would play the top team of the second half in a playoff to determine the league champion. With the first half finishing at the end of June and Fresno sporting a 5½ game lead, winning two of the three games at Salinas would nearly sew up the championship. Fresno put its ace, Pedro Reinoso, on the mound to start the series, and the Dominican had pitched eight solid innings when his shoulder began to hurt. Up 6–4, Werle turned to Masanori to close the game.

With the pitcher due to lead off, Salinas manager Kerby Farrell brought in Dave Allen to pinch-hit. "I underestimated him," Murakami remembers, and Allen hit a blooper single into left field. The next batter struck out before left fielder Chuck Knutson beat out a grounder into the hole for a single. With runners on first and second, Masanori lost the strike zone and walked first baseman Ken Free. "I was shaken. I faced the cleanup hitter with the bases loaded. My best curves were missing the strike zone for the second game in a row. The count went to two balls and a strike, so I decided to throw a fastball. It turned out to be a bases-clearing double—a walk-off loss. The loss was horrible."

That evening Murakami wrote in his diary, "Why do my pitches get hit? Why don't I have control? I don't understand now that I have no elbow pain. Don't I have the ability? I don't know. In short, I am just lame." Although Masanori had not formed close friendships with Takahashi and Tanaka, he missed them particularly that night. "Being so sad in a strange country was miserable. I could barely communicate with people, and I had no idea whom to speak with. There was nobody I could talk to about my feelings and emotions. I was feeling abandoned and extremely lonely. I felt very homesick. It was the first and only time I wished I was back in Japan."

Murakami decided to speak to Bill Werle. "When you came to Fresno in April and May," the manager told him, "you were confident with your pitching.

Now you are throwing to the wrong spots, worrying that you might be hit. That won't work. You have to take risks, and don't worry about the results. Just pitch in your normal fashion and don't worry about it. It is okay to be hit." Murakami agreed that he needed to be more confident, so he thought about his accomplishments. Even as a reliever he was among the league leaders in strikeouts and ERA. "There was nothing to worry about," he told himself.

The talk helped. Werle put him right back on the mound the following day as Fresno and Salinas battled into the twelfth inning tied 1–1. Masanori pitched a shaky twelfth, walking two batters, but held the Mets hitless and scoreless. After the Giants scored four in the top of the thirteenth, Murakami struck out the side to gain the victory. Werle turned to him four more times in the following week as Murakami worked on his form and confidence. At times he still struggled, no longer dominating all opponents. The Reno Silver Sox scored twice on him in 2 innings on June 13, but then over the next two days Masanori pitched 4⅔ no-hit innings with 5 strikeouts against the Stockton Ports. With the June 18 game against the Santa Barbara Dodgers on the line, Werle brought Murakami in with no outs and two men on in the eighth inning to preserve a 5–2 lead. It looked like Mashi had regained his form as he struck out the first two batters, but then shortstop Jim Jenkins drove the ball off the right field wall and circled the bases for an inside-the-park home run. The score now tied at 5–5, Masanori remained in the game for the next 5 innings, holding the Dodgers scoreless and striking out 7 more batters before giving up a solo home run in the top of the twelfth to lose the game. The usually demure *Fresno Bee Republican* baseball writer Tom Meehan could not resist Oriental allusions in the next day's lead paragraph, "Masanori Murakami may be a difficult name to pronounce but the Santa Barbara Dodgers are beginning to break through the veil of mystery which once surrounded the Nipponese rally nipper."[3]

The next evening Murakami was initiated into another difference between Japanese and American baseball. Fresno and Santa Barbara were locked in a tight game. In second-to-last place Santa Barbara had no hope of catching Fresno in the standings, but as farm teams of the Dodgers and Giants the two clubs were bitter rivals. With the Giants up 1–0 in the eighth and no outs, pitcher Pedro Reinoso tried to score from third on an infield grounder. Playing the infield in, the Dodgers threw home. Reinoso slid hard with his spikes aimed high. A scuffle ensued and Reinoso grabbed a nearby bat. With that the benches emptied. Unlike most baseball fights, which consist of a lot of milling around and a few shoves, this one became a true brawl as "fists flew for about five minutes."[4]

Stunned, Masanori stood wide-eyed by the bench. He had never seen anything like this. There were occasional fights in Japan, but with only a year in the minors he had not witnessed any, and Japanese fights usually involved just a handful of players shoving each other. "I had no idea what to do," remembers Murakami, "so I just stood in front of the bench."

As the fight broke up and his teammates walked past him back to the dugout, several gave Masanori hard looks. Unknowingly he had just violated one of baseball's sacred unwritten rules. The great Cubs shortstop Ernie Banks once called a player's failure to join a fight "the ultimate violation of being a teammate." Players were expected to back up and defend their teammates, even when the teammates were in the wrong. When a baseball fight begins, players in the dugout and the bullpen are expected to charge onto the field and join the brawl. "The player that didn't come out would lose a lot of respect from his teammates," noted Dave Collins, an outfielder who played sixteen years in the Major Leagues. "It's probably not a situation where he could ever work his way back into good graces. It's one of those things like cheating on your wife—it may be forgiven, but it will never be forgotten."[5]

Even those who abhorred violence or wanted no part in a particular fight needed to take the field. These men usually lingered on the edge of the brawls, pretending to scuffle or holding back opponents. Andy Van Slyke, a star outfielder during the 1980s, confessed, "A guy can walk out there, find somebody he knows, and try to look upset. I did that. I'd try to find somebody I knew and just go up and grab him by his shirt collar and say, 'Hey, how's the family?'" Staying on the perimeter of the fight and just talking was acceptable, as long as one pretended to be angry. The important point was that a player not stay on the bench as Murakami had done.[6]

"When the fight was over," Murakami remembers, "I was scolded that I hadn't come out to the fight." That evening Mashi not only learned about the etiquette of American baseball fights, but he also began to understand how American teammates supported one another. Seeing his teammates battle on the diamond allowed the young pitcher to free his own emotions.

In Japan Masanori was known as a quiet, polite young man, but compared to his American teammates, he was particularly mild-mannered. *Fresno Bee*

Republican sportswriter Tom Meehan remembers him as "a kind, gentle person, just really nice."[7] His natural demeanor had been reinforced by the ethos of Japanese baseball. The ideal high school and professional player in Japan was stoic. Players were expected to endure the intense training, abuse by their elders, and their own disappointments without complaint. Showing frustration was a loss of face, even in the professional leagues. Players who inappropriately lost their tempers were often disciplined by their teams and censured in the media.

When he first joined the Fresno Giants, the emotional intensity of the American players surprised Murakami. They were quick to anger and to release their frustrations. After a poor at bat, giving up a key hit, or losing a game, players would take their frustrations out on the bench, a water cooler, locker, concrete wall, whatever was near them. They would throw down their helmets or even their gloves—a shocking display to a Japanese player who was taught to respect and cherish his gloves as a samurai would his heirloom sword. Masanori realized, "These were not violent men, nor were they showing disrespect for the game; instead their acts exhibited how seriously they played baseball. After watching the fight, I began to show my emotions when I was frustrated."

It took just a few days before Murakami ignited. The lefty had come in to close out the second game of a doubleheader against San Jose. The Giants were leading 5–4 in the final inning when the leadoff batter singled.[8] Attempting to sacrifice, the second batter bunted the ball straight back to Murakami. Masanori "picked it up, looked to second and started to throw to first. He changed his mind and threw to second but it was too late and both runners were safe." The next batter also hit the ball back to the mound. Flustered from his mental error on the previous play, Murakami booted the grounder to load the bases with no outs. An infield single, a ground out, and a strikeout tied the score at 5–5. With the bases still loaded and 2 outs, Murakami had a 2-2 count on the batter as he threw the next pitch by him. To his shock, umpire John Raymer called it ball three. Catcher Larry Smoot pulled off his mask and began to argue. For the first time in his career Masanori joined the argument. Of course Raymer would not budge, but he allowed both Smoot and Murakami to remain in the game despite arguing balls and strikes, grounds for most umpires to eject a player. The next pitch was wide, forcing in the winning run.[9]

"After the loss to San Jose because of the umpire's mistake, I was so frustrated that I broke a chair," recalls Murakami. "I couldn't help it. I was told to pay the damage. but in the end I didn't have to. Later I broke a bat after being struck out. That time I was told not to waste anything. Since then I started using unbreakable things, such as a glove or a helmet. My teammates would yell and scream as they lost their tempers. Before long I started to imitate them, using those words they had taught me. I became so used to the American way, I started thinking that I should stay in the U.S. and not go back to Japan."

On June 27 the Giants traveled to Bakersfield for a Saturday doubleheader—one more win would clinch the first-half title. They lost the first game 1–0 and were down 4–3 in the fifth inning of the second game when Bakersfield loaded the bases with one out. Werle called for Murakami. "I threw a fastball for the first pitch, and, as I expected, the batter hit a ground ball to short for a double play. This was the best moment [for me] as a reliever." The following inning Masanori put away the Bears with his bat. After the Giants had tied the score, "it was my turn to bat with a runner on base. I felt really good and hit a double deep into right-center field. That was my first RBI for Fresno. And we got the victory. That was my best day with Fresno. The next day, we came back to Fresno. Everyone got dressed up in a suit and we had a victory party."

The outing at Bakersfield led to an apocryphal story that would be retold many times in many newspapers over the following two years.[10] Details, such as the name of the opposing team and the relevant inning, often changed, but the essentials of the story, as told here by Jack McDonald of the *San Francisco News-Call Bulletin*, remained constant.

"Murakami came in from the bullpen and there was a lengthy scene on the mound. Werle pointed to the scoreboard showing it was the ninth inning with one out and Fresno leading by only one run. The Reno club had runners on first and second. By gestures he [Werle] tried to impress on Murakami the gravity of the situation and how he wanted him to pitch to the man at bat. 'Low,' he said. Murakami nodded. Then Billy broke his wrist to indicate he wanted Murakami to throw a curve, his best pitch. Hoping he had gotten through to him that he wanted him to play for the batter. Billy started back to the dugout. Murakami called out after him. 'Okay to throw double play ball?' he asked. 'Sure, if you can do it,' said the surprised manager. And that's just what Murakami did throw to retire the side."[11]

In spite of some hardship, Masanori's time in Fresno was among the happiest times of his life. He was young, adventuresome, surrounded by new things and experiences, a celebrity and in a society more open than any he had experienced before. "I would wake up after noon and have breakfast. I had plenty of time until the night games. After day games I was often invited to dinner. I was not able to dance well in the beginning, but I was often invited to dance parties hosted by Nisei and Sansei, so I got better. It was dazzling when there were many young women! On holidays Mr. and Mrs. Saiki often took the family to the countryside by car. I enjoyed the huge natural areas that I could never have even imagined when I lived in Japan. Once we chased after wild rabbits in an orange field that Mr. and Mrs. Saiki owned. They told us that the wild rabbits would damage the crops so that they had to be hunted. It was my first time hunting, so I was excited, but they were very fast and nearly impossible to shoot. But it was so much fun!"

When asked about how Masanori and his two countrymen were adapting, Fumiko Saiki told reporters, "I thought that they would be homesick. Four months away from their home islands, they should yearn for something familiar, like fish. [But] the excitement of baseball keeps them diverted. They drink milk by the gallon. The milk here, they say, is richer than in Japan. They go for fried chicken, westerns on TV and John Wayne. Otherwise, they are very quiet, write letters a yard long, and ask where they can swim."[12]

The Fresno Giants as a whole were a serious bunch. They focused on baseball, on trying to advance to the big leagues. They were not much for partying but often went out in groups for meals and entertainment. The team was integrated, with a number of black and Hispanic players. Although there was little to no racial tension on the team, off the field the different races usually kept to themselves. Masanori had no close friends, mostly because of the language barrier, but he was often asked to join a group that was going out to dinner or on other excursions. He always said yes, wanting to experience as much of American culture as possible.

Manager Bill Werle told reporters, "He's a great kid. He's a model athlete, both on and off the field—and the team likes him. Our guys kid him all the time; it shows how much they do [like him]."[13] Masanori was not too shy to return the jokes. One afternoon pitcher Alex Bright's feet began to burn as he ran his pregame laps in the outfield. Returning to the bench, he removed his shoes and detected the telltale odor of wintergreen. Somebody had rubbed the liniment pitchers put on their arms on the inside of his cleats. According to Jack McDonald of the *San Francisco News–Call Bulletin*, "A chuckle down at one end of the dugout was a dead giveaway Murakami was the culprit."[14]

Slowly Murakami's English improved. Although he still had trouble expressing himself, by midsummer he could understand many of the conversations around him—as long as the topics were not too complex. He had little understanding, for example, of the race riots that were sweeping the country during the summer of 1964 or of the escalation of the Vietnam War. He could see the images on television and knew that his teammates were talking about the events, but he could neither read the newspapers nor fully understand the locker room conversations.

Murakami used road trips for sightseeing and experiencing America. In Santa Barbara he would wake up early and walk on its beautiful beaches. In Reno he went to the casinos with his teammates and gambled—almost always losing but having fun. He visited an amusement park with seventeen-year-old Ken Henderson and spent the day on rollercoasters and other rides. When the team traveled to San Jose, he would sometimes stay with Fumiko Saiki's sister Yoshiye Osaka and her family. On one visit they took him sightseeing in San Francisco; on another they went to Yosemite National Park. "That was the life I had," Murakami recalls; "for a twenty-year-old boy, it was just great. So it was natural that I started wanting to stay in the United States like that forever."

His father, however, had different ideas. Mashi's parents wrote often, and nearly every letter implored him to come home soon. The Murakamis had expected their son to be in the United States for just a few months. They now worried that he would remain in the foreign country. Cappy Harada tried to explain to Kiyoshi that Masanori was "well on the road to fame and fortune in the American majors," but the father remained steadfast.[15]

Masanori went through another rough patch on the mound during the month of July. From July 2 to August 2 he logged 24 innings during 15 games, giving up an uncharacteristically high 25 hits, 8 walks, and 8 earned runs.[16] During this period his 1.375 WHIP was 0.585 points higher than his WHIP during the rest of the season (0.79), while his 3.00 ERA was almost two runs higher than his 1.10 ERA for the other months of the season. Bruce Farris of the *Fresno Bee Republican* noted, "His usual pinpoint control was off and he was getting tagged regularly. He became both panicky and discouraged."[17]

The slump included many frustrating moments, including back-to-back losses on August 1 and 2 and the worst outing in Murakami's Minor League career. On July 10 Fresno and Salinas were tied 5–5 in the top of the ninth when a single, two questionable calls by the umpires, and another single knocked out starter Pedro Reinoso. Bill Werle brought in Murakami to work his magic, although he had given up 3 hits and 2 runs the previous night. Mets right fielder Eugene Orf greeted Masanori with a one-run single. Werle then decided to intentionally walk right-handed Jim Lang to let Murakami face lefty first baseman Dave Allen. The plan backfired as Allen hit a monstrous grand slam over the scoreboard in right-center field to give the Mets a 10–5 lead and chase Murakami from the game. The Japanese reliever's line score—0 innings pitched, 2 hits, 1 walk, and 3 earned runs—was his worst of the season.

Yet not all of his outings during July were poor, as he picked up two wins and several saves. The July 17 Friday night game against Reno became one of his memorable days in a Fresno uniform. The Giants had come back from a 4–0 deficit when starter Lou DeMar began to struggle in the eighth. A single, a walk, and another single tied the score and left two runners on base with no outs. Bill Werle signaled to the bullpen for Murakami. Exactly a week earlier Masanori had given up the grand slam, and he had pitched only a third of an inning since. But this time Murakami was in top form. He retired the next two batters without allowing a run to score, intentionally walked the third, and struck out the fourth to end the inning. In the top of the ninth he retired the side in order.

Murakami would lead off the bottom of the ninth, and with the score deadlocked Werle decided to let him bat. Salinas pitcher Gary Maloy attacked the Japanese reliever with a fastball, and Murakami turned on it, slamming a drive toward the left-center field wall. Left fielder Eddie Crawford gave chase, concentrating on the ball. Murakami sprinted toward first. At full speed Crawford approached the 385 marker on the outfield wall. He would get it! As he reached to snare the drive, a resounding thud filled the stadium. The ball and Crawford had reached the wall simultaneously. The ball rebounded off the wall into center field as Crawford crumpled to the ground. Murakami flew by second base. By the time center fielder Jay Johnson retrieved the ball and threw home, Masanori had crossed the plate. A walk-off home run! Or as the Japanese say, a sayonara home run!

But his teammates did not mob Murakami at home plate. Instead both dugouts had run to the outfield to check on Crawford, who remained flat on his back, unconscious. After about five minutes the outfielder came to and was helped to the dugout. He would be fine.[18]

Throughout the summer Bill Werle worked with Masanori on both the mechanics and strategy of pitching. With the language barrier it was not always easy. Werle told reporters, "My problem with Murakami is that when I try to tell him of a mistake or I want to have just a plain old chitchat with him, we can't understand each other."[19] Nonetheless, Werle was determined to teach his Japanese student how Americans played ball. Werle taught him the basics first: "If the batter is a lefty with an open stance, get the first two strikes with outside pitches; then the third can be either an inside pitch or a curveball out and away. To a right-handed batter with a closed stance, throw inside fastballs or curves, not outside balls." They also continued to perfect his change-up. Werle explained, "A change-up has to be thrown when the count is 1-0, 2-0, 3-0, or 3-2. As a cardinal rule, it must be thrown low. The change-up is most useful on a power hitter." When an instruction session was over, Werle would often say, "Now do it." And he would immediately have Masanori face live batters so he could practice his lesson. "I don't think that I would have been able to utilize the change-up so quickly if I had been in Japan," Murakami concludes. Following Japanese procedure, he would have had to master the pitch in practice to the coaches' satisfaction before being allowed to use it in a game.

Werle found his pupil to be a "real student of the game. He's always out there thinking. He moves the ball around well and makes relatively few mistakes for a rookie. He knows he can't overpower hitters, so he tries to out-think them."[20]

Murakami found the American strike zone lower than the Japanese. At first he was surprised when pitches he thought were strikes were called balls, but he soon adapted. "I found it easy to get strikeouts. I would purposely throw the first pitches a little outside. The batter would usually miss them or foul them off. I would mix my pitches up, high and low, then throw a fastball high and inside near his chest. If I knew he was waiting for another fastball, I would strike him out with my curve at the knees." Most observers agreed that Murakami's fastball had only average velocity. His real weapon was his curve. Thrown with a quick wrist snap, it "does not bend gradually like a roundhouse but darts sharply as it nears the plate."[21]

With Werle's instructions digested, Murakami became nearly unhittable in August. After the consecutive losses on August 1 and 2, Werle called on Murakami in the eleventh inning of the August 5 game against Modesto. With the score knotted at 6–6, Masanori dominated the Colts, giving up just 1 hit and striking out 4 in 4⅔ innings. In the bottom of the fifteenth Murakami was due up with the bases loaded and 2 outs. Despite the game's length, Werle had only used three pitchers and no bench players. The situation called for a pinch-hitter, but probably remembering Murakami's inside-the-park home run a few weeks earlier, Werle let Masanori bat. It was a gutsy, perhaps even stupid, decision. With a 1–1 count, the Japanese reliever silenced would-be critics with a clean humpback single to right-center field to win the game.

The win began an incredible run for Murakami—now commonly called "the Nipponese Rally Nipper" by the *Fresno Bee Republican*. From August 5 to 30 Murakami entered 11 games, pitching 22⅔ innings without giving up an earned run. He surrendered just 5 hits, walked 1, and struck out 35. During these 11 games he won twice and saved 5 games. His WHIP was a stingy 0.27.

In the midst of this streak the San Francisco Giants front office began to reconsider Murakami's future. "Murakami has pleased our organization with his work in Fresno," Jack Schwartz told the *Oakland Tribune*. "We are definitely interested in keeping him around."[22] Keeping Murakami might be difficult, Schwartz conceded. He told the *Oakland Tribune* that the three Japanese players "are property of Osaka Hawks of Japan's Pacific Coast League [*sic*], even though signed to Giants contracts. 'If we can iron out legal matters then we might be able to retain Murakami.'"[23]

Furthermore, the Giants needed to work out any deal for Murakami before October 16, when their forty-man roster was due. "Otherwise," Schwartz noted, "he'd be subject to the first year draft [and] any team could claim him. Scouts have asked me about him and I told them, 'You can forget Murakami. Either he'll come with us or return over.' After we brought him over and all, we'd be fools to let one of those jackanapes grab him."[24]

In mid-August Werle began sounding out Murakami about his future.

"When do you plan to go home?" he asked.

"Maybe September," Masanori answered. He had not heard from Nankai or Cappy Harada for months and had no idea when he was supposed to return.

"Do you want to continue playing here next year, or will you be playing in Japan?" Werle asked next.

"I don't know about that either," Murakami responded truthfully.

In late August Carl Hubbell began coming to the Fresno games to decide if the Giants wanted to acquire Murakami from the Hawks. Masanori put on a show. On August 21 he pitched 3 innings against the Santa Barbara Dodgers, facing the minimum 9 batters and striking out 7 of them. Five days later he needed just 12 pitches—9 strikes and 3 balls—to retire all three Stockton batters in the ninth for the save.

During a road trip to Reno on August 28 Werle asked Masanori if he could stay and play in the Arizona Fall League. "I feel like joining, but I cannot decide for myself," Murakami answered. "I will give you an answer tomorrow." That evening he telephoned his family in Otsuki. "Come home," they told him. He then called Cappy Harada in Tokyo to determine when he should return. "Since you are in the United States, you should watch the World Series and come home after that," Cappy advised. More than a little surprised by that response, Masanori then told Harada that he would like to stay for the fall season.

"I will negotiate it," Cappy said. "Please leave it to me."

"So," Murakami recalls, "I made up my mind that even if it was not fair to Nankai, while I was living in the U.S. I would experience as much as I could. I would go to the stadium tomorrow and tell Bill that I would join the Fall League. But the next morning when I went to tell Bill, he had other news for me."

"I was going to the Major Leagues!"

That night Murakami pitched his last Minor League game. Werle brought in Masanori during the sixth inning to protect a 6–5 lead. He pitched no-hit ball for the final 4 innings, striking out 10 of the 12 batters he faced. He was ready for new challenges.

CHAPTER 9

The San Francisco Giants were in turmoil.

When the franchise moved to San Francisco from New York in 1957, the Giants had just finished consecutive seasons in sixth place. The team was aging. The average age of the eight regular position players was thirty years, and five players remained from the memorable 1951 pennant-winning club. It was time to change.

And change they did. By focusing on the nearly untapped talent in Latin America and aggressively pursuing African American prospects, the Giants brought a group of exciting young players to San Francisco. With four rookies (two Latino, one African American, and one Caucasian), the average age of the 1958 starting lineup was just 25.25 years. The young team finished in third—well above expectations. Over the next few years the Giants supplanted the Dodgers as Major League Baseball's most integrated team. From 1958 to 1963 their lineups included twelve Latinos and nine African Americans. The starting lineup of the squad that Murakami would join consisted of four Latinos and three African Americans, and two more Latinos routinely came off the bench.

Not all were pleased with the Giants' diverse roster. Despite the team's obvious talent, the club tended to fade down the backstretch. In 1959, for example, the Giants led the league by 2 games with 8 left to play but collapsed to finish in third place. The following year the collapse came earlier. On June 12 they were just a half game behind the league-leading Pirates when three straight losses prompted owner Horace Stoneham to fire manager Bill Rigney. The team went into a free fall, finishing in fifth place. After the season J. G. Taylor Spink, editor of the *Sporting News*, investigated the cause of the breakdown. Players, team executives, and beat writers all told Spink that "the cause of the Giants' downfall [was] too many Negro players." The non-white players presumably disrupted the team's harmony and lacked the desire to win. The irony of this belief was that all but one of the Giants' top players were non-white. Without the very players blamed for the team's collapses, the Giants would not have been in contention.

During this era Willie Mays was the undisputed team leader. At the age of thirty-three in 1964, he was one of the older players on the roster and the only remnant of the Giants' pennant-winning teams of 1951 and 1954. He also may have been the best all-around player in the history of the game. By the time he retired at the end of the 1973 season, he had been an All-Star for twenty straight seasons, he had won twelve Gold Gloves and two MVP Awards, and he had led the National League at least once in nearly every offensive category. In 1964 the "Say Hey Kid" was still at the top his game and would lead the league in home runs and slugging percentage.

Mays was a quiet man, leading by example rather than motivating teammates with boisterous cheering or rousing speeches. He would rarely criticize players in public but instead would quietly take them aside to discuss an issue. He took special care of the team's two young African American stars, Willie McCovey and Jim Hart, and did his best to protect them from the caustic San Francisco press.

Many teammates found Mays extraordinarily generous and caring, but few outsiders saw this side of the superstar. Instead San Francisco fans and press often viewed him as aloof and pampered. On the road he usually ate his meals alone in his luxury hotel suite and flew first class when his teammates stayed two to a standard room and flew coach. Few, if any, of his teammates objected to the special treatment, but it drew the ire of the media and fans. Mays was also notoriously taciturn with reporters he did not trust and loath to bare his emotions, provide controversial quotes, or make political statements.

Orlando Cepeda, the Puerto Rican slugger, was Mays's opposite in nearly every aspect—except for hitting home runs. Between 1958 and 1964 Cepeda and Mays combined for 488 home runs—the best of any duo in the Majors. During these seven years Cepeda would win the 1958 Rookie of the Year award, make the next six all-star squads, and hit above .300 in six seasons (he hit .297 in the other). His big, happy, outgoing personality made Cepeda an instant celebrity in San Francisco. Fans loved his ever-present smile, which made "everything working on Orlando's face go up: the corners of his mouth, the corners of his eyes, even his hairline and eyebrows and ears." Cepeda seemed to enjoy living. He went to nightclubs, mixing with fans, listened to modern jazz and loud Latin music, and posed semi-nude for *Look* magazine. According to an article in *Sports Illustrated*, he "loves almost everything: Puerto Rico, America, girls, automobiles, large gold wristwatches, the Atlantic, the Pacific, money, sirloin steak, girls, fancy clothes. . . ."[1] To fans he typified a new generation of Giants baseball, young and hip, like their city.

With his vibrant personality and star status, Cepeda was the leader of the Giants' Latin contingent. Star pitcher Juan Marichal, shortstop Jose Pagan, and the three Alou brothers (Jesus, Matty, and Felipe, who was traded to the Braves after the 1963 season) formed the core of this group.

In the twenty-first century, when Latinos make up a vital part of American culture, it is sometimes difficult to fathom the difficulties facing Latino players in the 1950s and early 1960s. When they first arrived in the United States, few of the players spoke English, and few Americans spoke Spanish. Marichal recalls, "I didn't even know how to ask for a glass of water."[2] Furthermore, many white Americans would not even tolerate Spanish spoken around them.

For the Dominicans especially, the open racism and segregation in the United States was a shock. "When I was growing up in the Dominican Republic there was never any racism," Juan Marichal remembers. "Everyone was the same. It didn't matter what the color of your skin was. We never thought about it. . . . When I went to [the United States] for the first time . . . I was most shocked to see the different groups treated different ways, how everyone split up, whites, blacks, Latins. . . . I said to myself, 'Here I am in the biggest country in the world with that kind of prejudice.' It was unbelievable, terrible. I was young and excited and this was a big opportunity, and then I was confronted by all this racism. It got very discouraging at times."[3]

Faced with the language barrier and a different, often hostile, culture, the Latinos banded together both on and off the field. "We were very, very close," remembers Cepeda. "We were more than friends, we were like brothers," adds Marichal.[4] This Hispanic clique, hanging around the clubhouse listening to Latin music, laughing and joking in Spanish, just having fun, fostered resentment among the team's more conservative whites.

Leading this multiethnic team was an untested new manager. After the Giants' collapse in September 1959 and their poor 1960 showing, Horace Stoneham decided the team needed stronger leadership. He chose the scrappy, hard-nosed shortstop of his pennant-winning New York Giants, Alvin Dark, even though Dark had never managed before.

Alvin Dark was a forty-two-year-old Southern Baptist from Louisiana who hated to lose. His postgame tantrums were infamous. Once, after a tough 1–0 loss, Dark became incensed by two players as carefree as "a couple of hummingbirds, just laughing and having a good time." Grabbing a metal stool, Dark hurled it against the clubhouse wall. The thunderous impact stopped all conversation. The shock continued as the players watched blood spurt from Dark's hand. The tip of his little finger had become entangled in a joint under the stool's seat and had ripped off. As the trainer stitched the wound, players retrieved the missing digit and pickled it in a jar.[5]

Despite his temper, Dark was a God-fearing man who eschewed drinking, smoking—and when he could help it—swearing. He was politically and socially conservative—a supporter of Barry Goldwater who would sprinkle clubhouse speeches with Bible references.

Dark immediately clashed with the Latin players. In an attempt to break up the team's ethnic cliques, he posted a sign in the spring training clubhouse proclaiming, "Speak English, You're in America." He told the Latin players that white players had complained that they didn't understand much of the clubhouse conversation. The absurdity of the Alou brothers speaking to each other in a foreign language soon brought an end to the decree. Later Dark outlawed music in the clubhouse, a rule aimed at Orlando Cepeda's ever-present record player stocked with Latin music. Cepeda, in particular, felt that Dark had targeted him. The manager had openly questioned Cepeda's ability to hit in the clutch and insinuated that the Puerto Rican star exaggerated his injuries. Cepeda would become convinced that Dark was "trying to destroy [him] emotionally."[6] Later, in his book *High and Inside*, Cepeda would write, "When I first met him I thought Alvin Dark was an angel. He came on like a saint and fooled everybody. It did not take long for me to find out that he was the most vicious man I would ever meet in baseball. Without mincing words, I can easily and honestly say that Alvin Dark was a liar and a bigot."[7]

Under Dark's rule the Giants improved from fifth to third place in 1961, captured the 1962 pennant, and again finished in third in 1963. Both the

Associated Press annual poll and the Vegas oddsmakers pegged the Giants for another near miss in 1964, but Willie Mays began the season on a hot streak—hitting 6 home runs in the first 6 games and 17 by late May, while flirting with a .400 average.[8] The Giants found themselves in first place, a game ahead of the surprising Philadelphia Phillies, on May 28. With the strong start *Ebony* in its June baseball roundup proclaimed, "1964 looks like the year of the Giants."[9]

Then Lippincott published Jackie Robinson's *Baseball Has Done It*, a treatise on race relations in baseball that included extensive quotes from retired and active ballplayers. Among those quoted was Alvin Dark, whose comments, probably intended to show support for baseball's integration, made clear his Southern paternalist ideology and included a call to delay the forced integration of the South. "We from the South actually take care of the colored people," Dark explained, echoing statements by antebellum plantation owners, but integration was "being rushed too fast."[10]

If that had been Dark's last discourse on race relations, it might have been forgotten. Unfortunately for Dark and the Giants, a greater controversy lay ahead. In the meantime, through June and most of July, the Giants and Phillies traded days at the top of the standings. But the Giants were plagued by poor play. Mental mistakes cost them several games. Reporters openly questioned why such a talented team continually failed to reach its potential.

In the midst of a frustrating home stand *Newsday* reporter Stan Isaacs asked Dark why his team made so many mistakes. Dark, according to Isaacs, gave a surprisingly candid answer. "We have trouble because we have so many Negro and Spanish-speaking players on this team. They are just not able to perform up to the white ball player when it comes to mental alertness. . . . You can't make most Negro and Spanish players have the pride in their team that you can get from white players and they just aren't as sharp mentally. They aren't able to adjust to situations because they don't have that mental alertness." Dark conceded that some players, like Willie Mays and Jackie Robinson, were exceptions to his statement, but he singled out Orlando Cepeda as a prime example of his belief. A shocked Isaacs editorialized in his July 23 column, "All of sociology and the ideals that went into fighting the racist theories of the Nazis would make me think a man like Dark—neither unintelligent, nor with malice toward his fellow man—could not think such things. He does. So do others."[11]

News of the article reached the Giants when they arrived in Pittsburgh the following week. The minority players immediately gathered in Mays's hotel room. Most were outraged and wanted to act. Across the country African Americans were fighting for their civil rights. The passage and signing on July 2 of the Civil Right Act initiated protests, violence, and race riots throughout the summer. In Mississippi activists attempted to register the state's black population to vote, despite violent attacks and even murders by the Ku Klux Klan and other white supremacists. On July 18 the shooting of a black teen by an off-duty white policeman in Harlem ignited a full-scale riot that soon spread to Brooklyn and later Rochester, New York. In August race riots broke out in Jersey City and Philadelphia. Dark's racist comments could hardly have come at a worse time.

In the hotel room the angry players seemed to all speak at once. "Shut up! Just shut up!" yelled Mays.[12]

"You don't tell me to shut up. I'm not going to play another game for that son of a bitch," Cepeda shot back.

"Oh yes you are. And let me tell you why." Mays had already heard that Dark would be fired at the end of the season, so why "let the rednecks make a hero out of him?" Furthermore, Dark's intense competitive nature gave the team the best chance to win the pennant. For most of the players a share in the World Series proceeds would be a significant sum of money. The Giants had switched managers in midseason in 1960 and had quickly fallen from second to fifth place. No, Mays counseled, they needed Dark because he wanted to win and would continue playing black and Latin players if it would lead to victory. "He's the same as me and everybody else in this room: he likes money. That preacher talk that goes with it he can shove up his ass. . . . He helps us because he wants to win, and he wants the money that goes with winning. Ain't nothing wrong with that."

Cepeda and the other participants in the meeting took the field that night, but the team's morale was damaged. They split the four game set with the Pirates, beat up on the lowly Mets, and took 2 of 3 from the Reds before falling into a swoon and losing 10 of their next 16 games. Dark defended himself in an August 4 press conference, telling reporters, "I was definitely misquoted on something, and other statements were deformed [sic]." But the damage was done. On the morning Masanori Murakami joined the Giants, the team had fallen into third place, 6½ games behind the Phillies.

Not being able to read the newspapers or converse freely with his teammates, Murakami knew nothing about the controversies on the big league club. After the game against San Jose on August 30 Bill Werle and the Fresno Giants staff had given him airplane tickets to New York, where he would join the San Francisco Giants for a three-game series against the Mets. He would be staying with the team at the Roosevelt Hotel in Manhattan. As Masanori prepared to leave the locker room after his last game in Fresno, his teammates came over to say goodbye and good luck. Sensing a story, *Fresno Bee Republican* reporter Tom Meehan asked Murakami where he was going. "To New York," he blurted before Werle ushered him away. "I'm not at liberty to say," stated Werle. "Jack Schwartz, administrative secretary of the farm system, will issue a statement on any changes we may have coming up [on] Tuesday."[13]

Early the next morning Murakami flew from Fresno to San Francisco International Airport. He expected to be met at the gate by a Giants representative but found nobody waiting for him. With his broken English and bilingual dictionary Masanori navigated the airport and located his connecting flight to New York. Nobody was waiting for him in New York either. This posed a more difficult problem. He had never been to New York before and had no idea how to get to the Roosevelt Hotel. Luckily an airline pilot helped him get on the correct bus, and he arrived safely at the midtown hotel.

The difficulties continued at the hotel. When Murakami tried to check in, there was no reservation under his name. As he did not even know the name of the Giants' traveling secretary, he was at a loss. He sat down on a nearby couch and waited. Nobody seemed to be expecting him. "My body could be floating in the Hudson River tomorrow, and nobody would know I was even missing," he mused. After twenty minutes a man came up to him and said, "Are you the Japanese pitcher?" Eventually he got to his room.

Once upstairs, Murakami waited for somebody to contact him. Once again, nobody did. After two hours, feeling both hungry and neglected, he made his way back downstairs to the hotel restaurant. As he entered, Juan Marichal and Jose Pagan looked up from a nearby table.

"Hey, are you the Japanese pitcher?"

"Yes."

"Sit here."

A waiter handed Murakami a menu, but not being able to read it, he pointed at his teammates' large portions of roast beef and said, "Same thing."

Unfortunately he had neglected to notice the price. The bill with tip came to $12, his entire per diem. Welcome to the big leagues.

The telephone rang early the next morning, pulling Masanori from sleep. It was a reporter from *Hochi Sports* calling from Japan. His promotion to the Giants was important news in his home country, and the enterprising reporter wanted to get the scoop.

"What are you feeling?"

"Honestly, I am not feeling anything now because I never thought about wearing a Major League uniform. I am happy, but I'm more worried that I will not meet the expectations of the team."

"Are you used to living in the United States?"

"I'm used to everyday life and nothing is inconvenient, but I still can't communicate well. But I will never have a chance like this, so I will just do my best and hope to leave a record that I'm not embarrassed by."

"Did you learn any new pitching techniques?"

"Not especially. They just let me throw the way I wanted to. The practices are a lot easier here than in Japan."

"What are your plans?"

"I arrived here late last night, so I haven't met anybody from the front office yet, but I hear that the players will take me to the World's Fair, and I'm looking forward to it."[14]

After Murakami met the team in the lobby, they did indeed go to the World's Fair. Masanori recognized only a handful of the players but found them all friendly and welcoming. As they strode through the fair, a cadre of reporters and photographers followed Murakami. "Photographers were asking him to pose in front of every exhibit," Alvin Dark noted. "Murakami looked unhappy and apologized to his fellow players for making them wait as the photographers finished. . . . He's the most courteous and polite rookie I've ever seen!"[15]

Reporters and photographers in tow, the team went across the street to Shea Stadium. All the while reporters barraged the Japanese pitcher with questions. "I didn't understand fast-spoken English, so I was just smiling," recalls Murakami. "I was only thinking about my pitching."

The first task at Shea was to find Mashi a uniform. A staff member brought out a mountain of old uniforms. Masanori riffled through the pile and found number 10, his old number on the Nankai Hawks. He got dressed and had just taken the field for practice when the Giants' traveling secretary called him over and pointed to his undershirt. "Hey, what are you wearing? The Giants wear black, not navy blue." After some pointing, sign language, and a lot of effort, Murakami understood. The Giants had not issued him a regulation undershirt, so he had donned his old shirt from Fresno, and it was the wrong color. Unlike today, when players are allowed some latitude in their personal appearance on the field, in the 1960s the league strictly enforced uniform regulations. The undershirt would have to go. A search of the locker room, however, revealed no extra shirts in Murakami's size. Improvising, they cut off the sleeves so that the offending garment could not be seen, and Masanori retook the field.

During practice dozens of reporters swarmed around Murakami, peppering him with questions. Jack Hanley of the *San Jose Mercury* noted, "For fully an hour before the game, Murakami was photographed and interviewed more than any other rookie to appear on the big time scene."[16]

"Who are your idols?" one asked. Masanori scratched his head, looking puzzled. "Babe Ruth?" Somebody suggested.

"Babe Ruth good player," said Murakami. "Joe DiMaggio very good. I like him."

"How about pitchers?" another asked.

"Oh yes, I like pitching."[17]

The American reporters soon became frustrated with the language barrier. "Although Masanori, a handsome young man with a cherubic face and a glistening look about him, studied English for six years, he has trouble understanding and communicating," explained Bob Stevens of the *San Francisco Chronicle*. "But he tries, oh how very hard he tries, always flashing a shy, embarrassed smile when he doesn't get through. 'I, he said carefully, 'study English six years in Japan. But I don't get chance to speak it, so, please excuse me.'" Harry Jupiter of the *News–Call Bulletin* was more direct: "Masanori is serious, earnest, intent, sincere and all that—but he has a hell of a time with the English language!"[18]

Luckily dozens of Japanese reporters were on hand to cover the story. Sho Onodera, a Nisei who had served in U.S. Army Intelligence during World War II and as a monitor during the Tokyo War Crimes Tribunal and who now worked for the *Sankei* newspaper, stepped forward to interpret for Murakami. With Onodera's assistance Masanori "answered questions patiently and politely [although] . . . he kept asking his interpreter whether he was sure that the manager didn't object to his not participating in pre-game practice."[19]

All the attention prompted one observer to quip, "this guy better be good after all of this!"[20]

Minutes before game time Giants vice president Chub Feeney appeared on the field and with manager Alvin Dark approached Murakami. Waving a piece of paper in his hand, Feeney told Masanori, "Hello, Murakami. Welcome. This is our contract. We need you to sign so you can pitch." To Feeney's shock, Murakami said, "No."

Realizing that he needed help, Feeney turned to a nearby Asian reporter and asked him to act as an interpreter. As luck would have it, he had chosen a Nisei who spoke no Japanese. They soon located Sho Onodera, and Feeney explained that Masanori needed to sign a Major League contract to be allowed to play. Onodera turned to Murakami and translated. Murakami vigorously shook his head. A "spirited exchange in Japanese" began as Feeney tried to shoo away gathering reporters. Finally Onodera turned to Feeney: "He says he signed something already."[21]

According to *Daily News* columnist Dick Young, "A knot of American newsmen had gathered, and it was embarrassing. 'Let's go inside to your office and continue this,' said Feeney to manager Alvin Dark. So, off they went, with the interpreter."[22]

In the privacy of the office Feeney telephoned a Fresno official who confirmed that Murakami had only signed a release form from the Fresno club and still needed to sign a contract with the Giants. Together Feeney and Onodera explained the situation to their young pitcher, but he still hesitated. "Why didn't I sign that contract when he told me to sign?" Murakami recalls. "Well, I had already signed a contract before leaving Japan, and I was used to the Japanese way of doing things, where you only sign a contract once a year. Also, Mr. Saiki had told me to be very careful about contracts, and when he handed me this contract, I couldn't understand the contents." Feeney got back on the telephone and called Saiki in Fresno. After a brief discussion and an explanation that an American player needed to sign a release and contract every time he moved teams, Saiki told Masanori that he should sign.

"It was just fifteen or twenty minutes before the game was supposed to start and the roster had already been officially submitted when I finally understood and signed the contract. Immediately Chub Feeney got on the telephone and called the commissioner and told him that Masanori Murakami had signed the contract and could now play in the Major Leagues."

CHAPTER 10

"Attention, please, ladies and gentlemen. Now coming in to pitch for the Giants, number 10, Masanori Murakami!" Mets announcer Jack E. Lee's voice boomed over the Shea Stadium loudspeakers. The left-field bullpen gate swung open, and the young Japanese stepped onto the stadium's vibrant green grass.

The bright lights nearly blinded him—especially after the perpetual twilight of Fresno's John Euless Park. Four tiers of coliseum seating rose above Murakami. Shea was only five months old, finished just in time for the 1964 season and to be an attraction at the World's Fair held in adjacent Flushing Meadows' Corona Park. The stadium was a marvel. It was the first designed for both baseball and football and the first built without a single seat blocked by a support beam. Devotees called it "the most beautiful ballpark ever built" and "the ultimate in modern sports arenas."[1]

Masanori was calm. There were no butterflies. He had been nervous before the game, as reporters grilled him with questions he barely understood, but he had relaxed while warming up in the bullpen. In the sixth inning he had been sitting in the corner of the dugout, wondering if he could go to the bullpen to practice since he doubted that he would get into the game when Dark called out, "Hey, Mashi, why don't you go pitch in the bullpen?" "Okay. I will do," he said as he stood up and ran to the pen. Believing that he was just practicing after two days of inaction, Murakami threw about fifty pitches and had just declared that his arm felt good when a message came from the dugout. He was to pitch the next inning.[2]

Masanori walked slowly toward the mound, a wad of chewing gum in his mouth. The 39,379 fans were cheering, clapping, and whistling for him. Many were on their feet. They called themselves the New Breed. They were young, boisterous, brash, and fanatical about their Mets. "What is going on here?" muttered a veteran sportswriter. "Mets fans never cheer the opposing players," the writer explained to *Nikkan Sports* writer Kumio Sato. "They even booed Willie Mays when the starting lineups were announced."[3] The answer was simple. They knew they were witnessing history.

With the ovation Murakami's heart skipped a beat. He needed to remain calm and focused. He began to hum.

Ue o muite arukou
Namada ga kobore nai you ni
Omoidasu haru no hi
Hitoribotchi no yoru

(I look up as I walk
so that the tears won't fall
Remembering those spring days
But I am all alone tonight)

"Sukiyaki." It was the first tune that came to mind. It had no special meaning for Masanori at the time, but it was an apt choice. It would become symbolic of Murakami's career. Hauntingly beautiful and catchy at the same time, it was originally entitled *Ue o muite aruko* (I will walk looking up) and recorded in 1961 by Kyu Sakamoto. Rokusuke Ei wrote the lyrics in 1960 to express his despair after attending a failed rally to protest the Treaty of Mutual Cooperation and Security between the United States and Japan. The lyrics, however, are general enough to refer to lost love or any unfulfilled happiness. (In a strange coincidence, Ei sat in the stadium at that moment, watching Murakami.) When released in the United States in 1963, the song's named was changed to "Sukiyaki" (a hot pot dish), as the name was both familiar to many Americans and still distinctly Japanese. Like Murakami, the song was a trailblazer, becoming the first Japanese recording to reach the Billboard Top 100.

Resisting the urge to trot, Murakami continued his slow walk.

Ue o muite arukou
Nijinda hoshi o kazoete

Omoidasu natsu no hi
Hitoribotchi no yoru

Shiawase wa kumo no ue ni
Shiawase wa sora no ue ni

Ue o muite arukou
Namida ga kobore nai you ni
Nakinagara aruku
Hitoribotchi no yoru

(I look up while I walk
Counting the stars with teary eyes
Remembering those summer days
But tonight I am all alone

Happiness lies beyond the clouds
Happiness lies above the sky

I look up while I walk
So the tears won't fall
Though the tears well up as I walk
For I am alone tonight)

Del Crandall, the Giants burly catcher, met Masanori on the pitcher's mound. He tried without success to explain the Giants' signs before agreeing on the signals used by Fresno. The infielders approached and offered words of encouragement. Masanori nodded, not understanding, and began his warmup pitches as his teammates watched from behind the mound.

Murakami threw three-quarters overhand—not straight over the top, like many American pitchers of that time, and not true sidearm, but halfway between these two positions. At the windup, he brought his hands together high above his head as he faced the batter. He then pivoted sideways on his left foot, bringing his right knee up above his waist—nearly to his chest—as his arms fell to his sides. With all of his weight on his back left foot, he slung his right leg toward the plate and in a long, smooth motion, raised his left arm to shoulder height, and whipped it across his body toward the batter. He finished in a nearly upright position with his weight on his right leg and his left spinning forward until he reached a properly balanced

Fig. 1. Three-year-old Masanori held by his mother, Tomiko, with his sisters, Kyoko to the left and Haruko to the right. Courtesy of Masanori Murakami, may not be reproduced without permission.

Fig. 2. Pitcher for Hosei II High School, summer of 1960. Courtesy of Masanori Murakami, may not be reproduced without permission.

Fig. 3. Kazuto Tsuruoka, manager of the Nankai Hawks. Author's collection.

Fig. 4. (*opposite top*) Mashi on the mound at Candlestick Park as Tatsuhiko Tanaka and Hiroshi Takahashi watch, March 10, 1964. Courtesy of Masanori Murakami, may not be reproduced without permission.

Fig. 5. (*opposite bottom*) Shopping in Arizona with Tatsuhiko Tanaka and Hiroshi Takahashi, March 12, 1964. Courtesy of Masanori Murakami, may not be reproduced without permission.

Fig. 6. (*above*) Spring training at Casa Grande, March 1964. *From left:* Tatsuhiko Tanaka, Cappy Harada, Hiroshi Takahashi, and Masanori Murakami. Courtesy of Masanori Murakami, may not be reproduced without permission.

Fig. 7. Fresno manager Bill Werle. National Baseball Hall of Fame Library, Cooperstown NY.

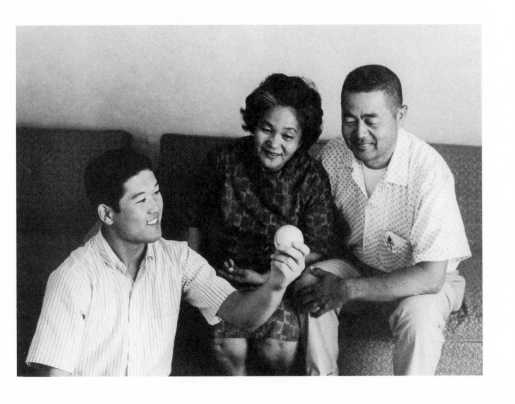

Fig. 8. Masanori with Kiyoto and Fumiko Saiki, 1964. Courtesy of Masanori Murakami, may not be reproduced without permission.

Fig. 9. San Francisco Giants manager Alvin Dark. © 2013 S.F. Giants.

Fig. 10. Masanori Murakami in Giants uniform. Author's collection, produced by Jaime Kent.

Fig. 11. (*opposite top*) Cartoon from the *San Mateo Times* featuring Murakami by Jack Matsuoka. Courtesy of Emi Young.

Fig. 12. (*opposite bottom*) At Haneda Airport, December 1964. *From left:* Secretary General of the Commissioner's Office Ko Ihara; Pacific League President Fujio Nakazawa; Masanori's father, Kiyoshi; Masanori; Masanori's mother, Tomiko; and Cappy Harada. Courtesy of Masanori Murakami, may not be reproduced without permission.

Fig. 13. (*above*) Returning to San Francisco for the 1965 season. © 2013 S.F. Giants.

Fig. 14. San Francisco Giants manager Herman Franks and Giants owner Horace Stoneham. © 2013 S.F. Giants.

Fig. 15. Mashi enjoying a hot dog. National Baseball Hall of Fame Library, Cooperstown NY.

Fig. 16. Mashi with Walter Osaka and his daughters (*from left*) Barbara, Mary, and Juli, 1965. Courtesy of Masanori Murakami, may not be reproduced without permission.

Fig. 17. Mashi before a game. National Baseball Hall of Fame Library, Cooperstown NY.

Fig. 18. Mashi with the Nankai Hawks, 1967. Author's collection.

Fig. 19. Masanori and Yoshiko Hoshino Murakami on their wedding day, December 5, 1967. Courtesy of Masanori Murakami, may not be reproduced without permission.

Fig. 20. Mashi and his parents, Kiyoshi and Tomiko, celebrating his hundredth career victory, 1979. Courtesy of Masanori Murakami, may not be reproduced without permission.

knees-bent fielding position. It was a graceful, pleasing delivery with little wasted motion.

In center field the colossal scoreboard summed up the game; at 175 feet wide and 80 feet tall, it was the largest in the Majors and the first to house a movie screen. It was the bottom of the eighth inning, and the Mets led 4–0. It had been a tight game, with starters Bob Hendley (Giants) and Al Jackson (Mets) battling until the Mets broke it open in the bottom of the seventh. With nobody on base and no lead to protect, Giants manager Alvin Dark reasoned it was a good time to baptize Murakami. Later Dark told reporters, "We were down, 4–0, so there was no pressure on him, although from watching him I don't believe pressure bothers him in the least." Dark continued: "I wanted to find out if he could pitch. They told me he could. . . . We felt all along he could help us. We wouldn't have brought him up otherwise. The fact Masanori is Japanese was no consideration at all to me when I decided to pitch him tonight."[4]

Charlie Smith dug into the batter's box. The Mets' slugger was having a tough season. Although he would lead the Mets with 20 home runs, he would bat just .238 and strike out 101 times (seventh highest in the National League). This night was no different. He had already struck out twice.

Smith had faced Japanese pitchers before. In 1961 the Yomiuri Giants had traveled to Vero Beach, Florida, to join the Dodgers for spring training. Then a Dodger, Smith had played against the visitors throughout the spring. "Those guys threw mostly slow breaking balls," Smith told reporters, "so that's what I was looking for."[5]

Murakami went into his windup and surprised Smith with a fastball on the outside corner of the plate. "Striiiiike!" announced umpire Ed Vargo, raising his right hand. The Mets' fans burst into applause as the old beat writer next to Kumio Sato widened his eyes and shook his head at the fans' reaction. Mashi came back with another fastball for the second strike. He threw the third fastball outside, hoping to get the swinging strikeout, but Smith held up. Then came the signature pitch—a curveball breaking sharply over the plate for a called third strike. One down.

Mets catcher Chris Cannizzaro came next and smacked a screwball into center field for a clean single. Loud cheers echoed through the stadium, but Masanori remained unfazed. Focused solely on his pitching, he later told reporters that he was unaware of the noise.

As Cannizzaro took a short lead off first, Murakami turned his attention to the Mets' first baseman, Ed Kranepool. The batter was six months younger than Masanori but already had nearly two hundred Major League games behind him. A Bronx native, Kranepool had been signed by the Mets straight out of high school with a staggering $80,000 signing bonus. Many believed he would be the next Lou Gehrig, but despite an eighteen-year career, he would never come close to that lofty comparison.[6] Four pitches later Kranepool swung and missed a fastball for strike three.

On the mound Murakami still seemed calm—even emotionless. "He knew he had a man to watch on first [but] he never showed excitement," noted Mets manager Casey Stengel. "He knows how to stand on the rubber." "We thought that he might be a little nervous," added Mets starting pitcher Al Jackson, "but he wasn't."[7] With two outs Murakami focused on shortstop Roy McMillian, who swung at the first pitch and grounded to short to end the inning. He had thrown just 13 pitches, 10 of them strikes, to polish off the Mets.

With the side retired, "Murakami, with a spring in his gait and a wad of chewing gum in his mouth, strode toward the Giants' dugout, [as] organist Jane Jarvis got into the swing of things playing the Japanese Sandman [a popular pre–World War II song written in 1920 by Richard A. Whiting and Raymond B. Egan and later performed by Benny Goodman and Artie Shaw]."[8] Knowing that they had just witnessed what Jack Hanley of the *San Jose Mercury News* called "a historic occasion for baseball and Japan," the Mets' fans rose to their feet to cheer for Murakami.[9]

After the game there were more interviews for Masanori, culminating with his being Mets' broadcaster Ralph Kiner's special guest on his famous postgame show, "Kiner's Korner." Even with a Japanese reporter to help interpret, the language barrier proved nearly insurmountable, and the interview was cut short.

Kiner began with an easy question, "Are you nervous?"

"Not so much," replied Masanori.

"What is your best pitch?" Kiner asked next.

Without waiting for the interpreter, Murakami jumped in with, "Koufax." Flummoxed, Kiner tried, "Who is your favorite pitcher?"

And he got the response to match his previous question: "Curve ball and a little bit change-up."

"I see," said Kiner looking puzzled. "Well, uh, Masanori, uh, thank you for being with us. Thank you very much indeed." Masanori and the interpreter nodded and smiled.[10]

Years later Murakami recalled that historic day. "During the game I was really excited and really into it. And after the game was over, I felt a sense of satisfaction. However, the moment I really became overwhelmed was the next day when I saw the newspaper and saw myself in there. I thought, 'Wow, I've really done something here!'"

Murakami's debut headlined the sports sections in both San Francisco and New York. The *San Francisco Chronicle* topped its Sporting Green section in inch-high bold letters: "Murakami Debuts; Giants Lose." Articles by Bob Stevens covered both the game and "Masanori's 1st Day in the Big Leagues," while a large photograph depicted Murakami signing autographs outside the Roosevelt Hotel. Bucky Walter's headline in the *San Francisco News–Call Bulletin* blared, "Murakami Pitches Way into History." Feature articles written by AP News and UPI and picked up by dozens, if not hundreds, of local newspapers spread the story across the country. Bob Stevens's emphasis on the debut's historical importance was typical: "History transcending even the importance of a costly defeat was made in Shea Stadium last night when Japan and the United States joined hands and played the game both countries claim as their national pastime. . . . The sight of the 20-year-old pitching pioneer, Murakami, making history for two great nations by working for the San Francisco Giants seemed more important. It was a moment that will live in faraway Japan long after this vital defeat has been forgotten."[11]

George Vecsey of *Newsday* noted the irony that Alvin Dark, who had just made headlines for his racist statements, would go down in history as the first manager to play an Asian in the big leagues. Dark, however, managed to stay in true form by sharing with the press a bon mot reference to the Japanese attack on Pearl Harbor when discussing Murakami's fastball. "I would say he's 'sneaky' fast although maybe you had better call it speedy fast. The people in Japan might not understand what I mean by sneaky."[12]

In reacting to Murakami's first Major League appearance, Dark was not alone in making lame ethnic jokes. Dick Young, the notoriously abrasive writer for the *Daily News*, entitled his article "Giants Spring Oriental Lefty but Honorable Mets Go, 4–1" and finished it off by sarcastically praising Mets fans for not unfurling a "banner reading: Remember Pearl Harbor." Prescott

Sullivan of the *San Francisco Examiner*, the cigar-chomping, rumpled veteran sports reporter who became the inspiration for Neil Simon's character Oscar Madison of the *Odd Couple*, wrote a long, rambling fictional account of an infant Murakami sitting on Lefty O'Doul's knee and receiving baseball instruction. The bizarre column is filled with pidgin English and bad ethnic puns, such as its calling the infant Murakami "the little nipper."[13]

In general, however, American reporters avoided the ethnic and racial jokes so common in depictions of Japanese baseball just a decade earlier. When the Brooklyn Dodgers went to Japan in 1956, for example, the *Sporting News* ran several cartoons depicting Japanese with the ugly, buck-toothed, squinty-eyed caricatures now known as Yellowface. Truly offensive depictions or descriptions of Murakami were noticeably absent from the media during his entire stay in the United States.

In Otsuki news of the hometown boy's historic achievement spread fast. "Neighbors just kept coming in to congratulate our family," Masanori's mother, Tomiko, told reporters. "Then when he pitched his first game, scores of people—many of them complete strangers—just wandered in to congratulate us. It was frightening to see so many people coming at once, but I was so proud that I almost cried."[14]

Tomiko Murakami told AP sportswriter Robert Liu, "I thought that it would be safer and more secure for him to go to college and become a doctor. . . . But he was stubborn . . . and refus[ed] to become a doctor. . . . He liked baseball and often played until long after his dinnertime so finally my husband and I gave in. My husband and I did not understand and like baseball at first so we bought simple baseball books to find out what it was about this American game that fascinated our son. Now we're beginning to understand and like the game and we only hope our son continues playing baseball and does not forget what we once told him—if you want to be a ballplayer, you will have to be the best in Japan."[15]

Over six thousand miles from New York on the Japanese northern island of Hokaido, Yoshiko Hoshino, the young woman who had escorted Masanori to Nara, was sitting quietly when a friend rushed over holding a newspaper. "Look! Murakami-san is in the newspaper!" There, in *Sports Shimbun*, was a large photograph of Murakami with a long accompanying article. Excited, they hurried out to the newspaper stand at a nearby train station to buy all the newspapers.

As Yoshiko found, nearly every major Japanese newspaper had reported on the debut. "Our dream has come true after thirty years of effort since the establishment of [Japanese] professional baseball," wrote a reporter in *Shukan Baseball*.[16] Masanori understood his importance to his countrymen: "I'm kind of overwhelmed by it all, but I'm glad I came through all right, especially because of every one in Japan."[17]

Surprisingly, however, it was not front-page news—even in the sports dailies. After all, few except for diehard baseball fans had heard of the twenty-year-old Minor League pitcher. Baseball historian Yoichi Nagata remembers, "I was a junior high student and an avid baseball fan. I knew it happened but I almost didn't care because it had nothing to do with my interest, Japanese pro baseball. In those years, Major League Baseball was not on my radar, probably wasn't for most Japanese. I don't think my friends and I talked about Murakami at school."[18] The day's sports headlines instead focused on a showdown between the rival Yomiuri Giants and Hanshin Tigers, locked in a tight pennant race. On the interior pages, however, many papers covered the debut and Murakami's story in depth. The most detailed coverage came in *Sankei News*. Although a business newspaper, it had the inside story from staff reporter Sho Onodera, who had acted as Murakami's interpreter prior to the game at Shea Stadium.

The American military newspaper *Pacific Stars and Stripes* featured Murakami's story all week long, and the weekly sports magazines ran lengthy articles on the debut and Murakami's background. *Shukan Baseball* even ran a detailed account of the debut as it was watched in San Francisco's famous Lefty O'Doul's Bar.[19] O'Doul, one of the few Americans in the Japan Baseball Hall of Fame, had helped establish Japan's professional league and had spent almost four decades promoting baseball exchanges between the United States and Japan. As Murakami threw his first pitch by Charlie Smith, O'Doul announced, "Tonight drinks will be my treat!" Looking over at the famous former ballplayer, the *Shukan Baseball* reporter noticed his eyes brimming with tears. At the end of the inning, as the bar patrons broke into applause, O'Doul stood. "I have been patiently waiting for this day for 30 years," he said. The crowd raised their glasses. "Congratulations, Lefty! *Ganbare*, Mashi!"[20]

Pacific League president Fujio Nakazawa summed up the general consensus: "It is wonderful for [Murakami] to join the Majors, as it shows the improvement of Japanese baseball. . . . I am looking forward to seeing how well he can do against Major Leaguers."[21] An unnamed editor of a Tokyo newspaper told sports columnist Art Rosenbaum, "The Murakami story will certainly be named one of the five major news events of 1964 from our view."[22]

But it was not to be. Murakami's debut as the Major League's first Japanese soon became overshadowed by the Tokyo Olympics and ultimately by a turn of events that would tarnish Masanori's achievement.

CHAPTER 11

Murakami mania swept through San Francisco in the week following the debut. For five straight days the *San Francisco Chronicle* ran articles on the young Japanese—most with accompanying photographs. Beat writer Bob Stevens covered his promotion, debut, and first day with the Major League team, and sports editor Art Rosenbaum featured or mentioned him in each column. The paper supplemented its exclusives with AP or UPI pieces on Masanori's background. Even political cartoonist Bob Bastian got into the act. The September 3 issue contained a cartoon depicting a confused batter staring out at a left-handed pitcher in mid-windup wearing full samurai armor. Beneath the caption, "The Giants' Imported Southpaw," was a breezy article declaring, "The San Francisco Giants . . . have in their quick autumnal decline written a glittering ineffaceable page of professional baseball history. They brought a Japanese player into the Big Leagues. . . . Furthermore, the new acquisition seems able to pitch, thus lending utility as well as novelty to the Giants line-up which has been suffering painfully from lack of the former commodity. . . . He looks like the best thing the Giants management has achieved this season."[1]

Other Bay Area papers, the *Pacific Stars and Stripes* and the *Sporting News*, gave Murakami similar attention. Alan Ward, writing for the *Oakland Tribune*'s Focus page, for example, used Murakami's popularity as a conduit to discuss the Japanese people's willingness to speak English as he urged readers to visit Tokyo for the 1964 Olympic games.[2] Even New York's *Daily News* ran a full page pictorial of the Japanese sensation in its Sunday, September 20, edition.

San Francisco's mayor, John F. Shelley, sent Masanori a congratulatory telegram. "On behalf of myself and all baseball fans, I welcome you as a citizen of San Francisco. Congratulations upon your first thrilling performance on the mound, which is but a hint of good things to come. We are proud of Japan's gift to San Francisco."[3] The Yamato Sukiyaki House, San Francisco's premier Japanese restaurant founded in 1948 by Kobo Ishizaki, also honored Mashi—by adding the Masanori Murakami Cocktail ("Three and you're out!") to the menu and sponsoring a Masanori Murakami Fan Club. Murakami got further good news on September 3, when the California League included him on the All-League team and named him the Rookie of the Year.

After Masanori's debut the Giants stayed in New York for three days before moving on to Philadelphia and then Pittsburgh. For the remainder of the road trip Masanori remained in the bullpen. Complete games by Juan Marichal and Gaylord Perry against the Mets and a second complete game by Marichal against the Phillies made his services unnecessary. But in four other games Dark used the bullpen liberally without calling on the Japanese left-hander. Twice in key situations Dark went to the ineffective thirty-one-year-old lefty Billy O'Dell, only to have O'Dell fail.

Watching from the sidelines, Mashi became frustrated. "I knew that I would not be used to protect a lead, but I thought they could let me throw when we were losing. Yet they didn't call me. I heard a rumor that I was only called up because of the race issue. I was embarrassed to throw only in the bullpen." With the inaction Murakami mania faded. By the end of the road trip the Bay Area newspapers no longer featured the new pitcher.

After Murakami had spent the summer in the low Minor Leagues, the Major Leagues were a dream. Gone were the long, tiring bus rides; the cramped motel rooms; the old, decaying locker rooms; and the meager meal money. Everything was now first class. They traveled by airplane, with coach buses picking them up on the tarmac. They stayed in the best hotels, complete with message cards inscribed "Welcome M. Murakami" and fruit baskets in the rooms. After the games there were impressive spreads in the clubhouse with hamburgers, fried chicken, salads, and even beer. Clubhouse attendants washed their clothes, shined their shoes, and transported their baggage. Travel per diem went from $3 with Fresno to $12 in the big leagues. "I felt like I had succeeded in the world!" says Murakami.

As the Giants stayed in New York, Philadelphia, and Pittsburgh, Murakami used his free time to tour the cities. As he expected to return to Japan after the season, it would be his only chance to see the East Coast. In New York he walked through the streets of Midtown; in Philly he visited Independence Hall and photographed the Liberty Bell. From each city he sent back stacks of postcards to friends and family in Japan.

Just as Americans had trouble with his and other Japanese names, Mashi had trouble remembering English names. He made a list of every player with his uniform number and carried it with him to help him learn.[4] Once he mastered the names on the list, he discovered that the players usually called each other by nicknames. Catcher Tom Haller was called Hatch; Dick Schofield was "Duck" because he walked like a duck; Ron Herbel was "Chicky" because of his big chin; and Hal Lanier was called "Maxi" because his father was a former Major Leaguer named Max. Some nicknames were sarcastic or mean and used behind a player's back. "My teammates often tricked me because I was not familiar with the situations and didn't understand the meanings. Somebody told me to call Frank Linzy 'Okie,' so when I met him in the morning I greeted him, 'Hi, Okie,' rather than 'Hi, Frank.' Linzy made a little disgusted look on his face. I didn't understand. My teammates had told me to call him that, so I simply did. Later I learned that he was from Oklahoma, and 'Okie' was the derogatory term for Oklahomans. It was very similar to being called a Jap. I had no idea. I just thought it was a friendly gesture. I kept calling him that until eventually he said, 'You Jap,' with a disgusted look, so I understood at last. But Frank knew that I had been tricked by my teammates and had no idea that Okie was a derogatory term, so he laughed it off."

Likewise some of the players called Willie McCovey "Donkey," probably because of his huge body and long face. "Right after I joined the team, I greeted him with, 'Hi Donkey,' as a friendly gesture. A sad, hurt expression came over his face, and he said, 'Mashi, please stop doing that.' I had no idea that he didn't like the nickname. I never used it again."

The Giants returned to San Francisco on September 8 for two games against the Los Angeles Dodgers. More than a hundred members of the Murakami Fan Club waited at the airport to welcome their hero home. "Seems like there was a mob of people waiting for him everywhere we went," noted a teammate.[5] With the Giants mired in third place, 6 games behind the Phillies and the Dodgers in seventh, 14 games out, little seemed at stake. But the fierce rivalry between the two teams ensured a hard series.

The first game, however, turned out to be a one-sided yawner. Don Drysdale held the Giants to just 5 hits as the Dodgers scored 7 off starter Bob Hendley. Down 8–0 in the sixth, Dark brought in Murakami to mop up.

Masanori took the mound and completed his warmup tosses. The last time he had stood there, it had been March and the stands had been empty; now 24,448 fans filled the seats. That unlikely fantasy had come true. He was now actually pitching in Candlestick Park in a real game.

Built on a twenty-five-acre spit on the west-side of San Francisco Bay, Candlestick has been called "the worst park in the history of Major League Baseball" and utterly "utilitarian and soulless, devoid of any amenities and charm."[6] The ballpark was plagued by bad weather, construction problems, and poor design. Fog would roll off the bay, obscuring fly balls and soaking the grass, making the players' feet wet and cold. To combat the chilly night air, architects had designed a radiant heating system featuring hot water running through pipes buried within the concrete floors under the seating areas. In practice, however, the pipes had been buried too deeply in the concrete, and no heat reached the chilled audience. Nobody had considered lines of sight when designing the stadium. When the ballpark opened on April 12, 1960, those seated in the press box could not see home plate, but some fans had an unobstructed view of the dugout toilet. The many problems led architect Alan Tesco to write an article for *Harper's Magazine* entitled "How Not to Build a Ballpark."[7]

Yet Candlestick's most notorious feature was the wind. "The howling winds whipped off San Francisco Bay and struck the Bayview Park Hill, just beyond the park's third-base side," writes historian James Hirsch. "The winds came over the hill, swooped down into the park, rushed across the outfield, caught the overhang of the stands along the right field line, swung back toward home, and blew past third. Candlestick was not so much a capricious wind tunnel as a ruthless vortex. At times, a player's shirt would be blowing one way and his pants the opposite."[8] Gusts of wind could carry infield popups over the outfield walls for home runs or, conversely, reduce powerful drives to easy outs. Towering fly balls could become an adventure, with players running around the field like circus clowns as the ball shifted directions. After a week reporters asked Murakami what he thought about Candlestick. "Cold" was his only response.[9]

On Murakami's first pitch in the infamous park, Dodger first baseman Wes Parker lined the ball just passed Mashi's ear and into center field for a single. Asked what he was thinking after the hit, Masanori laughed and told the reporter, "Something unprintable that didn't require any translation."[10] Murakami quickly regained his composure, struck out Nate Oliver, and retired both Drysdale and Parker on a "strike them out, throw them out" double play. Taking the mound again in the seventh, Mashi induced Maury Wills to ground to short, struck out Dick Tracewski, walked Willie Davis, and then ended the inning by striking out Tommy Davis.

The outing brought Murakami back into the news. Under the headline "Giants Lose to Drysdale," the *Chronicle*'s sub-headline stated, "Murakami Fans Four in Two Relief Innings." A companion article with a picture entitled "Murakami Unperturbed: The Hitter? Who Cares?" revealed that Masanori "didn't know the names of any of the opposition and his shoulder shrugs indicated he might not care either." He stated, "Pitching in relief, I usually go in without knowing which batter is at the plate. I just follow instructions from the manager and my catcher and try to get him out. I guess I've been lucky so far."[11] But more important, Murakami had proven to Dark that the inning in New York was no fluke. In three innings Mashi had allowed just 2 hits and a walk, and he had struck out 6. Dark now knew that he could trust the young Japanese import in important games. During the 1998 Japan Broadcasting Corporation (NHK) television documentary "The Trip of My Soul," Dark told Murakami, "You had great control. You knew where the ball was going and you knew how to pitch. . . . I could bring you in anytime and you'd throw strikes. That's the most important thing that I was looking for."[12]

Two days later Dark went straight to Murakami with the game on the line. The first-place Phillies were in town for a three-game series. A sweep would bring the Giants within three games of first place with twenty left on the schedule. Marichal started the opening game and pitched eight innings of four-hit ball. Unfortunately for San Francisco, the Giants could not score. In the bottom of the eighth Dark lifted Marichal for a pinch hitter. The strategy worked, with the Giants eventually loading the bases before Orlando Cepeda grounded out to end the inning. Still down 1–0, Dark brought in Mashi to face the top of the Phillies order. "I was itching with the desire to pitch. I was so happy," recalls Murakami. With his screwball working particularly well, he struck out left-handed Tony Gonzalez, retired Rookie of the Year Dick Allen on a ground ball, and forced Johnny Callison to fly weakly to center. It would be Mashi's only inning, as the Giants failed to score in the ninth and lost 1–0.

After the game reporters asked if he hoped to move into the starting rotation. "Every pitcher dreams of starting and I am no different," he stated through a translator. "But if Mr. Dark thinks I can help the club as a relief pitcher I'll be glad to stay there. Actually I shouldn't be thinking about a starting role because I don't really know if I'll last in the Major Leagues. After all, I've only pitched in three games totaling five innings. All I know is I'll have to try harder and maybe if I do well between now and the end of the season, I'll get a chance to start next year. Right now though, I can't worry about it. I'm too worried about just staying in the Majors. It's a lot tougher playing here because the players are all so good. I think I've been lucky so far but will have to work harder to do better."[13]

The Giants placed Masanori and the other rookies at the Benjamin Franklin Hotel, a modestly priced establishment in nearby San Mateo, about ten miles south of Candlestick Park. Built in 1927 as the town's top hotel, it had gradually declined and in the 1960s was used to house layover crews for United Airlines. Nonetheless, it had clean, comfortable, large rooms; a nice dining room and lobby; a recreation room; a swimming pool; and extensive grounds. It was a far cry from the Spartan Japanese baseball dormitories.

Masanori was rarely lonely during his short time in San Francisco. The Giants' front office reported that he received more than one thousand calls from organizations and fans asking about possible personal appearances.[14] On his off days members of his fan club or prominent Japanese Americans took him out to eat. At one luncheon held by his booster club, Mashi eschewed the provided interpreter and did his best to answer the audience's questions directly. Asked if he got upset when an umpire called an obvious strike a ball, he responded in English with a grin, "Oh, I say nothing. I just keep throwing strikes. Pretty soon umpire catch on."[15]

At the hotel Mashi became close friends with fellow rookie pitcher Dick Estelle. They spent hours in the hotel's recreation room playing ping pong, billiards, and pool. Estelle told *Chronicle* sports editor Jack McDonald, "Murakami reads American comic books a lot, but they are sometimes hard for him to understand. He also gets fan letters from American people, all wishing him success, and answering them with the aid of a Japanese-English dictionary is adding to his vocabulary."[16]

Masanori's English was improving rapidly. McDonald noted that Mashi "is getting along just famously. . . . He's a good mixer and has a fine sense of humor. Consequently, his teammates have been unstintingly cooperative and almost outdo each other teaching him new English words and American ways."[17] Relief pitcher John Pregenser told reporters, "We have had no problems communicating in English. He does have trouble with some words, but it's not that bad."[18] Relying on the phrases taught to him by the Latino walk-ons during spring training, Murakami even tried speaking Spanish. His attempts to converse with the Latino players in Fresno had led to the unfounded rumor that he could speak the language fluently. Matty Alou, however, confided, "He doesn't understand it real well, but enough to get along. We've been to several places and have no trouble communicating with each other."[19]

Mashi finally got his chance to save a game a week later against the Pittsburgh Pirates. After Murakami had pitched another perfect inning against the Mets on September 16, Dark gave him a true test two days later. Dick Estelle led the Pirates 3–1 going into the eighth inning. After a one-out double and walk, Dark brought in right-handed relief ace Bob Shaw, who promptly gave up an RBI double to Roberto Clemente. Still up by a run but with runners on second and third, Dark called Murakami from the pen to face left-handed pinch hitter Jerry Lynch. One pitch later Lynch popped harmlessly to first for the second out. Right-handed Donn Clendenon was due up next, but Dark decided to stay with Mashi. Working from the stretch, Murakami went into his windup and stopped. Home plate umpire Ed Sudol signaled a balk, and Bob Bailey jogged home from third to tie the game. Clendenon then singled up the middle, driving in Clemente for the winning run. Although Masanori would not be charged with either an earned run or the loss (the runners had been put on base by Estelle and Shaw), the defeat was his responsibility. Yet the press was surprisingly forgiving, and the next morning's papers contained no criticisms of Murakami's failure to protect the lead.

With the loss the Giants were now 8 games out with only 14 left to play. Nearly everybody—perhaps excluding manager Alvin Dark—believed the pennant race was over. A few days earlier Dark had proclaimed that with a hot streak the Giants could still catch the Phillies. He noted that many of the Phils' remaining games were against first-division teams (teams with winning records), while the Giants were scheduled to play second-division squads.

"And we're going all out to win them all!"[20] But few took him seriously. It was common knowledge that Horace Stoneham, who disliked Dark and was embarrassed by his racial comments, would fire the manager at season's end.

And then, just after Philadelphia had printed thousands of World Series tickets, the impossible happened. The Phillies began to lose. Plagued by injuries and using a three-man starting rotation, the Phils started the most famous and spectacular collapse in baseball history. From September 18 to 30 Philadelphia won just once in thirteen games. At the same time it looked like Dark's predicted hot streak might make an appearance.

After winning the remaining two games against the Pirates, the Giants flew to Houston to play three against the Colt 45s. In its third year of existence Houston was in the midst of seven straight seasons of losing baseball. It was currently in ninth place and should have been easy fodder for San Francisco. A sweep of the Colt 45s would put the Giants only four games behind the Phillies, but they would have to settle for two of three as they were held to just 4 hits in the opener. In the second game Masanori earned his first Major League save as he came on in the ninth to protect a 7–1 lead with two men on and no outs. In the words of the *Chronicle*'s Bob Stevens, "The unyielding Japanese lefthander wiped out the final three .45s."[21]

Under today's rules Murakami would not have been credited with a save for the outing. In the official rule, created by Major League Baseball in 1969, a save is awarded when a pitcher (1) finishes a game won by his club; (2) is not the winning pitcher; and (3) meets one of the following three conditions: (a) enters the game with a lead of three runs or less and pitches at least one inning; (b) enters the game with the potential tying run either on base, at bat, or on deck; or (c) pitches effectively for at least three innings. Prior to 1969 saves were not an official MLB statistic but were bestowed when a relief pitcher held a lead the remainder of a game.

The Giants moved on to Chicago, taking the first game easily behind Gaylord Perry's three-hit complete game. With the Phillies' continued losses, they were just 3½ games out of first place with 8 games left to play. Yet Cincinnati and St. Louis had also taken advantage of Philadelphia's collapse. Despite Dark's dismissal of these rivals, both the Reds and Cardinals had not lost for over a week and were entrenched between the Giants and Phils. The Giants had two more games against eighth-place Chicago and then would go back home to play the Colt 45s and Cubs again. Both the Reds and Cardinals would face the last-place Mets, sixth-place Pittsburg, and Philadelphia. A solid winning streak could bring the Giants to the top.

But it was not to be. "Giants Drop 2—And Out of Sight," proclaimed the *Chronicle* after the Cubs swept a doubleheader on September 27. The Giants flew home on September 28, 4½ games behind first-place Cincinnati, which had moved to the top of the standings with a five-game sweep of the Mets. Although not mathematically eliminated, the Giants would need a near miracle to capture the pennant.

During the trip to Chicago Masanori made an announcement. Despite pressure from his family and the Hawks to return to Japan, he would spend the winter in the United States "to practice the two things now closest to his heart": pitching and speaking English. "At home I learn English, but I don't have a chance to speak it. I stay here this winter with Japanese friends in Fresno and speak it every day. I learn that way."[22]

Back in San Francisco on September 29, just 4,749 people showed up to Candlestick to watch the Giants play the Houston Colt 45s. Nonetheless, for Murakami, "It was the most memorable day in my life." Neither team looked sharp as they traded runs through eight innings and entered the ninth tied at 4–4. Dark had Mashi throwing in the bullpen since the sixth inning and decided to use him in the top of the ninth. As Jeff Carter announced, "Now pitching, number 10 . . . ," the small crowd burst into applause and cheers. Masanori walked to the mound relaxed. No need to hum "Sukiyaki" anymore. This would be his seventh game, and he felt confident.

"I had begun to understand the American style of hitting. It was different from in Japan. On 1–0, 2–0, and 3–0 counts, batters looked for a fastball because most American pitchers wanted a sure strike. They were not aggressive enough to use a breaking ball like Japanese pitchers. In those counts I threw a curve or screwball to gain a strike, and they usually weren't ready for it." Murakami had dropped the change-up from his repertoire. Although he had worked on the pitch all season and found it effective in the California League, he feared that the stronger big leaguers would feast on the pitch. In a widely circulated interview he told Bob Stevens of the *Chronicle*, "The change-up no good. Relief pitcher come in, men on bases. Throw change. Boom! Long ball. No good."[23]

Mashi began by striking out shortstop Bob Lillis. Next, future Hall of Famer Joe Morgan, freshly called up from AAA, swung late and popped out near the third-base stands. The inning ended with a strikeout of slugger Jimmy Wynn. "I was pitching just like I was still playing for Fresno in A ball. Each time a Colt 45 fouled a pitch or swung and missed, the fans broke out in a cheer."

After the Giants went hitless in the bottom of the ninth, Murakami went back to work. Walter Bond popped to short, Sonny Jackson struck out, and Jim Beauchamp popped to short.

In the bottom of the tenth Mashi was due up with two outs. Two weeks earlier Murakami had complained after Dark had someone pinch-hit for him, supposedly pointing out to the manager, "I got five hits for Fresno and one was inside the park homerun."[24] This time Dark let him bat, only to watch him strike out, but the at bat allowed Murakami to take the mound again in the eleventh. It would be the first time Mashi had pitched in more than two innings since coming to the Majors. As he walked toward the mound, his teammates encouraged him, "Yes, Mashi, you can do it!"

After Rusty Staub flied out to right, catcher Jerry Grote hit a weak ground ball past the mound. Shortstop Jim Davenport ran in and slipped, allowing Grote to reach base. Pitcher Claude Raymond then laid down a sacrifice, moving the go-ahead run to second with two outs. Bob Lillis came to the plate to face Murakami for the second time, and minutes later a fly ball to left field ended the threat.

Matty Alou ended the game in the bottom of the eleventh with a lead-off "sayonara home run." It was his first home run in two years. The last, also hit against Houston, had come exactly two years earlier on September 29, 1962. "I felt like I was dreaming," recalls Murakami. "I was waving at the fans in the stands without realizing it. It was not until I came back to the hotel that I realized I was the first Japanese to win a Major League game. Once I thought about it, I could not stay calm. 'I did it! I did it!' I thought. I naturally picked up the phone and made an international call home. It was not a long moment, but it felt like hours until I reached Japan."

The next morning Mashi went into the team's front office at Candlestick Park. A letter from Yoshiko Hoshino with an accompanying picture waited for him. "She had not known that I would earn a win when she posted the letter, but it seemed to me that it arrived just in time to celebrate my first victory."

Masanori had not gone to the office just to retrieve his mail. Chub Feeney had explained that all first-year players not on the official forty-man roster were eligible to be drafted by other teams. To be on the forty-man roster Murakami would have to sign a contract for the 1965 season. Masanori longed to play another year in the Majors and had been discussing the possibility with his father on the telephone. Kiyoshi still demanded that he return to Japan as soon as possible and remain in his native country, but Mashi decided to follow his heart. With Kiyoto Saiki acting as interpreter and legal guardian, Masanori signed for the following season.

The dramatic victory against Houston seemed to inspire the Giants as they swept the Colt 45s and won the first game against the Cubs. On the morning of October 3, with just two regular season games remaining, they were only two games behind the first-place Cardinals. The Reds had slipped to second, just a half game back, and the Phillies had fallen to third, a game and a half back. Only one scenario would move the Giants into first place. If the Mets beat the Cardinals twice, the Phillies topped the Reds, and the Giants won the final two against the Cubs, there would be a four-way tie, with identical 92-70 records, at the top of the National League. The league announced that such a deadlock would force a playoff. The teams would be randomly paired off for a three-game series, with the winners meeting in a second three-game series to decide who would go to the World Series.[25]

Although the Mets did top the Cardinals on October 3 and the Phillies beat the Reds, the Giants were unable to help themselves as the Cubs thrashed them 10–7 to eliminate them from the race. The *Chronicle* noted that there were "two bright spots . . . two long homers by . . . Willie Mays . . . and another flawless performance by Masanori Murakami, 1⅓ scoreless innings this time, which caused the crowd to boo when he was taken out for a pinch hitter."[26]

On the final day of the 1964 season the Giants played "just for the exercise and with as much gusto as the fat men at a company picnic."[27] The Cubs knocked out starter Gaylord Perry in the third inning after pounding out 8 hits for 3 runs. With runners on first and third and no outs, Al Dark turned to Murakami. By now Mashi had proven himself to be the Giants' top reliever. He had pitched 11 innings, giving up just 4 hits, a walk, and no runs. He had also struck out 13 of the 37 batters he had faced. But on this final day of the season, as the *Chronicle* noted, "even Masanori Murakami, the only Major Leaguer to eat with chopsticks, discovered that nobody is perfect."[28]

Outfielder John Boccabella greeted Mashi with a single, scoring a run. A single by Ron Campbell and Dick Bertell's sacrifice fly plated two more, making it a 7–0 game. Masanori then settled down and retired the next eight batters before surrendering a single and his only home run of the season in the sixth.

As Murakami finished out the inning, Horace Stoneham called on the dugout telephone and asked Alvin Dark to meet him in the dressing room. According to Dark, the meeting was brief.

"I've got to make a change," said Stoneham.

"It's your ball club, Mr. Stoneham," responded Dark. "It's your prerogative. Thank you for giving me the chance to manage." That was it. After the game Stoneham held a brief press conference, announcing that Dark and his coaching staff would not return, except for third-base coach Herman Franks, who would manage the club in 1965.[29]

As the 1964 season ended, several newspapers saw Murakami's debut as a watershed event. In an article entitled "Jackie Robinson Did It for Negroes, Murakami May Do It for Japanese," the *Hokubei Mainichi* mused whether Mashi's success would initiate a flood of Japanese players coming to the Major Leagues. When asked if it was possible, Masanori responded, "I'm sure some of the players [in Japan] could make it here in the United States. If I can, I don't see why they can't."[30]

A *Sporting News* editorial summed up the situation nicely: "The significance of Masanori Murakami's appearance with San Francisco cannot be over emphasized. He is the first Japanese player to perform in a Major League game. Because of this, his work already has been closely watched. If he comes through in good fashion, it could be the first step in tapping a new source of talent. . . . Horace Stoneham . . . is ahead of the rest with Japanese talent. It could pay dividends for the Giants and could cause the rest of the majors to look to the Far East."[31]

Indeed Stoneham's Giants had already seized the opportunity. Another Japanese pitcher would be joining Masanori in the Arizona Fall League.

CHAPTER 12

Masanori's new roommate during the Arizona Instructional League turned out to be his former teammate from the Nankai Hawks farm team, Shozo Nishimura. Three years older than Mashi, Nishimura had been signed in 1961 after a year at Kinki University in Osaka. With the exception of a 1961 start that lasted only four innings and resulted in a loss, he had been unable to make the Hawks *ichi-gun* after four minor league seasons. He had pitched adequately in 1963, posting an 8-5 record with a 2.89 ERA in 109 minor league innings, but time was running out. Japanese teams did not allow players to languish on the farm team. Players who seemed unlikely to make the main squad were released.

In the wake of Murakami's success in the Majors, Cappy Harada had arranged to have Nishimura join the San Francisco Giants for the Fall League. Nankai was probably only loaning Nishimura to the Giants so that he could sharpen his skills under the direction of American coaches, but writers for both the *Sporting News* and the Associated Press assumed he had signed a Minor League contract with San Francisco.

Like Murakami, Nishimura did not fit the stereotype of the uptight Japanese. Whereas Mashi was adventuresome, friendly, but a bit quiet, the new Japanese ballplayer was a free spirit. "Sometimes," Murakami later admitted, "his behavior made me a little nervous." There was the time when he decided to strip down to his undershorts and a belly warmer while hanging up his laundry in the apartment building's courtyard. Another time, when the two Japanese pitchers were visiting Las Vegas, Bob Hope called them up on stage. As Hope was shaking their hands on center stage, Nishimura used his ring finger to tickle Hope's palm causing the famous entertainer to jump in surprise.

Despite the different personalities the two imports got along well. They shared kitchen duties—Murakami cooking and Nishimura washing (but often forgetting to use dish soap). They joined two American teammates on a desert hunting trip. Perched on top of an open jeep, they caromed through the desert, shooting at cacti, deer, and rattlesnakes with rifles and shotguns. It was great fun until Mashi's errant shot wounded a deer and it had to be dispatched with a knife. Masanori decided it would be his last time hunting.

Although Harada had told the press that Nishimura was "every bit as good" as Murakami, Nishimura did not impress the Giants during the Fall League. He entered five games (all in relief), was hit hard, and lacked control. In 11 total innings he surrendered 12 hits (including a home run) and walked 5 for a 4.91 ERA. Perhaps Nishimura would have adjusted to American baseball and improved if an unusual incident had not ended his season early.

In late October Nishimura went to cover first on a ground ball hit to the right of the first baseman. Instead of approaching the base from the infield side, Nishimura ran through the base path, colliding with the batter on his way to first. The 160-pound pitcher went airborne, hit the ground, and rolled three times. Springing up, he charged the batter, yelling, "Hey! What do you think you are doing!" in Kansai Japanese. Although the American did not comprehend the words, he understood the intent and readied for a fight. Mashi ran from the bullpen next to first base and separated the two players.

"Nishimura-san, stop it! You are no match for him. Look at his arms. They are as big as my legs!" Nishimura calmed down, and a fight was avoided.

A few days later, however, Nishimura's shoulder still hurt. An X-ray determined that he had a slight dislocation, but the examining doctor concluded that Nishimura also had tuberculosis. The pitcher found the diagnosis ridiculous and insisted that he was healthy, but he returned to Japan for further medical tests. The doctors in Kyoto found signs that Nishimura had suffered from the disease at some point but that it was no longer evident. With the proper certification of a clean bill of health, the pitcher returned to Phoenix at the very end of the season. It was too late, however, for Nishimura to regain his pitching form, and the Giants made no effort to place him in their Minor League system. He would return to the Hawks' farm team for the next two seasons before finally making the *ichi-gun* in 1967. His Japanese league career would be short, however, and he would retire after the 1969 season, having pitched in only 41 games.

Murakami, on the other hand, excelled in Arizona. "Murakami Continues Brilliance," proclaimed the *Sporting News*. Mashi started 8 games and relieved another 3. In 56 innings he surrendered just 45 hits and 5 walks— for an impressive WHIP of 0.89. He also struck out 41 batters. His 5 wins and 1.61 ERA were both the second-best in the league. Masanori did particularly well against the Dodgers, pitching 5 innings of no-hit ball with 6 strikeouts on October 28 and 7 innings of shutout, 3-hit ball in November.

On top of his heroics on the mound Mashi slashed 9 hits and gained 3 RBIs in 22 at bats for a .409 batting average. Although he was far from the required 130 plate appearances to be eligible for the batting title, his average was the highest in the league among batters with more than five at bats. Giants publicist Gary Schumacher proclaimed at the end of the Fall League, "It just could be that this kid is destined for stardom. There isn't anything in his statistics to indicate otherwise. And if he can give us one or two good innings each time he's called, we could have a very exciting year, indeed!"[1]

With Mashi's success San Francisco took steps to secure him for the 1965 season. On October 5, the day after the end of the Major League season, the Giants wrote a check to the Hawks for $10,000—the same amount stipulated in the teams' January 6 agreement for purchasing one of the visiting players' contracts. Instead of sending this check directly to Nankai's front office with an explanation that they were purchasing Murakami's contract, they handed the check to Cappy Harada. Harada, in turn, gave the check to Hawks' chief scout Yoshio Tominaga, who was visiting San Francisco on October 22. According to Harada, the scout was aware that the check constituted payment for Murakami's contract. Tominaga endorsed the check and deposited it in the Bank of Tokyo Trust Company. It cleared on November 16, 1964.

Realizing that the Major League contract for the 1965 season Murakami had signed on September 30, when he was still owned by the Nankai Hawks, might not be valid, the Giants asked Murakami to sign a second contract. Masanori contacted Japan for advice. His parents had repeatedly asked him to return to Japan as soon as possible, so Mashi was not surprised when his father did not support his staying in the Majors. Masanori was stubborn, however, and planned to ignore his parents' wishes. He was more concerned about receiving Nankai's permission. Prior to his leaving Japan, the Hawks had told him to rely on Cappy Harada, and the team had not contacted him during his stay with the Giants. Now, however, Mashi believed it important that he discuss his future with somebody from the Hawks' front office. He asked his father to have the Hawks telephone him in Arizona.

When the call came, Masanori could hear loud talking and the clinking of glass in the background. It was obvious that the Hawks' directing manager, Tsugihiro Iwase, was calling from a bar. The connection was poor, and the background noise prohibited a true conversation. Masanori tried to explain the situation, but Iwase kept repeating, "Come home," seemingly without listening to his questions. Mashi seethed. This was one of the most important decisions of his life, and not only would Iwase not discuss it, but he had also called from a bar as if the telephone conversation was barely worth his time. "At that point," Murakami recalls, "I lost my trust in the Nankai Hawks."

Murakami turned to Harada for advice, and Harada assured him that the new contract would be just for one year and had the blessing of both Iwase and manager Kazuto Tsuruoka. Ignoring his parents' objections, Masanori met with Chub Feeney, Jack Schwarz, and Harada in November and signed a second contract for the upcoming season.

The Nankai Hawks, however, had not given their permission for Murakami to remain with the Giants. Tominaga denied selling the Giants the rights to Murakami's contract. "It seems that Murakami wants to stay in the United States, but we expect him to be a force next season, so when I went to the States, I told him never to sign." Tominaga admitted receiving the check for $10,000 but claimed "that was not trade money" but a bonus given to the Hawks if Murakami made the Majors. "Before I left for the States, I had been told by [general manager] Iwase to receive this money, which had been promised to us." The Hawks also announced that Horace Stoneham was expected to come to Japan to negotiate for Murakami.[2]

In early December the Hawks declared that they were "recalling Murakami" and that he would return to Japan later in the month. Tsuruoka added that the young pitcher would play an important role on the 1965 Hawks. What the Hawks did not know, however, was that Mashi was coming home only for a short visit with his parents and to have his tonsils removed by his family doctor. He had no plans to play for Nankai in 1965.

CHAPTER 13

The Japan Airlines flight touched down at Tokyo's Haneda Airport just after 8:25 p.m. on December 17, rolling to a stop where a crowd of photographers gathered on the tarmac. A trio of Japanese movies stars, seated on the plane near Masanori, Nishimura, and Cappy Harada, noticed the waiting press and began preening themselves. Earlier in the flight one had rather rudely rebuffed Murakami's request for an autograph.

The movie stars descended the mobile staircase at the plane's rear exit just before the ballplayers, waving and smiling for the cameras. And they were ignored. As they reached the bottom of the steps, Murakami appeared in the hatchway. Dozens of flashbulbs lit up the evening. The actors turned and stopped, their mouths agape. Who was this young man?

The photographers jockeyed for better angles as Mashi, dressed in a blue blazer and "smiling with confidence," walked slowly down the twenty steps. He had changed in his ten months in the United States. His skin now suntanned, he had put on nearly ten pounds of muscle and in the words of one reporter, "looked very American."[1]

With photographers and reporters in tow, the travelers walked to customs. "*Genki rashiien ne!*" yelled out a reporter (You look good!).

"Oh yeah," Mashi answered.

"It was good that you got called up to the Major Leagues," another said in Japanese.

"Oh yes," Mashi responded again in English.[2]

Outside of customs Masanori's father and mother and the Hawks' Tsugihiro Iwase and Yoshio Tominaga waited to welcome him home. Kazuto

Tsuruoka was not present as he was vacationing in Europe. Behind them stood nearly eighty members of the media and fans. Taken aback at the size of the crowd, Masanori asked, "This is something that never happened to me in the Major Leagues. I'm a little embarrassed. What should I do?" Hawks officials then announced a press conference would be held in a nearby room at 9:30. According to a letter Cappy Harada later wrote to Chub Feeney, at this point Tominaga quietly asked Harada not to attend the press conference but to go straight home and avoid the press.[3] As Harada was still an adviser to the Hawks, he agreed, telling reporters that he had been diagnosed with leukemia and was tired from the long trip.

Masanori sat next to his father and mother in the center of the small room. In front of them stood a rectangular coffee table supporting a half dozen large microphones. The fifty reporters, squeezed together shoulder to shoulder, encircled the table and the family.

"I am playing for the Giants next season," Murakami told the crowd. "I signed for the 1965 season on September 30. Harada-san told me that he got Nankai's approval. The Giants paid the trade money to Nankai, and there is no trouble. I came back to Japan to get a throat operation and to pay a visit to Nankai. I'm going back to the States at the end of January. According to Nankai, they will try to make me wear their uniform next year, but I am a Giants player."

In a series of follow-up questions, Murakami told when and where he had signed the contract and his understanding of the agreement. "What would you do if Nankai does not allow you to go back to the States?" a reporter asked.

"In the end, I signed with the Giants, so I would just go to the States. That's all. I want to play in the States for another year. At any rate, I'm going there at the end of January. Besides, Nankai must have agreed with it."

Iwase, however, told the audience that Nankai had not agreed to transfer Murakami's contract to the Giants. "It is a fact that he signed in the presence of Saiki-san, on behalf of his parents, on September 30. But if he hadn't signed, then he would have been eligible for the draft, so the Giants made him sign to protect him. Although it is an official contract in the Major Leagues, it is not valid here. There is no problem because we have studied the system for a year with the commissioner. The rumor about the trade money is a mistake. In the United States they have an agreement to give money, like a private bonus, when somebody is moved up from the Minors to the Major Leagues.

That amount usually seems to be $10,000. Harada-san misunderstands that money as trade money. The Giants and Nankai have never exchanged any money whatsoever. Now that he's back in Japan, we would never return him. Murakami must understand how we feel."[4]

In a brief statement Yoshio Tominaga reiterated that the $10,000 was not trade money, noting that the amount would not have been enough to buy Murakami's contract, as the Hawks had paid him a $30,000 signing bonus on top of the costs of sending him to the United States.

Later that evening *Hochi Sports* asked Nankai president Shigeru Niiyama to comment. His statement was direct. "Murakami certainly is our player, and he will do his job here next year. Whatever the Giants said, it doesn't matter. If it gets too complicated, I will make it clear through the Commissioner."

Following the press conference the Murakamis took a train to a nearby hotel. A photograph, snapped by a shadowing reporter from *Hochi Sports*, captures the family's mood. Kiyoshi Murakami leans against the train's window with his hand on his forehead and eyes closed from weariness. Next to him Masanori sits thoughtfully, stroking his chin between his thumb and forefinger, a pose slightly reminiscent of Auguste Rodin's famous sculpture, *The Thinker*.

That night Masanori tossed and turned, sleep elusive. He believed he had Nankai's blessing when he signed with the Giants for the '65 season. Now everything was in doubt. "I felt like I was being cheated," he recalled later, "but I wasn't sure if it was by Harada or the Hawks." Jetlagged and worried about the Hawks' stance on his contract, he woke at 5:00 a.m. and spoke to his father about the situation. At breakfast several hours later, he looked glum, his eyes red and his face swollen from lack of sleep. A *Hochi Sports* reporter asked him why he had signed. "Harada-san said I had permission from Nankai to play for the Giants for one more year. There was nobody else to consult, so I had to trust Harada-san."

"What are you going to do?" asked the reporter.

"Since I have a contract to play next year with the Giants, I have to go back to America. There is no other way since I signed. Anyway, I want to play baseball in America. If I miss this chance, I will never have the opportunity to do it again."

Masanori looked out the window. Rain tumbled down. "I'm a rain man," he joked to the reporter. "When I left San Francisco, it was raining. When

I stopped over in Honolulu on the way here, it was raining. And today, it is raining. I have to carry an umbrella all the time."

As he finished up breakfast, he received a telephone call at the front desk. Returning to the table, his face was serious. "Iwase and Tominaga are coming to see me," he announced. "They will probably order me to stay in Japan."

Two hours later the Murakamis and Nankai officials met privately for an hour. Masanori emerged looking upset. "I don't want to say anything," he told the waiting reporters. "They just asked what was going on and when I signed the contract."

As part of the agenda for his return to Japan, Murakami had agreed to fly to Osaka the next day and meet with Hawks president Niiyama. First, however, Iwase wanted to see the disputed contract, which Masanori had mailed to his father and was now at their home in Otsuki. Josuke Nishino, a close friend of Kazuto Tsuruoka's, arrived with a car and whisked the family home. Tokyo's efficient highway system was still years in the future, so the car raced along curvy, bumpy local roads toward Otsuki as several cars packed with reporters tailed it. "It was like a car chase from a movie!" remembers Murakami. The harrowing trip left Masanori's mother motion sick, and upon arrival she was escorted to bed. Although he had been away for ten months, Masanori had no time to visit with his sisters or grandmother or enjoy the comfort of his childhood home. His father and he had to catch the 5:49 p.m. express train back to Tokyo. They retrieved the contract and immediately headed for the station.

In the meantime Iwase met with Fujio Nakasawa, the president of the Pacific League, at his Ginza office to explain the problem. Twenty minutes later Iwase left to meet with Yushi Uchimura, the commissioner of Japanese baseball. The two discussed the issue, and Uchimura counseled that the Hawks and Giants should work out the problem between themselves and not involve the two leagues' commissioners. Unfortunately that sage advice was ignored.

On Friday, December 18, Masanori, his father, Iwase, Tominaga, and Harada flew to Osaka to meet with Shigeru Niiyama and the Nankai Railroad Company's board of directors. Masanori would pay his respects and thank the board for the opportunity to play in the United States, while Iwase and Harada would present their versions of the contract dispute.

Niiyama had only recently taken over the presidency from Makoto Tachibana and was unfamiliar with the details of the initial agreement between the Giants and Hawks. Furthermore, Iwase and Tominaga had neglected to tell him that the Hawks had received a $10,000 check from the San Francisco Giants, causing one reporter to write, "I don't understand why they were hiding the $10,000 from Niiyama. If [they really thought] it was a bonus, why not tell him?"[5] Cappy Harada was convinced that Iwase and Tominaga understood the true reason for the payment but were embarrassed that they had unintentionally sold Murakami's contract for such a small amount.

Arriving at Osaka Stadium around midday, Iwase and Tominaga asked Harada to wait while they escorted the Murakamis to pay their respects to the board of directors. Nearly four hours later Tominaga returned by himself. "I asked him where Murakami and his father were," Harada later wrote to Chub Feeney. "I was told that they had already caught a train back to Tokyo." Instead of introducing the Murakamis to the board of directors, Iwase and Tominaga had brought them "into a closed-door conference with Hawks president Niiyama."[6] With the ruse the two officials had not only created the opportunity to tell Niiyama their version of the events first, but had also denied Harada the chance to have Masanori confirm his account of what had happened in the United States. "I was very disturbed about the way this was handled, but I . . . subsequently met with President Niiyama. . . . There were many red faces when I started to give President Niiyama all of the details." At the end of the meeting Niiyama asked Harada to return on Monday to discuss the situation further. According to Harada, Iwase and Tominaga, afraid for their jobs, conspired to prevent that meeting.

"The night of December 20th, Managing Director Iwase called me by telephone and asked me what I was planning to do on Monday, as if he did not know that I already had an appointment to see President Niiyama. I told him that I was making one stop at the Kabuki Theatre before going to Osaka Stadium, but instead of making the stop at the theatre I went directly to the stadium. When I arrived at the stadium, I asked Managing Director Iwase to inform President Niiyama that I was ready to meet with him at his convenience. Iwase said he would arrange for the meeting but, instead, he succeeded in keeping me from meeting with President Niiyama. I waited for five hours at the Osaka Stadium and, since there was no sign of either of the gentlemen showing up, I left for my hotel in Kyoto. While waiting to see President Niiyama, I discovered that Managing Director Iwase had dispatched Chief Scout Tominaga to the Kabuki Theatre to catch me and prevent me from going to see President Niiyama. I understand that he had waited at the theater for three hours for me to show up. Why did both Managing Director Iwase and Chief Scout Tominaga tried [*sic*] and succeeded [*sic*] in keeping me from meeting President Niiyama? According to reliable sources, they did not want to have me give President Niiyama details that will give their 'game' up. They have lied so much that they cannot make another move."[7]

After returning from Osaka, Masanori spent a few days at his parents' house before checking into a hospital on December 23 to have his tonsils removed. Every morning his contract dispute headlined the sports newspapers. Editors began calling the story "the Murakami Typhoon" and the "Murakami Incident" (*jiken*)—the word "Incident" was often used to connote a major crisis, such as the Mukden Incident (the 1931 Japanese invasion of Manchuria) or the "Marco Polo Bridge Incident" (which started Japan's 1937 invasion of China). The young Masanori had expected to return home a hero, not the center of a controversy. He felt angry, betrayed, and just confused. "I didn't know whom to trust. I felt that I couldn't trust anybody."

At 2:00 p.m. on December 26 Niiyama held a press conference at Osaka Stadium. Tsugihiro Iwase and Yoshio Tominaga were notably absent. Niiyama announced that upon close examination of the January 6 agreement between the Giants and the Hawks, he had concluded that San Francisco did indeed have the right to buy Murakami's contract for only $10,000. Furthermore, Niiyama conceded that the October 5 check from the San Francisco Giants to the Nankai Hawks for $10,000 fulfilled the requirement to purchase Murakami's contract. Masanori Murakami was legally a San Francisco Giant.

Now, Niiyama continued, we will try to get him back. As the agreement was originally negotiated between manager Kazuto Tsuruoka and Cappy Harada, the two would meet once Tsuruoka returned from Europe to see if the Giants would relinquish Murakami for the upcoming season. If those talks fail, Iwase and Tsuruoka would go to San Francisco to speak with Giants owner Horace Stoneham directly. If it was impossible to get him for the 1965 season, the Hawks hoped to negotiate Murakami's return for the following year.

Former president Makoto Tachibana admitted that when they had made the original agreement, "I didn't expect Murakami to join the Major Leagues. We also didn't examine the contract closely. I feel responsible for these two things. But Murakami has already signed [with the Giants] and we received the $10,000, so I think it is impossible to have him back this season. I think that it is better to concentrate on after next season."[8]

Niiyama's announcement must have thrilled Murakami, who remained in the hospital recovering from his tonsillectomy until December 31. As the New Year rolled in, he wrote in his diary, "The year of 1964 is now over. I think this was my best year ever. . . . There were many difficult problems at the end of the year, but it seems that things will be better. I want to think that this is because I am becoming a better player. I will have to start taking the first step again from tomorrow, the first day of the year."[9]

Kazuto Tsuruoka returned from his European vacation in time for the New Year and got right to work on the Murakami Typhoon. On January 4 he met with Cappy Harada. Not surprisingly, they agreed that the Giants now owned Murakami's contract but were unable to reach a compromise on Murakami's status after the 1965 season. The next day Masanori visited Tsuruoka's home under the pretext of wishing him and his family a happy New Year. For three hours they discussed the situation and their plans.

Asked his opinion about the contract dispute, Murakami told the press, "I'm not interested in the contract itself because it's business between the two ball clubs. My only wish is to play for the Giants and be a good pitcher. . . . I am fascinated by the way American baseball is played. It is on a larger scale and it is a lot different from Japanese baseball. . . . I really enjoy playing in the States. I'll do my best each time I hurl and make a better showing than last year." He added that he hoped to stay in San Francisco "for a long time."[10]

Soon after these comments were published, Tsuruoka's confidant Josuke Nishino visited the Murakami home in Otsuki and spoke "very frankly" with Masanori. As the Hawks had already announced at their December 26 press conference, they could not prevent Mashi from pitching for the Giants in 1965, but they wanted him to return to Nankai after the season. Tsuruoka would leave for San Francisco on January 17 to negotiate the deal, and Masanori was expected to cooperate with this plan. Although not pleased with the proposal, the young man felt that he had little choice but to agree.[11]

On the mornings of January 20 and 21 Tsuruoka and Iwase met with Chub Feeney and Jack Schwartz at the team's offices in Candlestick Park. The summit was short and unfruitful. "The meeting was meaningless," an angry Tsuruoka complained. "I asked about having Murakami back next season and they said, 'No.'" So "I asked to see Mr. Stoneham, but they wouldn't let me see him." Tsuruoka explained that Nankai had invested over $50,000 in Murakami and would never knowingly sell his contract for just $10,000. It had been a mistake, he conceded, and they would appreciate the Giants' allowing him to return after the 1965 season. "Murakami is a Giants player forever," was Feeney's terse reply.[12] Tsuruoka and the Hawks had run up against Major League Baseball's infamous Reserve Clause.

Instituted gradually in the 1880s to stabilize team rosters and prevent salary escalation caused by players selling their services to the highest bidder each season, the Reserve Clause effectually bound a player to a single team. By 1887 National League contracts contained a clause that gave a club the right to extend a player's contract for an additional year even if the player had not signed a new contract. From the clause's inception until the mid-1970s the "additional year" was applied to the end of each contract, thus binding a player to a team in perpetuity unless he was released or traded. Club owners fought any possible challenge to this clause—even rejecting a 1969 proposal for it to no longer apply to retired players over the age of sixty-five.

The Hawks' proposal challenged the underlying premise of the Reserve Clause—that a club controlled a player's contract in perpetuity. If the Giants created an exception for Murakami, they would set a dangerous precedent for a contract that excluded the Reserve Clause. Other players might insist on similar contracts, thereby opening the door to free agency.

The Giants did offer Tsuruoka a small compromise. At the meeting on January 21 they presented the Hawks with an agreement stating, "In order to preserve the present good will between the Japanese Base Ball League and the American Base Ball Leagues, if Player Masanori Murakami's contract is to be optionally assigned or assigned outright to a minor league team in the year of 1966, Player Murakami may, at his option, elect either to play with the American minor league club to which it is proposed to assign his contract or with the Nankai Hawks Base Ball Club of the Japan League. It is clearly understood that 1966 is the only year in which Player Murakami shall have this option. Further, the Nankai Hawks Base Ball Club, its officers, employees, stockholders, et al. agree to cease offering inducements to and otherwise communicating with Player Masanori Murakami and/or members of his family to persuade Masanori Murakami to violate his contractual obligation to the San Francisco Giants Base Ball Club."[13]

In other words, if Murakami was not talented enough to remain in the Majors, the Hawks could have him back. The proposed agreement did not prevent the Giants from trading Murakami to another Major League team or demoting him in 1965 or after 1966. In exchange for this small chance of retrieving Murakami, the Hawks had to affirm the Giants' rights to his contract. Not surprisingly, the Hawks declined to sign this rather one-sided "compromise."

Angered by the Giants' attitude, Tsuruoka returned to Japan, leaving Iwase in San Francisco to continue the negotiations. He arrived on January 25 on a 5:40 p.m. Japan Airlines flight and immediately held a press conference at Haneda Airport to report on the situation.

"If the Giants don't want to give him back, we also have something to think about!" (*kocchi nimo kangae ga aru*), Tsuruoka declared. Although the statement sounds innocuous in English, in Japanese it is a threat—often uttered in the heat of an argument or in samurai movies just before a showdown.

"So what will you do?" asked a reporter.

"We are still negotiating, so I cannot say," responded the manager. But he hinted that he might just ignore the Giants' claim on Murakami's contract and keep him in Japan. "If the Giants really want him, they will have to come and get him!"[14]

"Unless there is an amicable solution," announced President Niiyama, "we cannot allow Murakami to join the San Francisco Giants [for spring training]. "Under any circumstance, Murakami is not leaving for San Francisco unless he gets final permission from Mr. Tsuruoka."[15]

That evening Murakami met Tsuruoka at a *ryokan* near Jingu Shrine in Tokyo. They spoke for a long time. The manager explained the details of the contract dispute and exactly what had happened during the meetings with the Giants in San Francisco. It was the first time that Masanori had heard the full story. "After listening to the Hawks' side of the story, I started thinking that maybe they were right. After investing so much in me, they would not have given me up so easily. It was obviously a mistake, and both the Giants and I were taking advantage of it."

Over the next few days Masanori discussed the issue with his parents, who wanted him to remain in Japan. They were particularly worried about Major League Baseball's Reserve Clause. In their minds if their son returned to the Giants, he would probably remain in the United States for many years, if not forever. "My father was afraid that I would become American. It was shocking to my father, who lived in a small town between mountains in Yamanashi, to believe that his only son would live in the U.S."

They also discussed the obligation to Tsuruoka. It had been Tsuruoka who had recruited Masanori, mentored him, let him live in his own home, and given him the opportunity to study baseball in America and become the first Japanese Major Leaguer. For these acts Masanori owed his manager *giri*.

Giri is a notion that underlies much of Japanese social behavior and has no equivalent in Western culture. It is a complex and vague concept with many facets hailing from Japan's feudal past, but in this instance is defined as one's duties or obligations to somebody who has rendered services. *Giri* is usually owed to a social superior who has helped or guided a younger or inferior individual. Repaying *giri* to the best of one's ability is a moral obligation that often involves self-sacrifice.[16]

Masanori could see both the stress the contract dispute was causing Tsuruoka and his manager's desire to have him pitch for the Hawks in 1965. In his heart he wanted to return to San Francisco, but he knew that his *giri* toward Tsuruoka now made that choice impossible. "I was in Tsuruoka-san and Nankai's debt. . . . I could not be immoral." He wrote in his diary, "We decided that I would not go [back] to the U.S. I don't want to concern Tsuruoka-san anymore." Resigned to staying in Japan, he vowed to work hard for his manager and ignore his personal desires.

On Saturday, January 30, the same day as Murakami was supposed to leave for the United States to attend spring training, the young pitcher showed up at the Nankai Hawks training facility at Nakamozu. Practice began at 11:00 a.m., but Masanori arrived an hour earlier, changed into a Hawks uniform, and took the field to warm up. He looked tense, and his face became a complicated mixture of expressions when members of the media approached him. "I don't want to make a fuss," he told them. "I'm not a Major Leaguer. I'm an ordinary Nankai player. . . . Three days ago I forgot about the Giants. . . . [Now], I want to have a brand new start with Nankai, so that's why I came here."[17]

As practice began, Masanori approached Katsuya Nomura, the team's catcher, top player, and captain. He removed his cap, bowed formally, and introduced himself, "I am Murakami. *Kawai gatte kudasai.*"

Although *Kawai gatte kudasai* literally means "Please like me," it conveys a variety of complex meanings. It is a submissive statement, often said to a parent, teacher, or older colleague when one is asking for guidance. Murakami had, of course, met Nomura before. They had trained together, and Nomura had caught Murakami's Japanese league games in 1963. There was no need for Murakami to introduce himself. Instead he was making a symbolic statement. He was letting Nomura know that although he had been a Major Leaguer, he understood his place on the Hawks. He was just another young player at the bottom of the team's hierarchy and would not expect special treatment.

As the training began, Murakami relaxed. His face regained "his usual cheerful disposition" and he began telling jokes to his teammates. A reporter noted that Tsuruoka watched him "like a father looking at his own son." "No matter what happens," the manager told the reporter, "I cannot give him to the San Francisco Giants."[18]

Out of shape by Japanese standards, Masanori struggled through the practice and had to end early due to a muscle cramp, but he told the press, "It's been a while since I've had this good, clear feeling. It's nice to play baseball in Japan. . . . After wearing the Nankai uniform and training with my teammates, it feels so good. I will play for Nankai with all of my might."

On January 31, Tsugihiro Iwase returned to Japan and told the press at Haneda Airport that Nankai had retained an American law firm to challenge the authenticity of the release form signed in January 1964. In the meantime the Hawks would immediately sign a contract with Murakami for the 1965 season. Asked what would happen if the Giants challenged this second contract, Iwase boldly stated, "I am confident to win if the Giants bring it before a court."

The following day Murakami, dressed casually in a black sweater rather than jacket and tie, arrived at President Niiyama's office in Osaka Stadium at 2:00 p.m. Niiyama, Iwase, and Tsuruoka had been inside for three hours discussing the situation. Reporters already crowded the space outside the office. As Masanori approached, flashbulbs popped. Nervously he addressed the crowd. "I am not interested in playing for the Giants anymore." He took a deep breath and rubbed his face with his palms, temporarily hiding his eyes. "I would like to pitch for Nankai."[19]

The door to Niiyama's office opened, and a stern looking Tsuruoka shouted out, "Murakami!" Masanori entered and the door shut.

A half hour later Niiyama emerged. "Murakami has just signed," he announced as the press crowded around his office door. Masanori sat on a sofa. A small round table covered by a tablecloth and holding porcelain cups, half filled with tea, stood between the sofa and door. There was a moment of silence, then the reporters erupted, shouting questions simultaneously. Masanori lowered his head, looking exhausted, then snapped, "Stop it! It will not help if we dig it all up."

Before the reporters could ask another question, he continued. "I will write a letter to the Giants. I don't think they will grant my request so easily, but I will let them know that I have no plan to play in the U.S."

"Murakami, let's go," growled Tsuruoka. Standing up from the sofa, Masanori said sheepishly, "I will do my best if I consider myself a rookie. Thank you."

He followed Tsuruoka out, his broad shoulders drooping. His dreams of returning to the Major League shattered.

CHAPTER 14

The reaction in the United States to Murakami's signing a contract with the Hawks was nearly instantaneous. Aided by the time difference and an international telephone call from Cappy Harada to Chub Feeney, the Giants heard the news the same day. Feeney, who was traveling in New York, immediately went to see Commissioner Ford Frick.

The next day, February 2, Frick wrote Japanese baseball commissioner Yushi Uchimura. After outlining the facts of the dispute, Frick threatened, "If in the face of documentary evidence there still is insistence on the part of the Hawks baseball team in going through with this new arrangement and the breaching of the original contract, then as Commissioner of Baseball I can only hold that all agreements, all understandings and all dealings and negotiations between Japanese and American baseball are cancelled." Furthermore, "pending decision, I must hold that Pitcher Murakami has violated his contract and is placed on the Disqualified List insofar as American Baseball is concerned and that the Nankai Hawks are temporarily stopped from any negotiations with any members of Organized Baseball Leagues in the United States."[1]

Despite Uchimura's earlier advice to Iwase not to involve the commissioners in the dispute, the Hawks' actions had done just that. And Ford Frick always played hardball.

In Osaka, Nankai readied its challenge to the Giants' claim on Murakami. Working for the Hawks, San Francisco attorneys S. Lee Vavuris and Jack Riordan found several loopholes in the January 6, 1964, agreement that might allow Masanori to stay in Japan. The attorneys argued that to properly interpret the agreement between the Hawks and Giants, one must refer to an

October 28, 1962, bilateral agreement between Major League Baseball and Japan Baseball concerning loaning players between the leagues. Among other things, this 1962 agreement stated, "It is impossible for us [Major League Baseball] under Federal law to make a signed agreement between the clubs outside of the U.S. We cannot do this sort of thing as it may be considered as an International Cartel. Whatever agreement which would be made, will simply have to be an understanding." Thus according to Vavuris and Riordan, "It must be assumed that the alleged agreement of January 6, 1964, at most can be assumed to be an expression of understanding rather than a contract or agreement with legal validity and effect."[2] If that was the case, then the stipulation that the Giants could buy Murakami's contract was nonbinding.

The Hawks also noted that in the fall of 1965 Murakami was just twenty years old and thus still a minor. Under Japanese law he would need his parents' permission to sign a legal document such as his contract to play for the Giants in 1965. Nankai argued that his parents never granted their written permission, noting the parents' objections to their son's staying in the United States during the telephone and letter exchanges in September and October of 1964. It was only after Cappy Harada falsely, according to Nankai, told the Murakamis that the Hawks had agreed to extend Masanori's stay in the United States for one more year that the parents gave their oral permission.

The attorneys also noted that the eighth point in the 1964 agreement between the Hawks and Giants stated, "If any or all of the [Nankai] players shall become homesick or be unable to adjust themselves to living and playing in the United States and shall request to be sent home, they will be released unconditionally and returned to Japan."[3] This was in accordance with the 1962 agreement that stated, "We [Major League Baseball] cannot send a player to Japan without his voluntary consent" and later added, "The foregoing . . . applies to contracting both American and Japanese baseball players."[4]

In an attempt to take advantage of the homesick clause, Nankai prepared a letter for Murakami to sign.

Dear Mr. Stoneham

I am writing you to let you know that I will not be returning to the San Francisco Giants this year or any other year.

I am the only son in our family and I feel that my place is here in Japan with my family. Upon returning here, I have been treated very well. I did not realize until my return how much I missed Japan and its ways, and the thought of returning to the United States makes me homesick. I have come to the realization that I will not be happy in the United States and therefore feel that I must tell you that I am not returning. I am also thinking of getting married and this has also been a consideration in this decision.

Thank you very much for your many past courtesies. Yours very truly,

Masanori Murakami

When the letter arrived in mid-February, the Giants were flabbergasted. "All we know is that when the 1964 season ended Murakami said he was happy with us, he signed his 1965 contract, pitched for us in the Winter Instructional League in Arizona, and when he left for home told us he was looking forward to pitching for us again this year," Chub Feeney told the *San Francisco Chronicle*.[5] "It is hard for me," wrote Ford Frick, "to accept the belated argument of homesickness. The player certainly was not homesick while he was in the United States; he was not homesick when he returned to Japan and the development of homesickness while at home is a little hard to fathom."[6]

Horace Stoneham realized that the letter might not represent Masanori's true feelings. "There is no doubt in my mind the boy has been put under tremendous pressure in Japan," he told reporters. "They're putting on the pressure because they now have an internationally known ballplayer who would be their biggest drawing card."[7] Decades later Murakami revealed that the Hawks had drafted the letter and concocted the story, and he felt obliged to sign it. "I was definitely not homesick," Murakami wrote in his 1985 Japanese autobiography.[8]

Fortified with the arguments outlined in the legal brief, the Hawks once again tried negotiating with the Giants. Perhaps believing that language or cultural differences had contributed to the impasse during the previous meetings, this time Nankai sent two Americans to San Francisco. Joe Stanka, the six-foot-five pitcher from Oklahoma, would head the two-man delegation. Accompanying him was Carlton Hanta, the Hawaiian Nisei who had played for the Hawks from 1958 to 1961 and now coached their farm team.

On February 10 Stanka and Hanta met with Chub Feeney at the Giants' offices in Candlestick Park. Stanka, hoping to appeal to reason and sympathy, explained that the whole situation was "a real misunderstanding."[9] He reiterated the Hawks' position that they had never intended to sell the contract and asked the Giants to reconsider their stance while also pointing out that the "homesick" clause in the original agreement would allow Murakami to remain in Japan in any case. Feeney was unmoved. After forty minutes the meeting ended. "The situation is unchanged," Feeney told the press afterward. "We still feel that the facts and justice are on our side."[10]

Although the parties had planned to meet again the next day, Stanka canceled the second conference, informing Feeney that he would take the dispute straight to Commissioner Frick. "I'm very pleased with this development," said Feeney. "The case now is in the hands of the commissioner."[11]

Meeting with Frick on February 15 in the commissioner's New York office, Stanka unveiled an entirely new argument. The Hawks had been duped by Cappy Harada.

As both an agent for Nankai and a scout for the Giants, Harada had been seen as the ideal person to arrange the player exchange since he would presumably protect the interests of both clubs. Now Nankai was suggesting he had favored the Giants all along. The Hawks, through Stanka, kept most of their accusations vague but implied that Harada had purposely failed to inform them about the clause allowing the Giants to buy the contracts for just $10,000 apiece.

As Harada, acting as the Hawks' agent, had signed the January 6, 1964, agreement on Nankai's behalf, there was no proof that the Hawks' front office had understood or consented to all of the points in the agreement. Furthermore, the Hawks claimed that the signature of Tsugihiro Iwase on Murakami's release form, signed on January 13, 1964, was a forgery.

By comparing the signature on the release form with two verified signatures from Iwase, handwriting expert Donald Walker determined that the signatures were not penned by the same person.[12] "We don't know who signed the release," Joe Stanka told the press on February 23, "but we know it was not Mr. Iwase."[13] The implication, however, was that Harada had forged Iwase's signature to give the Giants rights to Murakami's contract.

The Hawks also argued that Harada had misled Murakami when he told the pitcher in the fall of 1964 that the Hawks had given their permission for him to sign a contract with the Giants.

About the same time as the Hawks released this new conspiracy theory, several Japanese newspapers and magazines published articles on Harada, painting him as an unsavory character. *Shukan Baseball*'s February 15, 1965, issue, for example, contained an article entitled "Nankai's Tsuruoka, Who Was Fooled by Cappy Harada: Managing People Criticizing Harada." An excerpt read, "There has been a dark rumor about this Murakami problem. It is about the character of Mr. Tsuneo Harada, who is the focal person of this issue. . . . It is said that his actions always made people distrust him." The article also reported nonsensical rumors that Harada had originally demanded kick-backs from Nankai as a reward for selling Murakami's contract to the Giants.

Harada responded angrily, defending his actions in the media and in private letters to the Giants. "I have nothing to hide or hold back regarding the Murakami matter," he told reporters.[14] "Various actions taken by the Hawks certainly prove that they realize Murakami is Giant property and since they cannot change the stand of the Giants, the Japanese ball club is now making false accusation of me, who acted in their behalf."[15] "The Hawks must realize that a contract is a contract and that agreements must be lived up to." Harada also met with his attorney, Frank H. Scolinos, to discuss bringing legal action against the Nankai Hawks for making false statements.[16]

Nankai's new argument, however, carried little weight with Ford Frick. On February 17, 1965, he wrote Japanese baseball commissioner Yushi Uchimura:

Yesterday, Mr. Stanka and another gentleman were in my office to discuss the Murakami case. They put up a prolonged argument in which they claimed that the club had been entirely misled in most of these negotiations largely by a Mr. Harada who was officially named by the club itself to represent them.

I listened to their story with a great deal of interest and with some sympathy, but there was nothing in the evidence they presented or the argument they made that would lead me to change my mind.

The facts are that they did enter into an agreement; the San Francisco Giants kept that agreement and followed it to the letter. At no time did they deceive or attempt to mislead the Hawk representatives in any of their negotiations. If the management of the Hawks was misled and was deceived that deception is traceable to their own appointed representative. . . . One does not penalize an innocent party to an agreement simply because the other party has been misled by his employee and associate. . . .

This office must hold that until the Murakami case is settled to the satisfaction of the San Francisco Club and other parties any further dealings, negotiations or agreements between Japanese baseball and American baseball are void.[17]

Directly after meeting with Stanka and Hanta, Frick had sent a letter to all Major League clubs outlining the facts of the Murakami dispute and informing them of his decision to sever ties with Japanese baseball.[18] The edict immediately elicited a response from Los Angeles Dodgers' owner Walter O'Malley.

O'Malley questioned Harada's honesty, asking, "Is Harada the same character who shortly after the Dodger trip to Japan did a term in Japanese prison for being a black market money operator?" And then O'Malley questioned the validity of the contract signed by him as he was a Giants' scout. O'Malley closed with, "My only interest in the whole episode is to let you know that I would not like to see the fine relations you have built with the Japanese over the years be destroyed."[19] Of course Murakami's being on the roster of the rival Giants and his being particularly effective against the Dodgers played no part in O'Malley's concerns.

Frick alleviated O'Malley's apprehensions, noting that Harada was an official agent of the Hawks with letters of authority to represent the club. He also cautioned O'Malley, "Please don't upset the apple cart by undue sympathy for the Japanese. Either we have good relations based on mutual honesty and the integrity of all agreements or we have none. The only way we can get along with the Japanese, I am convinced, is to make our position firm and stand with it. Their policy seems to be to recognize the agreements they like; ignore the ones they don't like; change the rules as they go along and use the Commissioner's Office simply as an accommodation."[20]

After being dismissed by Frick, Stanka and Hanta traveled to Washington DC to argue their cause before Senator Fred R. Harris of Oklahoma.[21] The appeal did little other than further annoy Frick and create rumors that the U.S. Department of State was becoming involved in the Murakami affair.

In Tokyo Commissioner Uchimura was also trying to end the crisis, despite being hospitalized with a bladder infection. Uchimura summoned Shigeru Niiyama to his hospital room on February 13 to inform Nankai that after reviewing the documents, he had decided that the Giants did indeed own Murakami's contract. The commissioner proposed that Nankai allow

Murakami to immediately return to the Giants and that he would negotiate with Ford Frick to have the pitcher returned at the end of the 1965 season. Niiyama, however, refused to compromise. We have "absolutely no intention of relinquishing Murakami," he announced.[22]

As the Nankai Hawks entrenched and blocked Murakami's return to the Major Leagues, Japanese public opinion turned against them. Articles in the Yomiuri, Mainichi, and Asahi dailies, Japan's three largest newspapers, argued that Nankai had indeed sold Murakami's contract to the Giants and needed to honor its obligation. It was selfish for the Hawks to jeopardize both Japanese American baseball relations and a young pitcher's career to extract themselves from their own careless mistake. The most damning comments came from the influential Sotaro Suzuki, Japan's foremost authority on American baseball, the organizer of Babe Ruth's 1934 tour of Japan, and a member of the Japan Baseball Hall of Fame. "The Nankai Hawks should live up to the agreement they signed with the San Francisco Giants. It is their fault if they were unaware of the reserve clauses in the agreement."[23]

Fans, interviewed by the press, clamored for Murakami's return to the big leagues. The comments of one fan were typical: "The Japanese people . . . were very proud of Masanori Murakami. We would like to see him pitch for the Giants. . . . It is a good opportunity to create good will between Japan and the United States."[24]

With the controversy swirling around him, Masanori became "exhausted by these hectic troubles." He wrote in his diary, "I feel like hiding somewhere far from this problem." Jack Russell of the *San Francisco Examiner* noted, "[Murakami] now is described as being 'confused.' One Japanese writer with the perception of a psychiatrist said, 'On the surface, he shows no signs of uneasiness, but below the surface he is very unhappy and upset.' Another writer, who describes Murakami as a 'very emotional' young man, hints that 'fans fear he may do something drastic.' When pressed for what he meant, the writer says the player might give up baseball at best, or be driven to 'something like hari kari.'"[25]

Throughout the off-season the Japanese media continued to hound the young pitcher. Reporters camped outside his home in Otsuki and followed him everywhere. "I felt like a criminal, like a murderer," Murakami remembers. A columnist for *Hochi Sports* was particularly offensive. While visiting Osaka, Murakami checked into a *ryokan*. Like most traditional Japanese inns, it had thin sliding doors and a communal bathroom. The *Hochi* writer rented the adjacent room, and Mashi was certain that the reporter spent the evening with his ear pressed against the thin wall. When Murakami left his room to use the toilet, the reporter followed. Returning to his room, Mashi repacked, and leaving his suitcase in the room, snuck to the front desk in his socks. He quietly explained to the manager that he needed to stay at another hotel but would like to leave his empty suitcase to trick the reporter. The manager agreed, and Murakami stole into the dark night.

To avoid the press Murakami would often visit Eikichi Hoshino and his family at their home in Osaka. Hoshino's wife would serve her specialty—grilled chicken wings—to the young visitor. Yoshiko attended a nearby college and would usually join them for dinner. She found Masanori kind and funny and soon forgave him for his boorish behavior during their visit to Nara the previous year. Around the New Year, they began dating. Although the relationship blossomed, both now agree that it had no bearing on Murakami's decision to stay in Japan.

With no compromise in sight and negotiations suspended, Commissioner Uchimura wrote an eight-page letter to Ford Frick on March 17, outlining the facts of the dispute and suggesting a possible solution. Uchimura noted that although the terms of the January agreement between the Giants and Hawks were clear-cut, the many extenuating circumstances made enforcing the transfer of Murakami's contract problematic. With Murakami unwilling to leave Japan, it was unlikely that he would ever play for the Giants again. Therefore Uchimura suggested that the Giants accept the compromise offered by Nankai in January—Murakami would play for the Giants in 1965 and then return to the Hawks at the end of the season. The Japanese commissioner urged the Giants "to accept this proposal in a spirit of tolerance and goodwill."[26]

Although the compromise seemed reasonable on the surface, it still threatened the sanctity of the Reserve Clause. The *San Francisco Chronicle* pointed out, "In order to comply with the Japanese request that Murakami be returned in 1966, the entire structure of baseball's reserve clause would have to be rewritten or thrown out altogether. Asked if he could legally make a deal that would permit Masanori's return to Japan, [Horace] Stoneham replied, "I would say definitely not."[27]

Frick responded almost immediately to Uchimura by telegram and then followed his initial message with a more detailed letter. "I am as anxious as you are to preserve pleasant relations. However, I must insist that the first step in solution of this case must be recognition of the contract. Unless agreements are completely observed any proper relations between American and Japanese baseball are impossible."[28]

From his hospital bed, recovering from a surgery, Uchimura told reporters that he was "deeply disappointed" in Frick's response, as the American commissioner "seems lacking in understanding that Murakami had signed the contract with the San Francisco Giants without fully knowing the details of the contract. Murakami and his parents fear that he [will] be retained by the Giants not only for the 1965 season but permanently. Mr. Frick should have shown more understanding of the anxieties of Murakami's parents."[29]

As the 1965 Major League and Japanese seasons began in early April, both teams refused to budge. Masanori continued to train with the Hawks at their minor league facility, but Uchimura had forbidden him from pitching against other clubs. His days consisted of endless drills, conditioning exercises, and throwing on the sidelines. "I began realizing how hard it was not to have a turn to pitch. I threw in the bullpen as much as I could. I also pitched batting practice every day. Yet I didn't have an objective, an actual game to practice for. That was tougher than anything else."

With his future uncertain and the constant media attention, the pressure built. Masanori began to drink. It began with an occasional "nightcap" to help him sleep but soon escalated to a nightly ritual. He decided if the stalemate continued into June that he would retire from baseball altogether and return to school or to follow in his father's footsteps as Otsuki's postmaster.

The 1965 season began poorly for the Giants. Two weeks into the schedule, on April 24, San Francisco had already fallen into eighth place. Among the team's problems was the lack of a reliable lefty in the bullpen. To fill the gap manager Herman Franks pulled Bob Hendley from the starting rotation, but the arrangement left the team without a left-handed starter. Fans and the San Francisco media clamored for Murakami's return, but publicly Masanori remained adamant. "I have no intention of going back to the United States to play baseball so long as there is no guarantee from the Giants that I will be returned to Japan after the 1965 season. I will not change my mind until I get that assurance."[30] Secretly, however, he longed to return to the United States. Equally entrenched, Chub Feeney responded that there was no possibility of the Giants returning Murakami to the Hawks after the 1965 season, and "Even if we were willing to make the guarantee, the commissioner wouldn't permit it."[31]

On April 21, just over a month from his last attempt to mediate the standoff, Uchimura penned another letter to Frick reiterating that Masanori was still a minor under Japanese law, making his father's signature necessary on any binding contract. Both the January 1964 release form and the contract with the Giants for the 1965 season lacked Kiyoshi Murakami's signature. "I . . . have met several times . . . with the father of Murakami. At each occasion of our meeting the father gave the same reply, saying repeatedly, 'The boy was sent to the States for study and study only and nothing else.' . . . However, . . . he may consent and agree to send the boy back to the States immediately, if and only when the Giants will agree to give him a definite and positive promise in effect that the boy will be sent back to Japan at the close of the 1965 baseball season."[32] It was exactly the same solution Uchimura had suggested a month earlier and Tsuruoka had suggested in January and the one the Giants had rejected each time. But this time circumstances had changed.

By the morning of April 26 the Giants had just lost 3 of 4 games, each by one run, to the laughable New York Mets, who would lose 106 games in 1965. The team desperately needed help in the bullpen. Later that day Horace Stoneham and Chub Feeney telegrammed Uchimura. "In spite of [the] bad faith and unwarranted action of [the] Nankai Hawks because we desire not to interfere with [the] career of [a] player if Masanori Murakami reports for 1965 season we will agree that at the end of the 1965 playing season we will give player Murakami the right to choose where he will play in 1966. This choice will be player Murakami's alone to make and if he elects to return to Japan he will be placed on the voluntary retired list of the San Francisco Giants."[33]

Frick followed the Giants' telegram with one of his own, as well as a letter calling the proposal "infinitely fair" but also suggesting that "you explain to your people that Mr. Stoneham's proposal is in no sense a sacrifice on contractual rights, nor is it intended as a compromise with the rules." By placing Murakami on the Giants' voluntarily retired list, the proposed solution would bypass the Reserve Clause, as San Francisco would still control the rights to Murakami's contract within Organized Baseball. "In other words," Frick told Uchimura, "he would be free to play baseball in Japan, but he would not be free to return to American baseball with any club other than the Giants."[34]

"We haven't changed our minds that Murakami belongs to us," Feeney told reporters, "but we're not mad at him, and they're not letting him pitch over there. We haven't guaranteed the Hawks that Murakami will return next year. As a matter of fact, we're hoping he'll stay with us."[35]

Asked what he thought of the Giants' proposal, Murakami told reporters, "I'm glad. I want to play as soon as possible."[36] Two days later Uchimura met with Niiyama of the Hawks, as well as Kiyoshi and Masanori Murakami. After cabling Stoneham to confirm details, the Hawks and Kiyoshi Murakami agreed to the proposal.

Despite his being at the center of the controversy, the Giants hired Cappy Harada to handle the details of Murakami's return. As an official at the American Embassy handed Masanori his visa, Harada exclaimed, "Thank God, it's over!"[37]

CHAPTER 15

A crowd of photographers, reporters, and schoolboys waited for Muraka-mi's May 4 Pan Am flight to arrive at San Francisco's International Airport. Flashbulbs popped as Masanori, in a fashionable dark blue pin-striped suit, stepped off the plane and did his best to answer questions flung at him in English while signing autographs for the young fans. Distracted, Mashi signed a baseball in kanji, causing a young fan to show it to a friend and ask, "What does *that* mean?"[1]

After clearing customs, Mashi held a short press conference and fielded a few questions through an interpreter. Was he happy to be back? Yes, "I'm very happy to be back in San Francisco and will try to help the team." What do you think of the new manager, Herman Franks? He didn't know him very well, as the previous season he had interacted mostly with Alvin Dark and pitching coach Larry Jansen. How did you keep in shape? A lot of running, practicing with the Nankai Hawks, and "trying to elude Japanese reporters." Have you lost weight? He confirmed that he had lost five pounds, "although he did not attribute that to being chased by reporters."[2]

Then came the question they were all waiting for: What are your plans for next season? Before leaving Japan, Murakami had announced that he would rejoin the Hawks after the 1965 season, adding "I would like to help Japanese baseball players with what I have learned in the United States, and also I would like to be with my parents. I have an obligation toward them."[3] No longer surrounded by his parents or Nankai Hawks officials, he now told the American reporters that he had not decided where to play but that "nobody is dictating to me what I will do."[4]

The next morning the *San Francisco Chronicle* ran Murakami's picture above the headline "Murakami Is Back" on the prestigious center column of the front page, just below the paper's name. The photo's caption read, "This young fellow arrived from Japan to save San Francisco yesterday. In a few days he will put on a Giant baseball uniform and strike fear in the hearts of enemy batsmen." Sports news rarely made the *Chronicle*'s front page, but San Francisco was once again caught up in Murakami Mania. Mashi's return headlined the sports sections of every Bay Area newspaper and was picked up by UPI and AP news.

The *San Mateo Times* ran a bizarre cartoon later in the week depicting Murakami pitching to a Los Angeles Dodger hitter as a Giants infielder played a *shamisen* while singing the song "Sukiyaki" and "I Left My Heart in San Francisco." The caption read, "If Murakami pitches like he did last year, Giants will go all-out to keep him from singing 'Sayonara' in 1966."[5]

Amid all the fuss Dan Hruby of the *San Jose Mercury* noted, "The publicity attendant with Murakami's winter-long hassle over whether he'd rejoin the Giants is more than a little unfair to the mild-mannered southpaw. He will have to be a combination of Carl Hubbell and Lefty Grove to even come close to accomplishing what some people now expect of him."[6] Mashi also had self-doubts. "Although I had pitched at camp with Nankai and kept working out, I was worried that I had not thrown in any games. I was very concerned that after all this attention and so much ado that people would laugh at me if I couldn't throw well."

The Giants were in St. Louis, finishing up an eight-game road trip and would return on Thursday, May 6. In the meantime Mashi settled in at the Benjamin Franklin Hotel and practiced at Candlestick Park. As he waited, Mashi worried that the contract dispute and his late arrival might cause some friction with his teammates or new manager, but there were no hard feelings. "Everyone welcomed me as if nothing had happened," he remembers. "It was a warm atmosphere, like welcoming back a friend after his having left the team just for a few days. I was happy about that." The team returned on May 6, Masanori's and Willie Mays's birthday. To celebrate, the players brought a cake to practice.

The front office immediately placed Murakami on the active roster and readied him for the big weekend series against the Los Angeles Dodgers. The rivalry between the clubs was always strong, but this season had already taken an ugly turn. A week before, on Thursday, April 29, the two teams' aces, Juan Marichal and Don Drysdale, had faced each other in Los Angeles. The previous season Drysdale had pitched against the Giants 5 times, winning 4 and allowing just 4 earned runs and 30 hits in 44 innings. As expected, the game became a tight pitchers' duel, with Drysdale limiting the Giants to just 1 run on 4 hits and Marichal allowing just 2 runs on 5 hits. With the Giants down 2–1 and 2 outs in the eighth, Willie Mays stepped to the plate hoping to ignite a comeback. According to Drysdale, Mays was "striding into the plate, looking for an outside pitch" when the Dodger right-hander threw a fastball up and in near his head, causing Mays to hit the dirt. Incensed, Giants relief pitcher Bobby Bolin retaliated by hitting Drysdale in the small of the back with a fastball the following inning.[7]

Following the game, Marichal complained to the media, "This stuff has to stop. We don't throw at hitters. Always they're throwing at us. I don't understand it. But I'll do something about it if it continues. . . . Next time, if he's pitching against me and he comes close—we'll see what happens. He'll get it. And real good, too." Told about the comments, Drysdale issued a challenge. "If Marichal throws at me or hits me . . . I'm going to get four Giants—and they won't be .220 hitters, either."[8]

As the Dodgers came to town on May 7, they were in first place, 5½ games in front of seventh-place San Francisco. Murakami pitched batting practice before the series opener on Friday night and was ready to relieve if needed for Saturday's expected showdown between Marichal and Drysdale. The duel, however, was postponed as Marichal had strained a groin muscle and needed an extra day's rest. Instead the indomitable Drysdale faced Ron Herbel, who surrendered 5 hits and 3 runs before being relieved with 2 outs in the first inning. Mashi sat and watched as the Dodgers won for the second straight day.

Over forty thousand fans came to watch Sunday's matchup between Gaylord Perry and Sandy Koufax. The two pitchers entered the eighth inning tied at 2–2 when Perry faltered. Two singles sandwiching a strikeout put Dodgers at the corners with one out. With the left-handed catcher John Roseboro due up, manager Herman Franks brought in Murakami. As Jeff Carter announced Mashi's name, the fans erupted. Their left-handed savior had arrived. He headed toward the mound, his head down—looking at the ground, trying to concentrate. "I trembled on the mound as I hadn't pitched here for a long time," he told reporters after the game.[9] Mashi's first pitch sailed up and in, hitting the burly Dodger catcher to load the bases. Rookie Jim Lefebvre, who would later make a name for himself in Japanese baseball, came next. Although a switch hitter, Lefebvre had trouble with left-handed pitchers. Mashi focused, and a few minutes later Lefebvre headed back to the dugout—caught looking at Murakami's signature curve for strike three. After Dodger manager Walter Alston brought in right-handed Lou Johnson to pinch-hit, Franks came to the mound to relieve Murakami. A now rested Juan Marichal came in to finish the inning and pick up the win as the Giants scored 4 in their next at bat.

Murakami's first appearance initiated a spate of media attention. The *San Mateo Times* ran a photograph of Murakami wearing a fireman's helmet posing with the town's fire chief. The caption read, "Relief pitcher Masanori Murakami gets in the mood for his role as a Giants' 'fireman.'" An accompanying article, "Murakami Debuts—What a Relief!," detailed his performance, while editor Jack Bluth's column, "Speaking of Sports," also focused on the Japanese reliever.[10]

Over the next few weeks Mashi reacclimated to pitching in the Major Leagues. Facing more power hitters, he threw more curveballs in the United States than he did in Japan. But at the same time he also had to increase his velocity, as Major Leaguers threw harder than Japanese pitchers. At times Murakami looked rusty. In a mop-up role against the Cubs on May 12, he surrendered a double and single, allowing two to score in $\frac{2}{3}$ of an inning. After two no-hit outings he blew his first save opportunity and was handed his first Major League loss by the Astros on May 22. Three days later, he was once again in a mop-up role while the Braves scored 6 and batted around against Mashi as they trounced the Giants 14–1. He told the Japanese press, "I can't exert all my strength to my body as I've caught a cold. . . . I can't somehow manage to throw hard."[11] Murakami ended May with a disastrous 9.00 ERA and 1.78 WHIP, giving up 9 earned runs, 14 hits, and 2 walks in 9 innings. He did, however, strike out 8. Despite their lefty reliever's struggles, the Giants had won 19 of their 30 games during the month and had moved into second place, just 3 games behind the Dodgers.

Even with his poor outings, Mashi remained popular with the media and fans. "Murakami is as popular as Mays," the Japanese magazine *Shukan Baseball* exclaimed.[12] His failures were quickly passed over while his better performances became headlines. "Nippon Twirler Saves S.F.," proclaimed the *Salt Lake Tribune* after Murakami notched a save against the Astros on May 16. After Mashi's second save on May 20 against the Cubs, the *Humboldt Standard*'s headline read, "Mays, Murakami Star in Win." The Bay Area papers continued filling their sports sections with human-interest stories on the Japanese import. When recently asked if his teammates resented the disproportional attention the media gave Murakami, Gaylord Perry responded, "Absolutely not. We had trouble filling the seats in those years. Murakami brought a lot of fans in, and that meant more money for the Giants to give us all better contracts."[13]

Spending five months in Japan had diminished Murakami's already shaky grasp on English. When he returned to San Francisco in May, he found himself struggling to communicate. Reporters complained that he "sounds rather like a coolie in a Pearl Buck manuscript." A number of scribes poked fun at his English, writing articles such has "An Interview with Masanori Murakami, Who Speaks a Little English, by a Columnist Who Speaks No Japanese" and "Mashie Back; English Is Still Hurling Curves."[14]

In a typical article, Tom Tiede related another reporter's supposed experience trying to interview Mashi.

"Can you speak English?"

"Anglish? Who me? No, no—me Japanese boy."

"He knows you're Japanese, Mashi," Willie McCovey chimed in. "He wants to talk to you about pitching."

"Pitcha? Me pitcha. Him pitcha, too?"

"Mashi, is the guy throwing his questions at you too fast?" offered coach Cookie Lavagetto.

"No, not fast thrower. Not Pitcha. Him newspaper fella."[15]

Mashi, however, seemed to have little trouble communicating with his teammates. The quality of Masanori's English depended on how much he wanted to speak to somebody. After being shadowed by reporters in Japan during the contract dispute, he had developed a dislike for the media, and his English often disintegrated when he was not in the mood to be interviewed—a point Tiede picked up. "As far as his lingual limitations go, they apparently go just as far as he wants them to. He answers 'velly solly' to a reporter's probing inquires, but understands perfectly when [Cookie] Lavagetto grunts at him through two pounds of tobacco in a one-pound mouth."

Teammate Gaylord Perry agreed, "I think he only spoke clearly when he wanted to."[16]

Language and cultural differences led to a series of good-natured practical jokes between Mashi and his teammates. "He was really fun-loving, so we had a lot of guys on the team who would kid around with him quite a bit," recalls outfielder Ken Henderson. "We constantly played little tricks on him, like taking his uniform out of his locker and watching him figure out how to get it back. Gaylord Perry would put rubber snakes in his locker to watch him scream. If the players were playing tricks on you, you knew that you were accepted. He would try to do things back at us too, so there was a lot of laughing back and forth."[17]

The most famous prank occurred in early June. Murakami and reserve catcher Jack Hiatt were warming up in the bullpen when Hiatt commented, "Mashi, it seems that you will be up again today. . . . I'll tell you something good," the catcher said with a smile. "When a pitcher is changed, the manager always comes to the mound. When that happens, you tell him this. . . ."

Murakami soon went in to pitch. After he had faced a batter or two, Herman Franks trudged out to the mound to discuss the next hitter. Catcher Tom Haller and some of the infielders gathered around. Looking down at his manager from the top of the mound, Mashi growled, just like Hiatt had taught him, "Herman, take a hike!"

Franks's eyes became huge. He then shot a puzzled expression at Haller. "What did you say, Mashi?"

"Herman, take a hike," Murakami repeated.

Franks seemed about to explode when the players on the mound burst into laughter. Then Franks smiled, realizing he and Mashi were the butt of a practical joke.

Returning to the dugout, Franks shared the story with the other players. It soon spread to the media. The story was picked up by the UPI news wire and appeared in newspapers across the country. "It was much talked about," Murakami remembers, "and I became famous as Mashi of 'Herman, take a hike.' The joke wasn't meant to harass me but as a way to help me bond with the American players." Masanori's sense of humor and gentle nature endeared him to his teammates. "He was, and is, one of the nicest guys you will ever meet," recalls Gaylord Perry. "If there is a more popular man on the club than the 21-year-old Mashi, I haven't found him," wrote the *Chronicle*'s Bob

Stevens. "And his legend is growing every time he speaks. For Masanori . . . speaks with humor, with depth of thought, and from behind a smile that makes you want to grab the nearest plane and fly to Japan."[18]

The weekdays in San Francisco were filled with practices and games nearly every night. There was little time for sightseeing or social events. Mashi spent his few free hours each day at the Benjamin Franklin Hotel, sitting poolside, playing billiards with teammates or in his room writing letters home to family, friends, and especially Yoshiko Hoshino. He wrote her weekly and when traveling sent her a postcard from each city, although sometimes his messages were only a line or two. Yoshiko wrote back often and the long-distance relationship flourished.

On weekends or when returning from road trips Mashi would stay with his Fresno host-mother's sister's family. Fumiko Saiki's sister Yoshiye had married Walter Osaka in 1954, and they were living with their three young daughters, Barbara, Mary, and Juli, in Santa Clara, just outside of San Francisco. There Masanori could converse with the parents in Japanese, get home-cooked meals, and enjoy a family atmosphere.

The Osakas were typical of many of the area's Japanese Americans. Both Walter and Yoshiye were Nisei—children of Japanese immigrants. Walter's father, Seikichi, came from Nishitagawa, in Japan's northwest Yamagata Prefecture. Although Seikichi's father held a middle-class managerial post, as a younger son, Seikichi would not inherit property or wealth. Therefore, soon after his twenty-second birthday, he decided to seek his fortune in the New World.

Seikichi boarded the *Tango Maru* in Yokohama and arrived in Seattle, Washington, on December 27, 1907. He was part of the influx of 30,824 Japanese coming that year, before the Gentlemen's Agreement curbing immigration went into effect. Like most Japanese immigrants, he began at the bottom—working as a fisherman, day laborer, porter, janitor, and eventually a launderer. A dozen years later he returned to Nishitagawa to be married. In April 1919, thirty-four-year-old Seikichi and his bride, nineteen-year-old Momose, returned to Seattle and started a family. Walter, the oldest child, was born in 1922 and was soon joined by William and Nancy. Seikichi worked hard to make a better life for his children. He purchased a dry-cleaning business and with Momose's help made $900 in 1939. His son Walter focused on his studies, making the honor society at Seattle's Garfield High School and enrolling at the University of Washington.

And then their lives were turned upside down. In mid-1942 the Osaka family, along with 7,400 of Seattle's Japanese Americans, was forcibly removed from their home and incarcerated at the Puyallup Assembly Area—a makeshift camp located about thirty-five miles southwest of Seattle. Most families had six or seven days' notice to settle their affairs before the evacuation. They were told to bring bedding, extra clothing, and personal effects but only what they could carry in a single bag or suitcase. Although his dry-cleaning business was not confiscated outright, Seikichi was forced to sell it at a ridiculously low price. On August 30, 1942, the U.S. government transferred the Osakas to the Minidoka Internment Camp, located in a remote desert area seventeen miles northwest of Twin Falls, Idaho. After a year Walter was able to leave the camp to enroll at a school in Minnesota, but his parents remained incarcerated until September 1945. Seikichi and Momose eventually settled in the Los Angeles area, while Walter became an engineer at Lockheed outside San Francisco.

"I remember when my parents told us that a young baseball player who had just come up to the Giants would be living with us," remembers Juli Osaka Tachibana, who was seven years old in 1965. "He had been at Fresno, and my auntie, Fumiko Saiki, was housing him there. We lived in a small white house—just three bedrooms; my sisters and I all slept in one room, and Mashi would sleep in our playroom. When Mashi first started staying with us, he was super polite and conservative and not much fun. After a while he relaxed and started playing with us kids. Then he became like a big brother."[19]

Like many siblings, they would sometimes bicker. "Mashi had a temper. When he would get angry, he would try to hold it in and his face would turn pink, so his teammates started to call him Pinky. He hated that. So sometimes he would tease me and call me Pinky when I would lose my temper. . . . The most annoying thing he did," recalls Juli, "was write on all of my toys. He was used to signing his name in kanji, so after he was called up to the Giants, he would practice his autograph in English on all of my stuff. His name was so long—Ma-sa-nori Mu-ra-kami—that it would cover the entire toy. He even signed my favorite stuffed animal!"

During off days the Osakas often took Mashi sightseeing, or Walter would take him fishing. They went trout fishing in Reno and deep-sea fishing out of San Francisco Bay. When they stopped by DiMaggio's Restaurant at Fisherman's Wharf, Masanori wanted to meet the Yankee Clipper. Walter explained that the restaurant was owned by Joe's brother and that Joe rarely visited, but they asked if the famous center fielder ever came in to eat. Of course DiMaggio just happened to be eating there that very day and came over to their booth to meet Mashi and the Osakas. He talked to Mashi about Japan and posed for photographs.

Murakami had always been a celebrity hound. He collected autographs and had brought over a large stack of *shikishi*, cardboard squares with gold boarders produced just for autographs, from Japan. Before games he would often approach players from opposing teams to ask for an autograph. Although some players may have thought the practice unprofessional, few turned down the Japanese pitcher's request. "I was probably the only Major Leaguer going into opponents' locker rooms and being welcomed. I was especially friendly with the Dodgers, our big rivals, and went into their locker room as if it was my own. They would just think, 'Oh well. That's just Mashi.' The atmosphere was like that." He was not above using his newly found celebrity status to add to his collection. When the singer Harry Belafonte came to San Mateo, Mashi asked Walter if he could arrange to meet him. Sure enough, Belafonte met Masanori in his dressing room after the show. Even with Mashi's limited English, the two talked baseball for half an hour.

Walter also taught Masanori how to drive. Juli remembers them "practicing parallel parking in front of our house in our old light blue Chevy sedan. For some reason I was in the back seat. I kept teasing Mashi, saying, 'I'm sacred. I'm sacred,' until he got really mad."[20]

The neighborhood boys often stopped by the Osakas' house to meet Mashi or ask for his autograph. Sometimes he took them to the back yard to play catch. "It was a dream come true to many of the young boys to meet a real pro baseball player," reflects Walter Osaka. "I think he had a positive influence on the younger generation. He was always gracious and very polite."[21]

Murakami took the family to games at Candlestick Park. "We would pass through the players' gate and park in the special section right next to Willie Mays's car," recalls Walter. "When I went along, it was a great event to visit the locker room and meet the players like Willie McCovey, Juan Marichal, Mays, and many others. One time Willie Mays greeted the kids by rubbing their heads. When the girls went to school and talked about how some player named Willie Mays greeted them, the boy classmates were really envious, especially since Juli was only seven and didn't really know who he was. At the ballpark we sat in the family section and sometimes got invited to the Giants' executive suites, with great seats, food, drinks, and other perks. So we enjoyed many games and special events thanks to Mashi."[22]

Mashi had regained his pitching form in early June. On the eleventh, the Pirates had already scored 5 when Franks brought in Murakami to pitch the third inning in another mop-up role. Mashi began by striking out Roberto Clemente, Willie Stargell, and Donn Clendenon. "My balls were sharp," Murakami recalled. "It had been about a half month since I had come back to San Francisco, and I no longer felt disadvantaged by my late start. I started with fastballs chest high, then went low with curves and screwballs. I also used the breaking pitches aggressively, throwing them even when I was behind in the count. I kept the same pattern the whole time." Back on the mound for the fourth, he then retired Bill Mazeroski, Gene Alley, and Jim Pagliaroni. His only trouble came in the fifth, when Bob Bailey doubled with one out. After inducing Bill Virdon to fly out, Mashi intentionally walked Clemente before striking out Stargell to end the inning.

After the game Mashi had an unusual encounter with the great Roberto Clemente. At Forbes Field in Pittsburgh the locker rooms for the teams were next to each other. As Masanori was leaving the visitors' locker room, Clemente emerged from the Pirates' clubhouse. "Hey Mashi," he called out. Surprised, Murakami stopped. They had never spoken before.

"Do you think that Mays is a great hitter?" Clemente asked.

Mashi answered as best he could in English that Mays was a great player—not only good at hitting, but also good in the field and on the base paths. "I have seldom seen a better player," he concluded and then thinking that it was not enough added, "Mays is famous in Japan too."

"What do you think about me?" Clemente demanded.

"You are a wonderful player," said Murakami, rather taken aback at the directness of the question.

"I am three years younger than Mays," Clemente bragged. "I get more hits than he does. I am faster. My arm is stronger. If you watch me play, you know I am not lying. I am the best player in the league."

"He was bursting with vigor," Murakami remembers. "The bragging continued, although in his eyes I was probably just a boy. He bragged endlessly to me as we stood in that corridor just outside of the locker rooms. I'm not sure if he was bragging just to convince me how great he was or if he was trying to intimidate me for the next time I faced him. But that's when I really realized the great pride of the top Major Leaguers.

"My first encounter with Pete Rose was similar. It was at Crosley Field in Cincinnati. Two years earlier he had been Rookie of the Year. Rose was practicing around second base when he called, 'Mashi, come here.' I didn't know him, so I went over, wondering what he wanted.

'Are you the pitcher from Japan?' he asked.

'Yes. I am Mashi,' I answered back.

'I am Rose,' he repeated twice and then added, 'The rookie king, Pete Rose, is me. Look at my arm.' It was as thick with muscle as a regular person's calf. 'Baseball is a sport played by this kind of body. Do you understand? Mashi, remember my time will inevitably come.'

"Obviously he was trying to intimidate me. The stars, like Clemente and Rose, had great fighting spirit. With opponents like these, the pennant race was a battle for survival."

CHAPTER 16

The pennant race was about to heat up as the Giants traveled to Los Angeles for a pivotal three-game series. As the games began on June 15, the Giants were in third place, 5½ games behind the Dodgers. Both teams looked for a sweep. Three losses would push San Francisco far behind, damaging their chances at the pennant even at this early date, while three wins would put them on Los Angeles's heels. All three games would be televised in San Francisco.

The first game would feature the much-anticipated next battle between Drysdale and Marichal. Newspapers in both cities rehashed the threats the pitchers had made the previous month, with the *Los Angeles Times* promising that the "meeting of the California rivals is bound to stir up trouble."[1]

Despite the rhetoric the 52,357 fans who packed Dodger Stadium saw a well-pitched, gentlemanly game. During the 2–1 Giants victory Drysdale did brush back third baseman Jim Hart a couple of times, and Marichal threw tight to outfielder Ron Fairly in the fourth after Wes Parker had launched a 410-foot drive over the center-field fence, but there were no beanballs, no tussles, and no trash talk following the game. The predicted trouble came from a different source.

Prior to the start of the series Herman Franks had received a two-page anonymous letter, written in pencil. The author ranted that Murakami should not be allowed to be in the United States "playing America's national game," as he probably had relatives who "fought against and killed Americans during World War II." If Franks continued to let Murakami pitch, the author promised, "You won't know where or when I'll shoot you, but I will." "This guy is just a crank who possibly did lose relatives or friends in the war," Franks told Bob Stevens of the *Chronicle*, "or possibly the guy was in the war himself and is an avowed reactionary."[2]

When the Giants reached Los Angeles, third base coach Charlie Fox contacted a cousin who worked for the local FBI office. Agents interviewed Franks at the Ambassador Hotel and collected the letter for evidence. "These cranks can be dangerous," an unidentified agent told Stevens. "We never take such letters lightly [and] we will make every effort to track this one down."[3] Unbeknownst to Mashi, agents watched over Franks and his Japanese pitcher for a short time following the threat. "Had I known about the letter, I probably wouldn't have been able to concentrate on my pitching," recalls Murakami. "Nothing happened in the end, so it was probably a simple harassment by an anti-Japanese person, but the manager's courage was amazing—he behaved so normally that I had no idea about the letter. I believed that I was welcomed not only by the Japanese Americans in San Francisco and Los Angeles, but also by all other Americans, so I never even noticed the security by the FBI."

Game two of the series featured Sandy Koufax against Bob Shaw. Shaw had pitched primarily in relief for the Giants the previous season, but Franks had added him to the rotation in 1965 and he responded nicely, entering the game with a 6–2 record and a 2.85 ERA. Despite erratic calls from home plate umpire Lee Weyer, Shaw pitched well again, giving up just 2 runs on identical plays. In both the fifth and seventh innings, Dodger shortstop Maury Wills beat out an infield hit, stole second, and then scored on a Jim Gilliam single. When Shaw was lifted for a pinch-hitter in the eighth, the Dodgers led 2–1. With left-handers Ron Fairly, John Roseboro, and Wally Moon due up for Los Angeles in the bottom of the eighth, Franks decided to risk his life and bring in Murakami.

Mashi induced Fairly to fly out to right and Roseboro to pop to second before walking Moon. Next up was the switching-hitting rookie Jim Lefebvre, whom he had struck out a month before in his 1965 debut. After getting two strikes, Mashi caught Lefebvre looking on a pitch right down the middle. But to his shock Weyer signaled a ball. Murakami "pointedly looked toward the bench," "spread his arms in despair and then heaved the rosin bag high to show his displeasure."[4]

Weyer yanked off his mask and started for the mound when catcher Jack Hiatt intercepted him. He didn't mean it. He doesn't even speak English, Hiatt pleaded. Weyer explained that he was not planning on ejecting Murakami, just warning him. By this time Franks had charged onto the field to prevent Weyer from tossing Mashi. After a quick conference play continued, and Lefebvre ended the inning with a fly ball to right field. The Giants failed to score in the ninth, losing by a final 2–1 score.

Murakami's outburst inspired the predictable comments that passed for wit in the 1960s mainstream media. The *Los Angeles Times* proclaimed, "Murakami was anything but an inscrutable Oriental when Weyer made a call he didn't like."[5] Prescott Sullivan of the *San Francisco Examiner* wrote a long column on the incident entitled "The Hon. Umpire a Thing of the Past." Sullivan told his readers, "Murakami is from Japan and in Japan they aren't supposed to do that sort of thing. Respect for the Hon. Umpire has been a distinctive—and amusing—mark of Japanese baseball since the sport was introduced over there. . . . No Japanese ball player would think of challenging the Hon. Umpire's authority nor dare to mock his judgment. The Hon. Umpire might be the blindest of Blind Toms and the dumbest of oafs, yet, like the Emperor, he could do no wrong."[6] Sullivan's claim was based more on the stereotype of Japanese blindly obeying authority than on fact. There are numerous examples of Japanese ballplayers questioning and even attacking umpires.

To some Japanese Americans the Rosin Bag Incident took on special meaning. A few days later, after returning to San Francisco, Mashi entered a Japanese restaurant. Some of the Nisei came over and shook his hand and congratulated him. Masanori was a little confused—after all the Giants had lost the game—until an older man explained in Japanese. All of his life he had been patient and did what white people told him. "If they told me to turn right, I turned right. If left, I turned left." During the war he had been sent to a camp and had lost his home and everything he owned. Afterward he started again with nothing, but he felt that he couldn't say anything because of the war with Japan. He just wanted to fit in. By throwing the rosin bag, Mashi had stood up for himself and not tolerated the injustice. Moreover, he had done it in the national sport of baseball and on television so that everybody could see a Japanese man standing up for himself. That had made the old man proud.

It was only then that Masanori realized the depth of his importance to the Japanese American community. Yet Murakami had no interest in politics or sociology. He had no desire to be a Japanese Jackie Robinson—a symbol for an ethnic group. "I never worried about things like that," he confides. "I was just here to play baseball and concentrate on my pitching."

After the series in Los Angeles, the Giants returned to San Francisco for a twelve-game home stand. As the Giants slowly gained on the Dodgers in the standings, Mashi emerged as one of the team's top relievers. Franks used him both as a mop-up man and as a late-inning lefty specialist.

Mashi was back in the mop-up role on June 22 against the Pirates. Willie Stargell had knocked out starter Gaylord Perry with a two-run homer with one out in the third when Franks brought in Mashi. With the Giants already down 5–0, Murakami retired the side and pitched the next five innings, surrendering five hits and a single run on Stargell's second home run of the night.

Four days later Franks brought in Murakami in a tight game against the Phillies. With the Giants down 5–4, Mashi struggled through the eighth inning, serving up a rare walk and a single before retiring the side. In the bottom half of the inning a Willie McCovey drive over the right-field wall tied the game. Mashi held the Phils scoreless in the top of the ninth, and the Giants pushed a run across in their next at bats to give Murakami his first win of the season. He was on the mound again the following night—this time mopping up in the ninth inning after the Phils led 5–0.

The home stand ended with two games against the Dodgers. The opener on June 28 would once again feature a showdown between Juan Marichal and Don Drysdale. The *Oakland Tribune* called the game "a zinging renewal of the brushback offense . . . [that] contained some of the finest corner-clipping control pitching of 1965." Both pitchers were on their game, but Marichal ended up on top, shutting out the Dodgers 5–0 as the Dodgers committed three errors. To the great disappointment of some members of the crowd, no batters were hit, but Drysdale did put one "under the chin" of rookie catcher Randy Hundley, who told reporters "he really humped up on that one. . . . I guess you noticed that I got away."[7] The win brought the Giants to just 2½ games behind Los Angeles.

Game two featured Bob Shaw against Sandy Koufax. Shaw did not last long. After the Dodgers had scored four, with one out in the top of the third and runners at the corners, Franks gave the ball to Mashi. The Japanese lefty wiggled out of the jam and led off the bottom of the third. He had already been up three times that season and another three in 1964 but was still looking for his first hit. Although Murakami hit well for a pitcher, he knew that Koufax completely outmatched him. "He was a great pitcher," recalls Mashi. "I was scared just standing at the plate. I could not imagine hitting his pitches. My batting was a waste."

With a 4–0 lead, Koufax would probably try to throw fastballs by Murakami. Sure enough, the first one came in straight and fast, right down the middle of the plate. Although Masanori knew it was coming, he couldn't get his bat on the ball. "So I gave it a thought. The second pitch would also be a straight fastball over the plate because he didn't think I would be able to hit it. I was kind of fast, so I would try a drag bunt. I could at least touch the ball. The second pitch was dead center straight, and I bunted it down the third base line. The third baseman had no idea that I would try a drag bunt. I ran feverishly and was safe by a hairsbreadth. The Giants bench cheered, and I was puffed up with pride." Asked after the game why he had bunted, Mashi joked, "Koufax has too good a fastball for me to hit the long ball."[8] Unfortunately Murakami's teammates could not capitalize on the leadoff hit as Koufax retired the next three batters in order.

Back on the mound in the fourth, Mashi ran into some trouble before surprising the Dodgers again. Jim Lefebvre, whom Mashi had dominated in their previous meetings, began the inning with a walk. Koufax sacrificed Lefebvre to second, a single by Maury Wills moved him to third, and a Jim Gilliam single brought him home. Willie Davis then grounded into a fielder's choice, putting Wills on third and Davis on first with two outs.

Wills was baseball's premier base stealer. He already owned the record for most stolen bases in a season (104 in 1962) and would challenge that with 94 in 1965. The Giants had not caught Wills all season. He had 9 stolen bases in 9 attempts against them, with the latest theft coming earlier that night against Shaw in the third inning. Davis was also among the game's top thieves. His 42 stolen bases in 1964 were the third-highest in the league.

As Murakami recorded his second strike on batter Ron Fairly, the runners attempted to steal a run. When in the stretch, a left-handed pitcher's back is to third base. To check a runner on third, he needs to look over his shoulder, leaving the runner out of sight when he returns to his ready position. Mashi peeked over his shoulder at Wills; then, as he turned his head back toward first base, Davis broke toward second. As soon as Davis began running, Wills dashed toward home.

The first-and-third double steal can work several ways. The runner on first can act as a decoy. If the pitcher throws to second, the runner stops short, allowing the runner on third to scamper home. The play can also rattle an inexperienced pitcher, causing him to balk or throw wildly. Reporter

Charles Einstein speculated that "Wills and Davis not only were playing [Murakami] for a nervous rookie but for his being an import from Japan and thus unschooled in the inner workings of clever baseball."[9] The ploy, however, failed. As Davis broke for second, Murakami calmly stepped off the rubber, faked a throw to second, wheeled and threw home, catching Wills after a brief rundown to end the inning.

Two innings later Koufax came to the plate with two outs. To Mashi's surprise Herman Franks trotted out to the mound and started giving him instructions on how to pitch to the weak-hitting Koufax—something about keeping the ball on the corners. Murakami nodded and struck out the pitcher. An exasperated Franks approached Masanori in the dugout. "No, Mashi. No," he said.

Murakami had misunderstood the instructions. Maury Wills would now lead off the next inning and if he reached base would undoubtedly steal and probably score. Franks had been telling Mashi to walk Koufax without making it look intentional so that Wills would bat with two outs and the slow Koufax on the bases in front of him. Luckily for Masanori, he retired Wills on a pop out the next inning.

Although the Giants lost the game, dropping them 3½ games behind the Dodgers, Mashi had pitched well. After catching Wills in the fourth, he was perfect—retiring 9 straight batters and striking out 3 before being lifted for a pinch-hitter in the bottom of the seventh.

Throughout July Franks continued to use Murakami both in the mop-up role and in tight games as a bridge to rookie closer Frank Linzy. Despite a woeful 5.56 ERA, it would be Mashi's most effective month of the season. In 7 games he held opponents to a .081 batting average and struck out 12 of the 41 batters he faced. A home run by Phillies outfielder Johnny Callison accounted for the sole run scored while Mashi was on the mound. Six other earned runs came when teammates Frank Linzy and Ron Herbel failed to strand runners inherited from Murakami.

Interest in the first Japanese to play in the Majors was not limited to California. As the Giants traveled to other National League parks, fans came to the stadiums to see Mashi, newspapers ran feature articles, and local Japanese American organizations honored him. When the Giants stopped in St. Louis on July 5 for a three-game series, two kimono-clad young Japanese women from the Dai Ichi Ban (Big Number One) Club presented Murakami with a lifetime membership during a pregame ceremony in front of the Giants' dugout. The club, which was still under construction, would be the first Japanese bath club in the United States. Facilities, expected to cost $250,000, would include a Japanese-style communal bath, massage room, restaurant, and Olympic-size swimming pool. Geisha imported from Japan would attend to members. The club was designed "strictly for men, with women allowed only at certain hours."[10]

Mashi gave his St. Louis fans reason to cheer in the final game, played on July 7. Bob Shaw faced the great Bob Gibson in a breathtaking pitcher's duel. After the Giants tied the score at one apiece in the top of fourth, neither team could push home a run for eight innings. In the twelfth inning Gibson was still on the mound when Dick Scofield singled home Jim Hart to put the Giants ahead. The Cardinals, however, came back in the bottom half of the inning to tie the game. With runners on the corners, only one out, and left-handed Tim McCarver due up, Franks removed Frank Linzy and gave the ball to Mashi. A weak pop-up to second base by McCarver and a strikeout of Carl Warwick ended the inning.

Gibson returned to the mound in the thirteenth and retired the first two batters. A single by Willie Mays and then a home run by catcher Tom Haller, however, put the Giants back up on top. With a 4–2 lead, Murakami ended the game with a perfect inning to capture his second win of the season. The next morning Harry Jupiter of the *San Francisco News–Call Bulletin* dubbed Mashi the "slinging samurai" for his sparkling outing.

The *St. Louis Globe-Democrat* also honored Murakami's victory with a feature article entitled "The Americanization of Masanori Murakami." This sympathetic piece by Robert Burnes discussed Mashi's winter contract problems, some of his thoughts on American baseball, and his language difficulties. Unlike many articles that poked fun at Masanori's English, Burnes told his readers that "nothing hurts him as much as people making fun of his attempts to improve. [A] writer in San Francisco," Mashi told Burnes, "asked me if I like American music. I say yes. I say I like Moon River. It comes out in paper Moon Livel. That not very funny." Burnes explained that to overcome his deficiencies, Murakami carried two dictionaries with him and studied every day. "You appreciate and enjoy this young man who is trying so hard to adjust," the writer concluded.[11]

After a three-inning mop-up performance against Philadelphia and two perfect middle-relief innings against Houston, Murakami gained his third victory of the season against the Reds on July 21. The teams were locked at 4 when Mashi took the mound in the top of the tenth. He retired 6 straight, 4 on strikeouts, before rookie Bob Schroder blasted a bases-loaded line drive off the right-field wall to win the game for the Giants. The following night Franks called on Masanori again to hold the Reds. He did—another no-hit inning.

A few days later the Giants' front office announced a special event. August 15 would be Masanori Murakami Day at Candlestick Park. Co-sponsored by the *Nichi Bei Times* and the *Hokubei Mainichi*, the event would conclude with a reception and buffet dinner at the Nikko-Sukiyaki at 5:00 p.m. following the afternoon game against the Phillies.

Mashi had become the pride of San Francisco's Nikkei. Juli Osaka Tachibana remembers, "He was really important to the local Japanese American community. Everywhere we went, they treated him like a celebrity." Her father, Walter Osaka, adds, "As his story spread among the local Japanese community, a lot of people wanted to meet him. We often had people come to our house and just sit and talk with Mashi."[12] Relatives of Atsuo Fukuda, Murakami's barber, begged their relation to save Mashi's hair clippings for them as keepsakes.[13] Even George Yoshinaga, editor of the Los Angeles–based newspaper *Kashu Mainichi*, who felt that Bay Area Nikkei were overdoing their adoration of Murakami, admitted, "I look over the Giants' box scores every morning in the metro papers to see if he pitched or not. When he does and turns in a good job, I find myself thinking, 'Isn't that wonderful?' and I get a warm glow of satisfaction."[14]

Americans have dubbed baseball the "national pastime," believing that it both represents and instills true American values. After being openly discriminated against, incarcerated, and then marginalized, many Nikkei drew pride from watching Murakami succeed in America's national game. He became a symbol of Japanese success in white American society.

"I didn't realize it back then, but many Japanese and Japanese Americans worked really hard to prepare the [Murakami Day] event. For the Japanese Americans who had struggled so much during and after World War II just because they were Japanese, having a special day for a Japanese at Candlestick Park was more impressive than I could have imagined. Furthermore, the game would be held on August 15, the day World War II ended for Japanese.

I wondered why they chose that day. Then I realized that the Japanese Americans had picked the date to celebrate peace between the two countries. So I was happy that they made that day Murakami Day—a glorious day for Japanese in San Francisco." Hearing about the event, Masanori's father Kiyoshi agreed, telling reporters in Japan "he believed it significant that his son was given his first big league starting assignment on the twentieth anniversary of the end of the Pacific War."[15]

Top seats for the game sold out immediately after the announcement, but the Giants reserved an entire section of the upper deck for readers of the two Japanese American newspapers. Best of all, Mashi would finally get a chance to start a Major League game.[16]

CHAPTER 17

Masanori stood, hands on hips, on the grass behind home plate. He shifted his weight impatiently from foot to foot as a dozen men in suits scurried around him. In a few minutes he would be starting his first Major League game, and he wanted to prepare for the challenge. At the same time he was excited to be honored and thrilled by the sports car, now covered by a white sheet and tied with a red ribbon, parked behind him. The newspapers had announced that Kikkoman International, the soy sauce company, would be giving him a brand new Ford Mustang convertible.

Nearly twenty-seven thousand fans had come to Candlestick Park for Masanori Murakami Day. The crowd included about a thousand Japanese Americans, over a tenth of the Bay area's Nikkei population. More might have attended if it had not been for the appalling news coming from Los Angeles. Four days earlier a routine traffic stop in the city's Watts neighborhood had escalated into a full-scale riot. For six days over thirty thousand African Americans battled police and National Guard units in the streets of Watts. Nearly three hundred buildings burned to the ground as opponents exchanged gunfire and snipers prevented firefighters from extinguishing the blaze. Over a thousand people would be injured and thirty-four would lose their lives. Fear that the unrest would spread to other cities and a fascination with events kept many Americans in their homes.

Soon the ceremony began. Officials presented Mashi with plaques from the Vallejo, California, Elks Club and the Japanese American community of northern California. Greetings, telegraphed from San Francisco mayor John Shelley and California governor Edmund G. Brown, Sr., were read over the

PA system, and Japanese consul general Tsutoru Wada gave a brief speech, telling the fans, "Baseball is just as much a part of our life in Japan as it is in the United States." Masanori's speech was short and to the point. "Thank you," was all he said.[1]

After the speeches, kimono-clad Judy Sugihara presented Masanori with the keys to his new car. By now whatever apprehension he had had about not preparing for the game had vanished. "I was so happy to have a car that I wasn't thinking about the game so much," he recalls. With a flourish the sheet came off, and Mashi looked down on his new . . . Datsun.

Masanori probably blinked with surprise. Where was the Mustang? At the last moment Consul General Wada had pressured Kikkoman International to give Murakami a Japanese rather than an American car to help publicize the nation's emerging automobile industry. Later in the season Murakami, with a big sigh, admitted to a reporter from the *Nichi Bei Times*, "I wish it had been a Mustang." Bringing a car to Japan involved large transportation and import duties, "but it would have been worth it for a Mustang," he added with another big sigh. Nonetheless, he hopped in the light blue Datsun with "GOOD LUCK MURAKAMI KIKKOMAN" stenciled across the driver's side doors and with a wide grin, waved to the fans and photographers.[2]

After the ceremony Masanori warmed up as Bob Courier, the Spaceman, flew across the diamond in a jet pack. Years later baseball writer and former beat reporter Charles Einstein would write, "Totally dependent on his teammates for schooling in the English language, he [Murakami] nevertheless wished to preserve the baseball custom of his homeland, under which the starting pitcher would greet the plate umpire with a courteous salutation. Came now in 1965 Murakami's one and only starting assignment, and his fellow Giants had primed him in advance. Striding out from the dugout to take the mound, Murakami paused and bowed to the plate umpire. 'Herro, you haily plick,' he said. 'How you like to piss up a lope?' The umpire, Chris Pelekoudas, found himself bowing back. 'I couldn't think of what else to do,' he explained."[3]

Like many of the reporters' "humorous" Murakami stories, Einstein's tale not only pokes fun at Mashi's poor English but also portrays him as a gullible rube—a common ingredient in most ethnic stereotypes and ethnic jokes. Also like most of the other stories, it is completely untrue. Murakami denies that the event occurred, noting that by August his English was pretty good, so he would not have asked his teammates for advice on what to say. Even if he had asked, he would have known that he was being set up, as he "had learned all of those words in spring training the year before." Furthermore, records indicated that Chris Pelekoudas was in Chicago that afternoon umpiring third base as the Cubs faced the Braves.

Instead of swearing at the umpire, Masanori merely took the mound and finished his practice pitches. Since the two games against the Reds in late August, Franks had used him often, and he had not pitched particularly well. Playing nearly every other day, he had entered 7 games, totaling 9⅔ innings, and recorded 2 saves. At times his signature sharp control was absent. He had walked 5 and thrown 2 wild pitches. He had also surrendered 6 earned runs. Yet today he felt ready, even though Gene Mauch, the wily Phillies manager, had stacked his lineup with right-handed batters. Star right fielder Johnny Callison would be the only left-hander to face Murakami.

It would be Callison who would get the first hit off Mashi. After he had retired leadoff batter Cookie Rojas, Callison and Dick Allen hit consecutive singles to put runners at the corners. He later told reporters that he "might have been overexcited about starting." Steadying himself, he then struck out both Dick Stuart and Alex Johnson to end the inning. The second inning went smoothly for Mashi as he struck out Adolfo Phillips looking and Pat Corrales swinging and forced Bobby Wine to foul out to third baseman Jim Hart.

In the bottom half of the inning Mashi came to bat with two out and runners on first and third. A hit would give him the lead and a chance for a win. He battled Phillies starter Ray Culp and pulled a pitch into right field. Callison, however, caught it for the final out.

As he took the mound to start the third, adrenaline rushed through Murakami. He had already struck out four, and Culp, the pitcher, would lead off. He should be able to strike him out as well, he thought to himself. "I got carried away," he remembers, "and that was not good." Trying too hard for the strikeout, Mashi overthrew and lost the strike zone, walking Culp. Rojas then ripped a single to center field. After Callison grounded into a fielder's choice, Dick Allen blasted a triple to center field, driving home the two runners. Giving Murakami surprisingly little leeway, Herman Franks brought in Ron Herbel to finish the inning. He fared little better, giving up a walk, three singles, and another two runs (one charged to Mashi's ERA).

After being knocked out, Masanori showered and watched from the press box as the Giants made an impressive comeback. In the bottom of the third

Jim Hart hit a grand slam to put the Giants ahead 4–3. Murakami breathed a sigh of relief. "I was so happy because I didn't want to lose on the anniversary of Japan's defeat in World War II. It would have been like being defeated all over again."

In the fifth Willie McCovey hit a three-run "off-the-plate home run." With Matty Alou on second and Mays on first, McCovey hit the ball straight down. It bounced off the plate straight into the glove of Phillies pitcher Bo Belinsky, who nonchalantly fielded the ball and "fired it something like 40 feet over the head of the first baseman" into right field. Alou scored easily and Mays barreled home just ahead of the relay throw. Catcher Pat Corrales, however, believing that he had tagged Mays before he touched the plate, began arguing with umpire John Kilber. Completely forgotten, McCovey continued to circle the bases. Finally eyeing him rounding third, Corrales heaved the ball down the line, well beyond the bag and into left field. McCovey jogged home for the Giants' ninth run. Two innings later McCovey hit a true 400-foot home run over the center-field screen to push the score to 13–4. In the end the Giants would win 15–4, and in the words of Charles Einstein, "It was hard to remember that Murakami had started at all."[4]

Indeed Mashi's anti-climactic performance on his well-publicized day led a reporter who had traveled all the way from Tokyo to spice up the story. The Japanese tabloid reported that Mashi was in the midst of a torrid romance with Judy Sugihara, the attractive young lady who had presented Masanori with the keys to his new car before the game. According to the story, Miss Sugihara, who was the daughter of the president of Kikkoman International, had "begged her father to give her athlete-boyfriend a car for a present on his day." When told of the story by Japanese American reporters, Murakami responded, "It's a shame how they make up stories about big-name players, just to sell more copies of their paper."[5]

The Japanese tabloid was not the only newspaper interested in Mashi's romantic life. Several American reporters suggested that the Giants find Masanori an American girlfriend to make him want to stay in the United States, and a few others, picking up the false report on Judy Sugihara, wrote that he was already deeply in love. The truth, however, was far less interesting. "I never thought of having a girlfriend, nor did I have the time to have one during the baseball season," Mashi later told *Shukan Baseball*. "I went to dinner with a lot of people—five or six—but not on a date." Cultural differences, as well as Yoshiko Hoshino, kept Murakami unattached.[6] "I think the girls here are very open," he told American reporters. "They live alone in apartments. I don't understand this. Maybe in Japan if a girl lives far away from her parents, she lives in an apartment. Here a girl lives in the same town as her parents—almost the same block—but she lives in an apartment. If she wants to go out—[she just goes] out! In Japan she must ask her parents [first]. I think that's better."[7]

With all the attention he received on Masanori Murakami Day, reporters began pressing Mashi on his plans for the 1966 season. "I don't know yet what I will do. It is very good here with the Giants, very nice," he stated in early August. "I've enjoyed playing in the United States very much. The people have been good to me, and I have had no serious problems," he added directly after his start.[8]

"The Giants [players] would like nothing better than to have the personable lefty back," reported the *Hokubei Mainichi*. "He is one of the best-liked players on the club with his happy disposition, and as far as communication is concerned his teammates say there is absolutely no problem. His English is more than proficient, his mates claim."[9]

Mashi bonded with the other two youngest players on the team, nineteen-year-old Ken Henderson and twenty-year-old Bob Schroder. Henderson recalls, "Masanori had such a great personality and a great sense of humor. He was really fun-loving, so he was well accepted. He was always eager to learn, asking questions. He was very inquisitive and anxious to learn about so many different things. He wanted to know what American baseball was about. What the big leagues were like. What should I be doing? What is the right etiquette? We would walk the streets of New York City, and he would go into certain stores just to see how people merchandised things. He would go to different restaurants to find out about different cuisines."[10]

Henderson and Gaylord Perry had taught Murakami to play gin rummy. He picked up the game easily and soon became very good. On road trips the team would often leave one city after a night game and travel through the night to the next destination. Unable to sleep on the short flights, the three would play cards for hours. Perry, who would later admit to throwing the spitball and doctoring baseballs with illegal substances such as Vaseline, would sometimes need his cunning to beat Mashi. Murakami would usually take a window seat; Perry would take one on the aisle, and they would leave the middle seat open to play cards. One night Henderson, walking down the aisle, asked Masanori how the game was going. "Ah, he beat me too much. He beat me too much!" he replied. Perry had just taken about a dozen straight games. "Masanori, look in your window!" exclaimed Henderson. The Japanese pitcher's cards were reflected in the window and Perry could see them all.

While on the road, ballplayers have little time for leisure. Days are filled with practice, nights with games and travel. Mostly they eat, sleep, and play baseball. Masanori would occasionally see a movie with Henderson and Schroder. His favorites were cowboy films, and he would stop everything when *Rawhide* came on the television. "But I didn't go out with the team members a lot," remembers Murakami "because there were always people coming to fetch me." On nearly every road trip local Japanese would come to the hotel, introduce themselves to Masanori, and take him out to see their town. One time when the Giants were in New York, for example, a couple of Japanese Americans telephoned him at the hotel.

"We came from Boston to watch you play. If you have time, why don't we show you New York?" Without hesitating, Mashi said, "Okay!" They were complete strangers, and now Murakami muses, "I could have easily been kidnapped!"

They brought Masanori to the Statue of Liberty and other landmarks before closing out the tour with a drive through Harlem. In 1965 the area was not the mecca of African American culture that it had been in the 1920s or the thriving commercial and cultural district of today. It was a neighborhood characterized by poverty, decay, and racial tension that had erupted the previous summer in deadly race riots. It was also a common destination for the more adventurous tourists, who wanted to see "the ghetto" through the rolled up windows and locked doors of their automobiles.

Even for a foreigner like Murakami, who could not read the newspapers and had no interest in politics, the racial tensions of the times were impossible to escape. When a Japanese reporter asked what he thought of Willie Mays, Mashi began with a surprisingly candid comment. "Generally speaking, in the United States black people are kind of looked down upon, but I personally don't regard them as such. He [Mays] is a very good person. He gave me a lot of advice. . . . He also cheered us young people on; he was always thoughtful of the young players and helped us a lot." When asked the same question about Murakami, Mays told American reporters, "He's a good boy. He's learning all the time. He likes to give you the impression he doesn't understand English and he doesn't know one hitter from another, but he knows what he's doing."[11] Besides, "language has nothing to do with our friendship. Murakami and I are good friends, so good that we may not need a language between us."[12]

Sometimes the Giants' captain would invite teammates to his home for dinner parties. Japanese rarely entertain business associates, or baseball teammates, in their homes. Instead men will invite associates to a restaurant or club. Masanori, therefore, found these invitations particularly enjoyable. Mays's home at 54 Mendosa Avenue in the predominately white, but heavily Jewish and Catholic, Forest Hill neighborhood was called "the most extravagant bachelor's pad in San Francisco." Built on a steep slope that overlooked the Golden Gate Bridge, the two-story ultra modern house was relatively small, containing just seven rooms in 2,106 square feet but was decorated with the opulence of an eighteenth-century French noble. Thick, expensive gold carpet covered the floors; fine Austrian white drapery framed the windows. Six of the seven rooms contained a television set.[13]

One afternoon Mays invited some of the Giants and their families over for a barbeque. Mashi sat in the yard talking to his teammates. "It was a relaxed atmosphere, and I felt very comfortable, as you do with old friends. Willie told me to come with him and we went into the house, up to his bedroom on the second floor. He went to his closet, opened a drawer, and pulled out a pair of cufflinks with diamonds and rubies on them. "Here," he told me, 'I want you to have these.'"

Although Mays had little trouble purchasing the house on Mendosa Avenue in 1962, he told Murakami of the difficulties he had encountered when he had tried to buy a home in a white neighborhood in 1957. Real estate agents would not return his calls, homes were taken off the market when he showed interest, and an offer was flatly refused on the grounds that selling to an African American would lower neighborhood property values. Later in his life Murakami realized that Mays was warning him that although the baseball fans loved him, as an Asian he might still encounter discrimination in the United States.

After Mashi's poor start against the Phillies, reporters asked Herman Franks if Murakami would get a second chance. No, responded the manager. He was the club's top left-handed reliever. "It's not that Mashi did so badly, it's just that he's much more valuable in the bullpen."[14] In the upcoming series against the Dodgers, Mashi would prove Franks right.

The Dodgers arrived in San Francisco on August 19 for a four-game series. The California press had been hyping the games all week, calling them "the Fight for First Series" as Los Angeles's NL lead had slowly dwindled. By the start of the first game, the Dodgers had actually fallen into second place, a half game behind the Milwaukee Braves. The Giants, a half game behind Los Angeles, hoped to leapfrog into first.

The opener featured Don Drysdale against forty-four-year-old Warren Spahn in his last year of professional ball. The grueling game lasted four hours and eleven minutes before the Dodgers scored three in the fifteenth to capture the victory. It might have been over much sooner if Murakami had held the visitors in the seventh inning. With a 3–2 lead, a runner on first, and one out, Franks brought in Mashi to relieve a tiring Spahn. He struck out Willie Davis looking but then surrendered a double to catcher John Roseboro that tied the game. It was only the third time all season that Masanori had not protected a lead. The next morning the headline of the *Bakersfield Californian* blared, "Dodgers Draw First Blood in Big Series." As most baseball fans know, more blood would flow later.

On the surface the second game seemed uneventful. Bob Shaw pitched a complete game as the Giants won easily, 5–1. The newspapers reported no beanballs or altercations, but an exchange occurred that would have violent consequences. In the fourth inning Maury Wills faked a bunt but pulled back the bat at the last moment, hitting catcher Tom Haller in the process. It was an old but effective trick, and umpire Al Forman awarded Wills first base on catcher's interference.

The following inning Franks ordered Matty Alou to attempt the same ploy. Alou pulled the bat back at the last instance but failed to hit Roseboro. The pitch, however, struck the catcher firmly in the chest protector. "You weasel bastard!" Roseboro cursed at Alou, followed by a threat. Hearing the comments, Franks and Juan Marichal berated Roseboro from the Giants dugout. Expletives and threats flew back and forth, ending with Roseboro yelling at Marichal, "The next time something like that happens, you're going to get hit in the head with the ball!"[15]

Tempers seemed to calm during Saturday's game. Another thriller, the Giants led 3–2 with one out in the seventh when Roseboro homered off starter Bob Bolin to put the Dodgers on top 4–3. Franks immediately brought in Mashi to keep the game close, and he struck out pitcher Bob Miller and Maury Wills to end the inning. He would only pitch to the two batters, as Franks removed him for a pinch-hitter in the bottom half of the inning. The Giants would go on to tie the game at four before eventually losing in the eleventh inning. The win put Los Angeles back in first place, a half game ahead of the Braves and a game and a half above the Giants.

The matchup on Sunday, August 22, between Sandy Koufax and Juan Marichal brought 42,807 fans to Candlestick Park to witness one of the most infamous moments in baseball history. Trouble began with the first batter. Leading off, Maury Wills laid a bunt down the first baseline, beating the throw for a single. After advancing to second on a ground out, he scored on a Ron Fairly double. Marichal apparently took exception to Wills's "cheap hit," and when he came up again in the second inning, the Giants' ace knocked Wills to the ground with a high, tight fastball before retiring him for the third out.[16]

Willie Mays led off the bottom of the second. To pay back the Giants for knocking down Wills, catcher John Roseboro signaled Koufax to come in high and tight to Mays. Koufax, who as a rule did not throw at hitters, fired a fastball well over Mays's head instead. Although harmless, the pitch satisfied baseball's unwritten rule that a knockdown pitch had to be answered. With the inside pitch to Wills revenged, at least symbolically, the teams were even, and play should have continued normally.

But the following inning Marichal threw a tight fastball to outfielder Ron Fairly. Marichal later claimed that it was not intended as a brushback pitch, but the Dodgers saw it as a clear violation of baseball etiquette—Koufax's pitch to Mays was supposed to have ended the knockdown pitches. Dodgers screamed at Marichal from the dugout. With Koufax unlikely to respond, Roseboro vowed revenge.

Marichal led off the bottom of the fourth inning with the Dodgers ahead 2–1. Knowing that Koufax would not throw at an opponent, Roseboro decided to punish Marichal himself. The first pitch came down the middle for a strike. Roseboro tossed the ball back to the mound. Koufax wound up and delivered a ball, inside and low. Roseboro received the pitch, then deliberately dropped the ball just behind Marichal's back foot. Picking it up, Roseboro fired it back to Koufax, grazing Marichal's ear.

"Why did you do that?" yelled Marichal. You better not hit me with that ball!" Roseboro's response was a stream of curses and comments on Marichal's mother's virtue as he took a threatening step toward the Giant. Marichal shoved the catcher aside, raised his bat above his head with both hands, and swung down, striking Roseboro on the head. The catcher fell to his knees, blood streaming from the wound. Marichal struck twice more before Koufax, third base coach Charlie Fox, and umpire Shag Crawford intervened.

Players from both teams charged to home plate—some to prevent further conflict, others to exact revenge. A season of tension between the teams boiled over. "Aroused to the point of blind fury, Marichal continued to swing his bat menacingly until forced away by Dodgers and teammates." Giants rookie shortstop Tito Fuentes jumped into the fray, wielding his own bat. Dodgers outfielder Lou Johnson threw punches at any Giant he could reach. Others pushed, shoved, wrestled, and punched. Mays also rushed into the melee, straight for Roseboro. But instead of delivering a blow, the Giants' captain, "with tears in his eyes and blood splattered on his uniform, held Roseboro's shoulders, restraining him."[17]

Murakami had been watching the game from the bullpen. He had seen Roseboro drop the second pitch and then looked away for a moment. Shouts brought his attention back to the plate. Marichal had already hit Roseboro, and other players had just reached the fray. Mashi and the other relief pitchers rushed from the bullpen. "Everything happened before I knew it. All the players ran out from both benches immediately. Mays was the first to run out. He ran to Roseboro and held him back from attacking Marichal. Koufax was running to home plate. Marichal's friend, Fuentes, was jumping into the group, waving his bat. Mays's uniform had turned red with Roseboro's blood. It was crazy." As he reached the edge of the fight, somebody pulled Mashi aside. "You're a pitcher," he said. "Stay away from the fighting so you don't get hurt."

Following the instruction, Murakami stayed near the edge of the conflict, pulling an occasional shirt. "I was trying to think of something to say, but I couldn't think of anything, so I just milled around the crowd of fifty players." The brawl lasted about fifteen minutes before order was restored. Crawford ejected Marichal from the game, and Roseboro was helped off the field, his gash bandaged, and driven to the hospital for observation.

Undoubtedly rattled, or at least distracted, Koufax returned to the mound, walked two batters, and then gave up a home run to Mays. The Giants now led 4–2. Franks brought in Ron Herbel to pitch, and he shut down the Dodgers for five innings before running out of steam with one out in the ninth. A hit batsman followed by a single, put Wes Parker on third, Jeff Torborg on first, and brought Franks to the mound. With left-handed Wally Moon coming to the plate, Franks brought in Murakami. Dodger manager Walt Alston countered by pinch-hitting with right-handed rookie Don LeJohn.

Coming into the game, Mashi felt perfectly calm. Although the brawl had been terrifying to watch, the altercation had not involved him personally, and he bore no hostility toward the Dodgers. He focused on LeJohn, who bounced a ground ball back to the mound. Murakami fielded it, faked a throw to third to check Parker, and threw to Hal Lanier at second base to start a game ending double play. But Lanier, hurrying to make the play, dropped the ball. All the runners were safe and Parker scored. The Dodgers now trailed by only one run, had runners on first and second with one out, and had the top of the order coming up.

The dangerous Maury Wills entered the batter's box. There would be little chance of the speedy shortstop hitting into a double play, while a successful bunt could load the bases. But "Murakami retired Wills on a windblown foul fly that Lanier snared near the Giant bullpen, then caught Jim Gilliam looking at a called third strike" to end the game.[18] Looking back nearly fifty years later, Mashi would list saving the famous Marichal-Roseboro game for the Giants as one of his favorite memories in Major League Baseball.

The Giants emerged from the "Fight for First Series" just a half game behind the Dodgers, but the brawl, and Marichal's subsequent eight-game suspension, seemed to sap the team's drive. Embarking on a seventeen-game road trip, they lost four in a row in Pittsburgh, another to the lowly Mets, and then two of four in Philadelphia. Yet when they reached Chicago on September 3, they were just a game behind Los Angeles, which had suffered a similar losing streak.

After dropping the opening game against the Cubs, the Giants started to win. They began with the remaining three in Chicago and then took two from the Dodgers in Los Angeles. When Murakami retired Wes Parker on a fly ball to right field to save the Giants' win on September 7, San Francisco moved into a first-place tie with the Dodgers. The following night's win against Houston gave them sole possession of the top spot for the first time during the 1965 season. "This club is going to win the pennant," predicted Warren Spahn. "Did you see them out there today? They were making some great plays. That's the way it is with pennant winners. It's what's commonly called momentum. The players get to believing they're going to win and they do. This club has just gotten that attitude in the last week or so, but they've really got it now."[19]

The Giants' winning ways continued as they swept two from the Astros, four from the Cubs, and then four more from Houston. When they finally dropped a game on September 17 to the Milwaukee Braves, they had won fourteen in a row and were comfortably in first place with a 3½ game lead over the Dodgers. Rebounding from the loss, the Giants won the next three, increasing their lead to four games, with just a dozen left to play.

Willie Mays was the driving force behind the winning streak. Although his batting average dipped a few points during the fourteen games, he pounded out seven home runs, with a .722 slugging percentage. Teammate Warren Spahn noted that with the game on the line, Mays swung for the fences and invariably came through. "What impressed me was the way he went for the home run each time. A guy might settle for a base hit, but he was trying to tie it up. . . . The way he did it makes me wonder how good he could be if every time was a crisis."[20]

Out of the bullpen Murakami was superb. "The Giants never would be leading the pack now into the pennant stretch without him," wrote Jack Hanley in the *San Jose Mercury-News*.[21] After the start against Philadelphia until September 20, Mashi entered 14 games, pitched 22 innings, and surrendered just 15 hits, 5 walks (plus 3 intentional passes) and 2 earned runs. He also struck out 32 batters and picked up 4 saves. The raw statistics translated to a 0.82 ERA, a 0.91 WHIP, a 6.4:1 strikeout-to-walk ratio, and a .185 batting average against him.

Murakami was particularly effective against the rival Dodgers. Pitching in five of the six times the teams met after August 1, Mashi gave up just 1 hit and no runs in 5 innings. He also struck out 7 of the 18 batters he faced. "He's deceptive," an unidentified Dodger told the *Oakland Tribune*. "At first you don't think he's fast. Then he gets the ball over before you know it."[22]

On September 21 the annual San Francisco Giants' late-season collapse began. They lost two to third-place Cincinnati, then two of three to Milwaukee. Meanwhile, the Dodgers went on their own winning streak. When the Cardinals came to town on September 27, the Giants and Dodgers were deadlocked at the top of the National League with identical 91-64 records.

"So we just start all over, even with the Dodgers," Herman Franks mused, "with seven games to play."[23]

The Giants, however, continued to lose—often in spectacular fashion. They dropped two of three to the Cardinals, including a 9–1 loss to rookie pitcher Larry Jaster and a 8–6 loss highlighted by Bob Shaw's serving up a grand slam to opposing pitcher Bob Gibson. In each of these games the previously slick-fielding Giants made 3 errors. Shirley Povich of the *Washington Post* noted that the Giants "have been playing ragged baseball . . . [and] have suddenly become error-struck and as a pennant contender are more than faintly resembling the Mets."[24]

By September 30 the Giants had fallen two games behind the Dodgers when the Reds came to town to finish out the season with a four-game series. At first it looked like the Giants might bounce back. Juan Marichal had pitched seven strong innings when he turned the game over to Mashi in the eighth with the score tied at 2–2. Masanori was still pitching well and had not allowed an earned run in his last seven outings. After recording an easy first out, Murakami faced the dangerous power hitter Frank Robinson. Mashi started him off with a curve that failed to break. Robinson "smashed it high into the left field bleachers, but foul."[25] Murakami tried again. Once again the curve stayed flat, and Robinson slammed it down the left-field line. This time the ball stayed fair, and the Reds took the lead. Luckily the Giants staged a comeback, tying the game in the bottom of the eighth. After Mashi retired the Reds in the ninth, Orlando Cepeda gave Masanori his fourth win of the season with a walk-off "sayonara" home run. The next morning the *Chronicle* celebrated the rare victory with a large picture of Cepeda jokingly trying to land a kiss on a reluctant Murakami's cheek.

Despite the win the Giants gained no ground on the Dodgers, who had now won thirteen straight games. The next day sealed the Giants' fate. The onslaught began right away as starter Bob Bolin gave up two singles and two home runs before recording the second out of the first inning. Franks brought in Mashi to finish the first and hopefully help the Giants get back into the game. Tired from two innings the night before, Murakami was chased from the mound in the second after he surrendered a two-run homer to Pete Rose and a double to Vada Pinson. By the end of nine innings the Reds had pounded out 17 runs off eight different Giants pitchers. The following day, October 2, the Dodgers clinched the pennant.

Disappointed and fatigued, the Giants emptied out their lockers and packed up their belongings after beating the Reds in a meaningless game on October 3. Mashi gathered his things thinking that it might be the last time he would be in this room. He had brought a stack of *shikishi* with him and asked his teammates to sign the white cardboard squares with a felt-tipped marker. There was no end-of-the-season party or team meeting. Players drifted from the locker room after subdued goodbyes. Some told Mashi, "See you next season"; others said, "Goodbye." It was time for Masanori to decide his future.

CHAPTER 18

After clearing out his locker, Masanori went to the home of Walter and Yoshiye Osaka. Somebody had suggested that it would be rude if he returned to Japan during the Japan Series, as his arrival would disrupt its media coverage. The series pitted his own Nankai Hawks against Tetsuharu Kawakami's Yomiuri Giants. It would be a clash of philosophies—Kawakami's samurai-inspired control baseball against Tsuruoka's more American approach. Kawakami had recently excised all foreign players from the Giants, while Tsuruoka's team featured three American stars. The best-of-seven series would start on October 30 and run through the first week in November.

In the meantime Masanori stayed in California, sightseeing with the Osakas, visiting the Saiki family in Fresno, and attending various events and banquets. On October 6 the editorial staffs of the *Nichi Bei Times* and *Hokubei Mainichi* hosted a dinner in his honor at the Tokyo Sukiyaki. "I don't like newspaper reporters," Mashi told his hosts, before quickly adding, "I mean newspaper reporters in Japan. Why, some of them just talk to you a few minutes and then make up a whole interview several columns long. I blame them for my not being in better condition when I reported to the Giants last May. [Last winter] it got so bad that I didn't want to go home before 10:00 p.m. because usually some reporters would be waiting for me. I usually went to the movies and even to bars once in a while."[1]

A week later the City of San Francisco held a ceremony for Masanori on the steps of City Hall. Mayor John Shelley had planned to present Mashi with the "Key to the City," but politics intervened. Prior to the event the mayor and the city's board of supervisors began debating who had the authority to issue the coveted foot-long skeleton keys. The issue was unresolved by the morning of the ceremony, so Murakami had to be content with a framed copy of a resolution signed by both the mayor and the supervisors stating that "as a pioneer Masanori Murakami has set a fine example of sportsmanship and ability and that the City and County of San Francisco was proud to have him call San Francisco his second home." Mashi also received a certificate of appreciation from the San Francisco Junior Japanese American Citizens League for his cooperation with community programs. In his brief acceptance speech Masanori "stated his desire to return to San Francisco; however, he was noncommittal as to his future."[2]

During his stay in San Francisco, Murakami and Chub Feeney of the Giants negotiated the terms of a contract for the 1966 season. "The minimum salary in those days was about $6,000, but I had been paid $15,000 in 1965. For the next year they proposed another $15,000 contract. But while we were talking, I balked, and they said, 'Okay, $20,000.' Finally they went up to $30,000 for the next year, plus they would bring my parents over to the States for a month." Kiyoshi Murakami, however, was not intrigued by the invitation, responding, "I saw enough of foreign countries during the war."

Throughout the fall the Bay Area press ran articles on Murakami's contract status and where he might continue his career. Sid Hoos of the *Hayward Daily Review* summed up Giants fans' fears that Mashi "could again be the focal point in a tug o' war between Organized Baseball and the Japanese Empire." When asked what he would do, Masanori's answer remained constant: "My parents want me to play in Japan, but I have yet to make up my mind."[3]

One perceptive reporter wrote, "The 21-year-old Murakami is a young man torn between two loves: his homeland of Japan and his adopted country—the United States of America. Secretly Murakami yearns to pitch for the San Francisco Giants. If he does, he will have to turn his back on his own country's professional league. But Masanori is a smart boy and will probably weigh many factors before he makes a decision."[4]

Mashi's choice would not be dictated by money. Although the Giants' offer of $30,000 was roughly twice the average Major League salary, the Nankai Hawks would undoubtedly offer a similar amount. Other factors would weigh more heavily on the young man.

Masanori had little desire to leave the Giants. Despite the language difficulties, he had made a number of close friends. "[They are] very great men," he told a reporter. "Very fine friends. I like them very much."[5] He enjoyed the easygoing American lifestyle and found the relaxed atmosphere in the Major Leagues better suited to his personality than the rigidness of Japanese baseball. Mashi also enjoyed the American ballparks and fans. "I liked the way the fans cheered the team and players. Most of the time Japanese fans were very quiet back then. As the only Japanese in the league, I felt that the American fans treated me very warmly even in the away ballparks."

In an interview with the *Nichi Bei Times* Murakami explained that he would like to continue playing in the Major Leagues, where the game was faster and the caliber of play higher than in Japan. "I've learned more about the game here than I could ever learn in Japan. [Because of my late arrival], I finally rounded into shape early in August. I certainly would like to pitch one full Major League season, just to see what I can do."[6]

In Japan, on the other hand, Mashi would probably move into the Hawks' starting rotation. Even after two seasons as a relief specialist in the United States, Murakami still wanted to be a regular starter. "I like to start," he told an Associated Press reporter. "In relief, one bad pitch and it goes out, earned run goes up and it does not look good. If I start, one bad pitch does not look too bad afterwards."[7] In 1966 Japanese baseball still did not use relief specialists. Pitchers who could not crack the rotation were generally assigned the mop-up roles, while top starters were often brought in to save close games. It was therefore common for a Japanese team's ace to start every four games and also pitch an inning or two during the games between his starts.

The most compelling reasons to return to Japan had little to do with baseball. Now twenty-one years old and no longer a minor in Japan, Masanori did not need his parents' permission to return to the United States for the 1966 season, but his parents missed him greatly and had repeatedly asked him to come home. As he told the American press, he would make his decision only after consulting with his parents. The primary reason for returning to Japan, however, was his continuing loyalty to the Hawks' manager, Kazuto Tsuruoka. The sense of obligation, or *giri*, that had caused Mashi to sign a contract with Nankai the previous winter still remained and had actually grown stronger once Tsuruoka allowed Mashi to return to the Giants for the 1965 season. Turning his back on Tsuruoka to follow his desire to play for the Giants would be difficult.

In late October Tsuruoka was preparing the Hawks for the Japan Series.

The showdown with the Yomiuri Giants featured the Hawks triple-crown winner Katsuya Nomura against Yomiuri home run king Sadaharu Oh. On paper the two teams were remarkably even, and fans expected a tight seven-game series. Nankai had a plethora of good pitchers, including American Joe Stanka and Mashi's minor league roommate Toshihiro Hayashi, who had just finished a 17-3 season with a 2.25 ERA. Tsuruoka, however, decided to begin the series with his former ace, Tadashi Sugiura. Although Sugiura had won all four games in the Hawks' 1959 sweep of the Giants, injuries had limited him to just eight starts in 1965. The plan backfired. Sugiura lost the first and final games as the Giants won the series in five meetings.

On November 6, the day following the Hawks' defeat, two announcements shocked Nankai fans. First, Tadashi Sugiura announced his retirement. "I want to assume responsibility for the two defeats in the Japan Series and I also am doubtful about my right arm in the future. The young pitchers will not make headway if an old pitcher like me continues to be in service."[8] More surprising, however, was a similar announcement from Kazuto Tsuruoka. "I have managed the Hawks for 20 years and I want to make room for another man." Tsuruoka told reporters that he had made the decision prior to the Japan Series. He planned to remain in professional baseball and would consider managing in Japan's Central League. Head coach Kazuo Kageyama would take over the Hawks' helm.[9]

The following day Murakami left San Francisco on Japan Airlines. Before boarding, he gave a final statement to American reporters. "I honestly don't know what I'll do. I will talk things over with my family and then make up my mind. It is hard to leave San Francisco after being here so many months and making so many friends. I know one thing. If I ever decided to leave Japan, I would like to make my home in San Francisco. The people are friendly and everyone here treated me just fine."[10]

As Mashi's flight was called, the Osaka girls "hung onto his legs and hands and walked with him down a hallway to the plane. When Murakami pulled himself away at the door entrance, the middle sister, Mary, said to him, 'Kiss me.' Murakami bent down and complied. Then he ambled away, as everybody yelled, 'Sayonara!'"[11]

The following afternoon at Haneda International Airport, a "swarm of newsmen and photographers" met Mashi at the gate. One paper exclaimed, "The press conference at the airport rivaled the reception for Princess Meg."

He greeted his parents and a group of Nankai officials before addressing the reporters. "I haven't made up my mind yet. I want first to talk with Hawks officials and my parents." Then, according to one reporter, "Murakami dropped a tiny bomb. 'Now that Tsuruoka-san is not manager of the Hawks, I feel more free to make a decision.' This brought more worried looks."[12]

Masanori spent the next few weeks at his parents' home in Otsuki and visiting the Hawks and friends in Osaka. There were no welcome-home parties. There was nothing to celebrate "because I was not happy," recalls Murakami. He spent hours discussing the decision with his parents. Now that Tsuruoka was no longer the Hawks' manager, one of the primary reasons for returning to Japan had been eliminated. Mashi felt far less loyalty to the Nankai organization, which had treated him poorly throughout the contract dispute the previous winter. Although his father still firmly believed he should stay in Japan, his mother was beginning to thaw.

In mid-November Masanori and his father visited the office of the Japanese baseball commissioner. The league had not yet replaced Commissioner Yushi Uchimura, who had retired in May. Instead a three-man committee, chaired by Toshiyoshi Miyazawa, managed the organization. The visit was partially a courtesy call to thank the office that had made his season in San Francisco possible, but Murakami also needed to know what his official status would be if he decided to go back to San Francisco in 1966 and return to Japan at a later time. Miyazawa explained that if Masanori returned to Japanese professional baseball at a later time, he would still remain the property of the Nankai Hawks.[13]

Then on November 17 Mashi received news that would ultimately decide his fate. At 3:00 a.m. that morning newly appointed Hawks manager Kazuo Kageyama had a heart attack and was found unconscious on his living room floor. He was rushed to a hospital but died within an hour. Three days later, on November 20, Tsuruoka accepted Nankai's plea to renounce his resignation. He would return to lead the Hawks immediately.

Throughout the fall the Giants waited to hear from Murakami as Bay Area newspapers speculated about the final decision. "We've talked to him and we have a 50–50 chance to keep him right now," Horace Stoneham told the *San Francisco Examiner*.[14] Believing that the parents' objections were the primary obstacle to resigning Mashi, Chub Feeney sent Kiyoshi a letter on December 6:

We were extremely happy to have as fine a boy as your son as a member of our team. He is both a fine pitcher and a very fine person. He is extremely well liked by his teammates, our management and the many baseball fans of San Francisco. He has reflected great credit on his family and his country while in the United States.

We sincerely hope that he will pitch again for the Giants in the future and assure you that every care will be taken of him if he does.

I had hoped that you and your wife would visit this country and see for yourself your son as a pitcher and would hope that, if Mashi returns here, you will pay us a visit.[15]

Feeney followed the letter a week later with an official contract for the 1966 season. Both would arrive too late to make a difference.

With Tsuruoka back at the Hawks' helm, the issue of *giri* reemerged. Kiyoshi still felt that his son's obligation to Tsuruoka outweighed the selfish desire to play ball in America. Masanori understood. "I was brought up in the countryside, where people were very close to each other and cared for each other. We valued the bonds between people that made it very natural for me to think that way." After Tsuruoka had allowed Mashi to return to the Giants in 1965, the obligation toward him had increased. Masanori knew that Tsuruoka expected him to return to the Hawks and felt morally bound to pitch for his old mentor. Besides, after his having spent two years abroad, his parents truly missed him and wanted him nearby. Surprisingly, at least to an American mind, Mashi's budding relationship with Yoshiko Hoshino did not enter into the decision.

On December 6 Murakami began serious contract discussions with Nankai, and a week later, on December 14, he signed. Initial reports had his 1966 contract at $83,333, but that was soon corrected to the actual amount of $40,000.

At a press conference Mashi announced, "I finally decided to play for the Hawks a couple of days ago. This is strictly my own decision although the Hawks officials have been advising me to play in Japan. . . . I'm not sure how much I can do in Japanese baseball because I've been away from home for nearly two years. But I believe that my career in the United States will surely add to my confidence."[16]

On hearing the news, Chub Feeney told reporters, "I'm very sad. If in the future, whenever it might be, he wants to return, we would welcome him back."[17] Horace Stoneham wrote Mashi directly:

I am sorry that you won't be back with us next year, but the decision to remain in Japan was one you had to make for yourself, and I wish you the best of luck and success with your new club. You were a very fine pitcher for the Giants, and I am sure you also found it a very interesting experience. Your personality and ability was reflected in the high regard in which you were held by your teammates, the fans in San Francisco and all the members of the Giants' organization. You will be remembered here with pleasure. You have reason to be proud of your career here, as the first Japanese player in the Major Leagues. It was an honor for yourself and for your country, and I am sure it made a deep impression upon the fans of Japan.[18]

A short time later Josuke Nishino, Tsuruoka's friend who had counseled Mashi during the previous winter, invited Masanori to dinner. They dined on *fugu* (blowfish) in Yokohama and then stopped in a small local bar for a few drinks. Sitting in a corner booth with a long couch, they drank scotch and talked. After a few drinks Mashi stretched out on the sofa and closed his eyes. "I was very relaxed and started quietly singing 'I Left My Heart in San Francisco.' Tears fell from my eyes and rolled down my cheeks."

Nishino saw the tears.

"Oh, you wanted to stay in San Francisco that much. I will speak with Manager Tsuruoka for you. I can convince him to let you go back to the United States next year. But you have to come back to Japan the following year."

"But," recalls Murakami "I refused his kind proposal. I strongly felt that I should not trouble people any more. I indeed had regrets. I wanted to stay in San Francisco, but I could not. If I went back to the States, I would have lost the relationship with Tsuruoka-san because I would have betrayed him. So I fulfilled my obligation to Mr. Tsuruoka and forever carry a sense of regret with me. Yet if I had returned to the Giants, I would have realized my dream but would have to live with a sense of betraying Mr. Tsuruoka. I am still proud of the decision I made."

AFTERWORD

Once Murakami announced that he would stay in Japan, his popularity soared. He posed with Central League MVP Sadaharu Oh for the New Year's Day cover of *Sankei Sports*. *Asahi Graphics*, a pictorial news magazine, placed Mashi on the front cover of its January 28 issue. Inside a short article discussed his home life in Otsuki, noting that he was a friendly, modest young man who had returned to Japan to honor his parents' wishes. In addition to numerous other print and television interviews, he did an in-depth interview with Yomiuri Giants ace Masaichi Kaneda for the January 24 issue of *Shukan Baseball*. After asking about Mashi's experiences in the Major Leagues, the elder Kaneda advised him to be careful of injuring himself in spring camp by training too hard, as after two years in America his body would not be ready for Japanese practices; not to drink too much or womanize; and most important, "ignore your Major League pride and remember that you are just a young Japanese player."[1] After the interview Kaneda brought Mashi to meet a famous pop star at her home—an honor unimaginable to him two years earlier. She told Masanori that he was cute.

As Mashi reported to Kure in late January for spring training, he decided to try something different. Up until then he had pitched with a low three-quarters delivery—not throwing sidearm, nor straight above his shoulder, but about halfway in between. During the off-season he had read a critique of his delivery and became convinced by the author's argument that he could become a more effective pitcher if he adopted an "over-the-top" delivery. The over-the-top delivery actually offers no advantages over a three-quarters motion, but anxious to succeed, Mashi decided to follow the advice.

As Mashi was Japan's only Major Leaguer, the fans, media, and teammates expected him to become Nankai's new ace and dominate Japanese opponents. Dan Hruby of the *San Jose Mercury* remarked, "The Japanese . . . seemingly expect him to throw a no-hit game every time he mounts the pitcher's rubber."[2] Some suggested that as a starter he might win twenty games. In a rare instance of bravado Mashi proclaimed "he would try to start going for a strikeout record."[3]

Reporters clustered around him in training camp as Mashi tried to master his new delivery. The transition was not going well. With the new release point, he had lost the pinpoint control that had made him famous in the United States. He expected that to return with more practice. More troubling was the tightness he felt in his left shoulder. The unfamiliar motion was putting stress on the joint and undeveloped muscles.

In early March Murakami started his first preseason game at Koshien Stadium against the Hanshin Tigers—Osaka's more popular Central League franchise. The outing began well as Mashi held the Tigers hitless for the first three innings, but in the fourth, Tigers cleanup hitter Kazuhiro Yamauchi, whom Mashi had induced to pop up three years earlier in his Pacific League debut, smashed a towering home run to score the game's first run. The following inning Murakami seemed to "run out of steam," as Hanshin pounded him for 3 hits and 2 runs before Tsuruoka removed him from the mound.[4]

Mashi fared no better in his next exhibition start. On Sunday, March 13, the Hawks faced the Yomiuri Giants at Osaka Stadium in a rematch of the 1965 Japan Series. Murakami lasted just four innings, giving up 3 runs on two long balls. Coach Carlton Hanta remembers Japanese batters especially bearing down against Mashi. A hit off Murakami was effectively a hit off a Major Leaguer, proving the batter's ability to compete at the highest level.

Whereas the American press had overlooked his poor outings, the Japanese media pounced on him. One newspaper proclaimed that Murakami had betrayed his fans and Japanese baseball with his feeble performances. Even the usually supportive *Pacific Stars and Stripes* headlined its baseball news with "Some Fans Bewildered As Murakami Is Shelled" and "Mashi Fails Again As a Starter." A writer from *Asahi Shimbun* sympathized, noting that Murakami was "under considerable pressure" and that "the fans expect too much of him."[5]

When the Hawks opened the 1966 season against the Tokyo Orions on April 9, Tsuruoka relegated Murakami to the bullpen. In the first month Mashi appeared in 10 games, winning 2 without a loss and posting an outstanding 1.75 ERA. The statistics, however, belied serious problems. He continued to struggle with his mechanics and had trouble finding the strike zone. In 20½ innings he had walked 10 batters and struck out just 11. He had also given up 19 hits for a 1.41 WHIP—well above the 1.16 league average. Worse still, the pain in his shoulder had increased.

From May onward the season spiraled downhill. "Somehow I just wasn't able to reach my peak. My curves wouldn't break and my fastball lost its zip."[6] By the time Masanori lost his first game on June 8, he had pitched in 33 innings and surrendered 29 hits, 16 walks, and 12 runs. His WHIP had ballooned to 1.49 and his ERA to 3.27 (the league ERA was 2.88). Fans became increasingly hostile. On June 5, after Mashi failed to protect a 1–0 lead and was removed before recording an out, the fans began yelling, "Go back to America." The comment was both ironic and painful. "I was not doing well, so I was very unhappy," recalls Murakami. "When people were making negative comments and yelling, 'Go back to America,' I couldn't help thinking, That's what I want to do! It was you guys who wanted me to come back!" Frustrated with his poor performances, Mashi began throwing his glove at the dugout wall or kicking over clubhouse furniture when yanked from a game.

Members of the media and especially those from *Hochi Sports* attacked Mashi for "picking up bad American habits."[7] They blamed him for his temper tantrums, calling him unprofessional. They blamed him for chewing bubble gum when pitching, calling him too casual. They blamed him for being *tengu*.

Tengu are common spirits in Japanese folklore, recognized by their human-like faces with ridiculously long noses. They are disruptive magical creatures bent on causing trouble and in some stories are the ghosts of particularly arrogant people. Today the term describes a person who is conceited and too proud after becoming successful due to luck rather than hard work. It is also associated with a Japanese who has achieved unusual success in a foreign country—probably a reference to the shared long noses of *tengu* and Westerners. Murakami, who was virtually unknown when he left Japan in March 1964 and became a celebrity in the United States, was easy to criticize as *tengu*.

"I didn't feel I was *tengu*," Murakami told *Stars and Stripes* reporter Mike Berger in 1968. "They [the reporters] didn't like me because I spoke directly and because I chewed gum. They said I was impolite; that I must eat my sushi with Worcester sauce" (a habit practiced only by non-Japanese and especially Americans). "How could I forget the Japanese way of doing anything, even if I was stupid?"[8]

Hochi Sports, which had always been particularly nasty toward Murakami, claimed that his Nankai teammates worried when he took the mound as "he lacks speed and his control is poor." They also "wonder how he ever was good enough to pitch for the San Francisco Giants."[9] Fans became increasingly hostile, jeering each time he took the mound. Some would yell, "*Bai koku do* [Traitor]!"—a particular nasty insult in the postwar period that implied a betrayal of Japan for personal gain. The abuse became so bad that his teammates began avoiding him. According to one reporter, "Mashi eats by himself, and is often the last player to leave the field, the locker-room, the hotel lobby."[10]

Throughout the season American newspapers followed Mashi's troubles. He remained a popular player, not only in the Bay Area, but also around the country. Small-town papers from Waterloo, Iowa, to Oneonta, New York, routinely reprinted AP and UPI articles on his difficulties in Japan, while the San Francisco media carried more in-depth stories. Many, like Dan Hruby's "Bring Back Murakami!" longed for Mashi's return to the Giants to bolster their meager bullpen.[11]

By mid-June Tsuruoka had demoted Mashi to the mop-up role. "He hugs the bench more and more, pitching only when Manager Kazuto Tsuruoka gives him the rare nod," an AP article noted.[12] In the second half of the season, however, Masanori slowly regained control of both his pitches and his life. His shoulder began to feel better, the media attacks subsided, and he became one of the Hawks' top relievers. In the final three and a half months of the 1966 season Murakami resembled the pitcher who had played for the Giants. He entered 30 games, pitched 63⅓ innings, and surrendered just 51 hits and only 9 walks. He struck out 50—about 20 percent of the batters he faced. During this time his WHIP fell to 0.95 and his ERA to 2.98. According to a UPI article, "He has gained the respect of his teammates as a stopper, particularly against left-handed batters."[13]

As Murakami improved, the Hawks cruised to the Pacific League pennant. Once again they would face the Yomiuri Giants in the Japan Series. The Giants featured a switch hitter and three left-handed hitters in their starting lineup, including Central League home run and RBI king Sadaharu Oh.

To counter the threat Nankai would need particularly strong left-handed pitching, but Murakami was the team's only southpaw. Leslie Nakamura of the *Pacific Stars and Stripes* speculated, "Murakami . . . could be the hero to help win the Japan Series."[14]

But there would be no storybook ending for Mashi's first season back in Japan. Tsuruoka gave the ball to Murakami in 5 games, but the Giants hit him hard. In 9⅓ innings he allowed 7 runs on 8 hits and 4 walks with 4 home runs. Yomiuri took the series in 6 games. As one reporter succinctly put it, "By any measurement of what Japanese fans expected, Mashi has been a flop."[15]

Despite Mashi's miserable season, the San Francisco Giants wanted him to return to the Majors in 1967. In November Chub Feeney mailed Murakami a contract. Under the Reserve Clause to retain their rights to Murakami, the Giants were required to send a contract or he would become a free agent, but the offer was more than a legal formality. "We'd like to have him back," Feeney told the press. "I think we might have won the pennant last season if Mashi had been in our bullpen. We've been led to believe that Mashi became disenchanted with baseball in his country this past season when he pitched for the Nankai Hawks. But we still fear family ties will again be the deciding factor and he'll remain in Japan."[16]

"I would like to pitch for the Giants again but I am on Nankai's roster," Murakami responded. "Nankai still has rights to me."[17]

There was little chance of the Hawks' relinquishing Murakami's contract, despite his troubles. "It's out of the question," snapped Hawks' president Shigeru Niiyama when told that the Giants wanted Mashi back.[18]

In the wake of Murakami's success in the Majors, American teams realized that Japan provided an untapped resource of potential players. Bill Veeck, the maverick owner of several American League teams from 1946 to 1981, exclaimed, "Murakami showed that Japanese players are not bums. . . . There is at least one player on each team . . . who could play in our major leagues," and he predicted that Japanese players would soon be prevalent on all big league rosters.[19]

To prevent American teams from raiding the Japanese leagues and set guidelines on international rights to players, William Eckert, the recently appointed commissioner of Major League Baseball, traveled to Japan after the 1966 season to meet with new Japanese commissioner Toshiyoshi Miyazawa. Together they forged the United States–Japanese Player Contract Agreement, usually called the Working Agreement, which bound members of each league to honor the reserve clause and contracts of the other league. The agreement altered Murakami's legacy. Instead of becoming a Jackie Robinson–like figure, initiating an influx of Japanese players into the United States, his brief stay in the Major Leagues had the opposite effect of slamming the door on future Japanese imports.

Masanori's misery continued in 1967. He stayed with the overhand delivery, and the ache in his shoulder persisted. Once again he was unable to crack the Hawks' starting rotation and was banished to the bullpen. Yet even in this familiar role he pitched poorly. Tsuruoka brought him into 41 games, where he threw 80⅓ innings and posted a 4.03 ERA—the worst on the team's regular staff and a full run above the Pacific League average. With his decline on the mound, Mashi faded from the American news—the updates on his career all but disappear after the start of the 1967 season. In Japan, although the fans and press continued to razz him, the abuse was not as bad as the year before. Expectations were significantly lower. This was in part due to Mashi's poor performance in 1966 but was also helped along by his old rivals, the Los Angeles Dodgers.

In October and November 1966 the Dodgers came to Japan for an 18-game tour. They played seven games against the Japanese champion Yomiuri Giants in an exhibition international World Series and twelve games against Japanese all-star teams. Mashi pitched in three of these games and did not fare well, surrendering 8 hits, 2 home runs, and 4 runs in 8 innings. The Dodgers, however, also failed to impress. Playing without star pitchers Sandy Koufax and Don Drysdale, who had refused to make the trip, Los Angeles lost the series to the Giants four games to three, and tallied an overall record of 9-8-1. It was the worst performance by a visiting Major League team since the tours began in 1908. To the Japanese the conclusion was obvious. There was no longer a significant talent gap between the American and Japanese leagues. As a result many stopped viewing Murakami's success with the Giants as evidence that he was superior to most Japanese players. Instead they saw his success in the Majors and inability to succeed with the Hawks as further proof that the Japanese leagues were on a par with the Majors.

For Masanori 1967 did have a bright spot. Since his return to Japan he and Yoshiko Hoshino had continued dating. "The newspapers portrayed him as a very bad person, and it was very effective," she recalls, "but I knew better. He was just a very nice, decent Japanese man." That season the relationship became more serious, and on December 15 they were married.

Kazuto Tsuruoka presented the couple with a full-length mirror, telling them that it served a dual purpose: "Your wife can use it for dressing in kimono; you use it for practice pitching."[20] The manager also instructed Yoshiko to always send her husband off to the ballpark with a smile, even if they had been fighting, and not to say anything negative to him in the morning. If she had bad news—for example, if somebody had died—she was only to tell him after he came back from the game. Embarrassed by his poor performances on the field, Mashi did not invite any of his American friends, even the Saiki and Osaka families, to the wedding.

Murakami boarded the train for the familiar trip to the spring training camp at Kure, determined to improve in 1968. "I was ashamed to be with my wife this spring," he told *Hochi Shimbun*, "because I was a failure."[21] By the end of spring training, however, the pain in his shoulder had returned. Moving back to Osaka, he tried acupuncture and cortisone injections, but neither provided relief. In early April he began taking the train to a clinic in Kyoto for electrotherapy treatment. Each day a now pregnant Yoshiko would meet him at the train station when he returned from the clinic. Seeing his new bride's smiling face provided inspiration. He would work hard, overcome the injury, and make her proud. By the end of the month Mashi was ready to rejoin the Hawks.

While sidelined with the injury, Mashi had made a decision. He would return to the three-quarters delivery he had used with the San Francisco Giants and abandon the attempt to throw over the top. "Throw any way you like," Tsuruoka snapped when told of the change.[22] "I felt he'd given up on me," Mashi recalls "but at the same time, I felt *Yoshi* [all right then]! I'll show them."[23]

Murakami practiced the old familiar motion, added a lower release point, developed a slider, and started to win. He began the season in the bullpen but soon moved into the starting rotation for the first time in his career. On July 9 he won against the Nishitetsu Lions to begin a streak of twelve straight victories. Not long after he pitched a four-hitter against the Kintetsu Buffaloes on July 30, Tsuruoka told the press, "He has much better control and the ball is more active, too."[24]

In typical Japanese fashion Tsuruoka used Mashi to both start and close games—often with little rest in between. On August 30 he had Murakami pitch the final 3⅔ innings in an 8–6 win over the Tokyo Orions. The following day Mashi came in from the bullpen again, this time in the ninth to pitch 2⅔ shutout innings before the game ended after the twelfth inning in a 2–2 tie. Murakami was back on the mound the next day as well—as a starter. He beat the Orions 5–1, throwing a complete game while surrendering just 6 hits and going two-for-four (with a double) at the plate. During the three days he had pitched 15⅓innings, won twice, and given up just 10 hits and 1 run. A Japanese sportswriter noted, "Nankai is surprised by Murakami's courage and his new spirit."[25]

In Japan many believe a ballplayer will slump in the season after he weds. But Masanori openly credited Yoshiko with his success. "When I see my wife, I have spirit," he told reporters. Soon the Japanese media were focusing on Yoshiko. "My wife thinks it's wonderful to be interviewed," Masanori added.[26] One newspaper ran a feature article entitled "The Goddess of Victory."

Murakami ended the 1968 season with a stellar 18-4 record, a 2.38 ERA, and a 1.02 WHIP. He was sixth in the Pacific League in wins, second in ERA, third in WHIP, and first in winning percentage. A headline from a Tokyo sports daily summed up the development nicely: "After Three Difficult Years, a Smile Comes to Mashi."[27] He had finally reached his potential and emerged as the star Tsuruoka had envisioned when signing him straight out of high school.

Nankai had high hopes for Murakami in 1969. The team's top pitchers were aging, and at twenty-five, Mashi looked ready to become the Hawks' ace. He worked hard during camp, trying to improve both his mechanics and stamina through strenuous workouts, but "A week before the season started, my elbow began to hurt. I had simply pitched too much." Once again Masanori left spring training with an arm injury. He struggled through the 1969 season, his elbow never really healing. Bouncing back and forth between the bullpen and the starting rotation, Mashi finished with a 7-9 record in 119 innings. His 4.54 ERA was far above the 3.23 league average.

After the 1969 season Masanori and Yoshiko traveled to the United States on a delayed honeymoon. They visited San Francisco, Reno, Phoenix, and Disneyland, but Mashi also spoke with Horace Stoneham and the Giants' management about his future. "I still want to return to the Giants," he told American reporters "but first they must negotiate my release from the Nankai

Hawks." The press reported that Murakami would join the Giants for spring training if San Francisco could secure rights to his contract. Negotiations with Nankai, however, were unsuccessful.[28]

Murakami would remain in the Japanese leagues for the next thirteen seasons, pitching for the Hawks, the cross-town Hanshin Tigers in 1975, and Tokyo's Nippon Ham Fighters from 1976 to 1982. He stayed in the Hawks' starting rotation from 1970 to 1972, amassing a 36-35 record with a 3.71 ERA and making the 1971 all-star squad before returning to the bullpen for the remainder of his career. He never duplicated his success of the 1968 season but had several strong years as the Fighters' long reliever. During the 1977 and 1978 seasons he saved 16 games and won 19 in relief with a 2.70 ERA. When Mashi announced his retirement in 1982, he had pitched 18 seasons in Japan, won 103 games, saved another 30, and posted a respectable 3.64 ERA.

At the end of the 1982 season Masanori met with Nippon Ham Fighters manager Keiji Osawa and general manager Osamu Mihara. He was now thirty-eight years old and had pitched in only two innings (surrendering three hits and two runs) during the year. It was time for Mashi to retire. The organization offered him a position as the assistant pitching coach for the farm team, but the pay was poor. Instead he accepted his release. He was now no longer held by the Japanese reserve clause. He was a free agent, able to play where he wished.

Murakami immediately telephoned his old teammate Tom Haller, now the general manager of the San Francisco Giants, to ask for a tryout. Haller agreed. Mashi could come to the Giants' 1983 spring training camp in Phoenix to compete for a roster spot.

The homecoming intrigued many, and the story was featured not only in the San Francisco media, but also in the *Sporting News* and picked up by numerous small papers across the United States. "Guess Who's Back?" was the large headline in the sports section of western Pennsylvania's *Monessen Valley Independent*.[29] "I'm not too old," Murakami told the press. "I can pitch. Gaylord Perry and Phil Neikro are still pitching. My body is very young. My legs and arm are not getting old."[30]

Yet Mashi's dream of returning to the Giants remained unfulfilled. He pitched well during spring training, but just before the team headed north, Haller brought him to his office to explain that he would not make the final cut. "I understood the situation. He had to go with younger pitchers. But

I'm glad I gave it one last shot."[31] After twenty years on the mound Murakami's career was over.

Masanori decided to spend the season in San Francisco anyway. He spent most of his days in uniform at Candlestick Park, training with the Giants and pitching batting practice. Yoshiko, his fourteen-year-old daughter Maho, and his twelve-year old son Naotsugu came to join him. The children attended American schools, became fluent in English, and grew to share their father's love for the Bay Area.

At the end of the year they returned to Japan. Murakami spent a few years as a baseball commentator before returning to uniform as a pitching coach for the Fighters, Hawks, and Seibu Lions. In 1990 he reentered the broadcasting booth as a commentator for NHK and began writing baseball columns for *Daily Sports* and other publications.

By the early 1990s the American public had almost forgotten about Mashi. His name occasionally showed up in baseball trivia quizzes but rarely in newspapers or sports magazines. Japanese baseball suffered a similar fate. Major League franchises stopped touring Japan in 1984. Instead MLB sent over allstar squads to face their Japanese equivalents. The American media gave a collective yawn and rarely bothered to report game results. At the same time the success of former Major Leaguers like Randy Bass, Boomer Wells, Bob Horner, and Warren Cromartie in Japan implied that the Japanese leagues were far below big league standards. Bob Klapisch of the *Bergen County Record* summed up the prevailing American view of Japanese ball in the lead paragraph of his article, "Japanese Baseball Is Better Than You Think." "Admit it," he wrote, "Japanese baseball is a joke to you. It is played in microscopic stadiums, is populated with sub-170-pound players, none who throw harder than 80 mph. Go ahead, be honest: You're an American baseball supremacist."[32]

But all that changed in 1995, when a young Japanese fireballer named Hideo Nomo grew frustrated with being overused by his Japanese manager. After pitching for the Japanese Olympic team in 1988, Nomo signed with the Kintetsu Buffaloes and in his first season won the 1990 Pacific League's Rookie of the Year, Most Valuable Player, and Sawamura Awards. He remained Japan's top pitcher for the next three seasons until 1994, when the Buffaloes' new manager, Keishi Suzuki, decided to toughen up his ace. Following the old "samurai baseball" philosophies of Ichiko and Suishu Tobita's Waseda University teams, Suzuki forced Nomo to finish his starts to improve his fighting spirit. In a July 1 game against the Seibu Lions he refused to relieve a wild Nomo, requiring him to pitch the entire game despite his walking 16 batters and throwing 191 pitches. Soon afterward Nomo's shoulder began to ache. Suzuki's solution was to send his ace to the minor league for more practice, proclaiming, "The best way to cure a sore arm is to throw more." Within a few weeks, the injury escalated, and Nomo was out for the season.[33]

At the end of the 1994 season Nomo teamed up with agent Don Nomura to escape Suzuki's control and realize his dream of playing in the Major Leagues. Nomura had found a loophole in the standard Japanese player contract. The contract clearly stated that a retired player wishing to rejoin Japanese Professional Baseball would belong to his former club, but it did not specify who would own the rights if the player chose to play outside of Japan. Nomo promptly announced his retirement from Japanese baseball and began shopping his services to Major League teams.

In early 1995 the San Francisco Giants contacted Mashi and asked him to escort Nomo to the United States to meet with their management. The trip and subsequent meeting went well, but ultimately Nomo signed with the rival Los Angeles Dodgers.

Nomo, of course, became an instant success, starting the 1995 All-Star Game and winning the National League Rookie of the Year Award. Both the United States and Japan were soon caught up in Nomomania. Millions of dollars were made on Nomo T-shirts, jerseys, pennants, trading cards, and figurines. The public clamored for information about the taciturn superstar. Hundreds of reporters covered his games, while dozens followed his every move, camping outside his apartment and even rummaging through his garbage.

The frenzy brought Murakami back into the limelight. American reporters became interested in Japanese baseball, wondering how a foreign league considered to be of AAA caliber could produce a player of Nomo's quality. They soon rediscovered Mashi and retold his story as part of their longer articles on Nomo. In Japan Nomo's starts were broadcast on television. Already working for NHK, Murakami became the color commentator for these games. Reporters on both sides of the Pacific wanted Mashi's opinions about pitching in the Majors and the challenges Nomo was facing.

In midsummer Murakami returned to the United States to cover Nomo's start at the All-Star Game in Arlington, Texas. He joined the festivities, playing in the annual Old Timers' Game and making public appearances. After the all-star break, he traveled to San Francisco, where the Giants held a second Masanori Murakami Day. The visiting Los Angeles Dodgers altered their rotation so that Nomo would start on the historic day. Following the ceremony to honor the first Japanese in the Majors, the second import stole the show by holding the Giants to 1 hit while striking out 11 in a complete-game shutout. On that night there was no doubt how far Japanese baseball had come.

Since 1995 over forty Japanese have followed Nomo to the Major Leagues. Asked about the pressures on these players to stay in Japan, Murakami responded, "Baseball players should choose the best place to compete and now that is MLB. They shouldn't think about loyalty to a Japanese team. Baseball is a business and players should get as much in salary as they can, as interest in their skills rapidly fades."[34] Mashi has continued his role as a commentator, writer, and unofficial adviser to many of these young men. He has become a bridge between American and Japanese baseball—an unofficial ambassador. In 2004 the Ministry of Foreign Affairs of Japan recognized his unique position and contributions by awarding Murakami a Certificate of Commendation on the 150th anniversary of U.S.-Japanese diplomatic relations for "strengthening the friendship and goodwill between the two countries."

Now retired, Murakami works with a number of charities. In 2013 he became the first former athlete to be appointed as a goodwill ambassador for the United Nations High Commission for Refugees. He hopes that his prominent role in baseball will encourage Japanese to give more generously to help the unfortunate around the world.

In his role as a celebrity Mashi gives many speeches. Most have the same theme: pursue your dreams. He tells his audiences, "I really wanted to play in the United States, but I honored my obligation to Mr. Tsuruoka and came back. As a person, I think I did the right thing. I am still proud of doing that. But at the same time, I have a lot of regrets. I think that for my life, I should have stayed with the Giants. You only have one life, so it is important to do what you want to do. It doesn't matter what other people say about you. As long as you follow the law and don't hurt other people, you should try to live your life without regrets and follow your dreams."

APPENDIX: MASANORI MURAKAMI STATISTICS

MASANORI MURAKAMI CAREER STATISTICS

YEAR	TEAM	W	L	ERA	G	GS	CG	SHO	SV	IP	H	R	ER	HR	BB	SO	WHIP
1963	Nankai	0	0	4.50	3	0	0	0	0	2.0	2	1	1	1	2	2	2.000
1964	Fresno	11	7	1.78	49	1	0	0		106	64	28	21	6	34	159	0.925
1964	Giants	1	0	1.80	9	0	0	0	1	15	8	3	3	1	1	15	0.600
1965	Giants	4	1	3.75	45	1	0	0	8	74.1	57	31	31	9	22	85	1.063
1966	Nankai	6	4	3.08	46	2	0	0		96.1	80	34	33	10	25	66	1.090
1967	Nankai	3	1	4.03	41	1	0	0		80.1	72	36	36	11	26	60	1.220
1968	Nankai	18	4	2.38	40	19	9	1		177.2	141	54	47	18	40	90	1.019
1969	Nankai	7	9	4.54	31	14	3	0		119.0	139	64	60	19	32	47	1.437
1970	Nankai	11	11	3.25	32	24	9	2		191.1	167	79	69	18	52	75	1.145
1971	Nankai	14	15	4.10	38	31	13	0		234.2	233	122	107	36	63	78	1.261
1972	Nankai	11	9	4.28	33	19	6	1		147.1	156	79	70	20	46	57	1.371
1973	Nankai	2	4	5.21	23	8	0	0		65.2	75	42	38	8	25	27	1.523
1974	Nankai	1	2	1.82	10	2	1	1	0	24.2	13	7	5	1	3	10	0.649
1975	Hanshin	2	1	5.12	18	1	0	0	1	19.1	24	14	11	4	7	8	1.603
1976	Nippon Ham	1	0	3.74	32	1	0	0	0	53.0	61	24	22	7	15	17	1.434
1977	Nippon Ham	7	4	2.32	61	0	0	0	6	112.1	96	36	29	7	19	78	1.024
1978	Nippon Ham	12	11	3.03	57	2	0	0	10	130.2	125	54	44	12	29	59	1.179
1979	Nippon Ham	5	3	4.20	45	0	0	0	11	98.2	101	50	46	16	30	42	1.328
1980	Nippon Ham	2	3	4.70	37	0	0	0	2	67.0	70	39	35	12	28	31	1.463
1981	Nippon Ham	1	1	4.43	17	0	0	0	0	20.1	28	13	10	1	9	10	1.820
1982	Nippon Ham	0	0	9.00	2	0	0	0	0	2.0	3	2	2	0	1	1	2.000
MLB Totals		5	1	3.43	54	1	0	0	9	89.1	65	34	34	10	23	100	0.985
JP Totals		103	82	3.64	566	124	41	5	30	1,642.1	1,586	750	665	201	452	758	1.241

Source: BaseballReference.com.

MURAKAMI GAME LOG WITH FRESNO, 1964

DATE	OPPONENT	RESULT	IP	H	ER	BB	SO	COMMENTS
April 24	@ Santa Barbara	W, 7–5	5	0	0	3	9	Win (1–0)
April 27	@ Santa Barbara	L, 11–8	⅔	0	0	0	1	
April 29	Stockton	W, 4–3	2⅔	1	0	0	6	
May 7a	San Jose	W, 4–3	⅔	0	0	0	0	Win (2–0)
May 12	@ Modesto	W, 7–4	1⅓	0	0	0	2	
May 14	@ Modesto	W, 7–1	2⅔	2	0	0	5	
May 19b	Reno	W, 3–2	7	6	1	2	14	Win (3–0); Japan night
May 22	@ Stockton	W, 3–1	1	0	0	0	1	Win (4–0)
May 28	Santa Barbara	L, 3–1	2	1	1	0	4	
May 29	@ San Jose	W, 6–3	3⅔	0	0	1	4	Win (5–0)
May 31b	@ San Jose	L, 2–1	3⅓	?	0	?	2	No box score
June 5	Bakersfield	W, 7–5	2⅓	0	0	2	2	
June 6	Bakersfield	W, 9–5	2⅔	2	0	0	4	
June 8	@ Bakersfield	L, 5–3	1⅓	2	2	2	2	Loss (5–1)
June 9	@ Salinas	L, 7–6	⅓	3	3	1	1	Loss (5–2)
June 11	@ Salinas	W, 5–1	2	0	0	2	4	Win (6–2); strikes out side in thirteenth

June 13b	Reno	L, 6–3	2	3	1	0	3	
June 15	@ Stockton	W, 2–1	2⅔	0	0	1	3	
June 16	@ Stockton	W, 7–4	2	0	0	0	2	
June 18	Santa Barbara	L, 6–5	5	5	2	0	9	Loss (6–3)
June 21b	@ San Jose	L, 6–5	2+	?	2	?	?	Loss (6–4)
June 25	Modesto	L, 3–0	1	2	1	0	2	
June 27b	@ Bakersfield	W, 6–4	2⅔	1	0	?	4	Win (7–4)
July 2	Stockton	W, 10–7	3	4	1	0	4	
July 3	Stockton	W, 9–2	0					
July 5a	Santa Barbara	L, 6–5	⅔	1	0	1	1	Loss (7–5)
July 8	Salinas	W, 5–2	⅓	0	0	0	0	Save
July 9	Salinas	W, 8–5	2	3	0	0	3	Gives up 2 unearned runs
July 10	Salinas	W, 12–5	0	2	3	0	1	
July 13	Reno	W, 8–5	⅓	1	0	0	0	
July 17	San Jose	W, 6–5	2	0	0	1	2	Win (8–5); hits HR
July 21	Modesto	T, 9–9	6	7	2	1	11	
July 23	Modesto	W, 16–11	2	2	1	1	3	
July 25	Salinas	L, 5–1	?					No box score
July 26	Salinas	L, 4–2	2	3	0	1	0	

Date	Opponent	Result	IP					Notes
July 28	Reno	W, 11–4	1⅔	0	0	0	3	
July 30	Reno	W, 3–2	1	0	0	0	1	Win (9–5)
July 31	Reno	W, 12–3	0					
August 1	@ Stockton	L, 5–4	?	?	?	?	?	Loss (9–6); no box score
August 5	Modesto	W, 7–6	4⅔	1	0	0	4	Win (10–6); gets winning hit
August 12	Santa Barbara	L, 4–3	2	1	0	0	3	Loss (10–7)
August 13	Santa Barbara	W, 5–3	1⅓	0	0	0	2	Save
August 14	Santa Barbara	W, 9–2	1⅓	0	0	0	1	
August 15b	@ Bakersfield	L, 1–0	1	0	0	0	2	
August 18	Salinas	W, 2–1	1	0	0	0	2	Win (11–7)
August 19	Salinas	W, 8–6	1⅓	2	0	0	1	Save; 1 unearned run
August 21	@ Santa Barbara	W, 5–3	3	0	0	0	7	Save; fans 7 of 9 batters faced
August 22	@ Santa Barbara	W, 8–5	1⅓	1	1	0	1	
August 26	Stockton	W, 3–1	1	0	0	0	2	Save
August 29	@ Reno	W, 6–5	4	0?	0	0?	10	Save; strikes out 10 of 12 batters faced
Totals			106	64	21	34	159	11 wins, 7 losses, 1.78 ERA

Sources: *Bakersfield Californian* and *Fresno Bee Republican*.

1964 MURAKAMI MLB GAME LOG

DATE	AGAINST	RESULT	IP	H	R	ER	BB	SO	HR	DECISIONS
September 1	NYM	L, 4–1	1.0	1	0	0	0	2	0	
September 9	LAD	L, 8–1	2.0	1	0	0	1	4	0	
September 11	PHI	L, 1–0	1.0	0	0	0	0	1	0	
September 16	NYM	L, 4–0	1.0	0	0	0	0	1	0	
September 18	PIT	L, 4–3	0.2	1	0	0	0	0	0	BS (1)
September 22	HOU	W, 7–1	1.0	0	0	0	0	0	0	S (1)
September 29	HOU	W, 5–4	3.0	1	0	0	0	3	0	W (1–0)
October 3	CHC	L, 10–7	1.1	0	0	0	0	2	0	
October 4	CHC	L, 9–2	4.0	4	3	3	0	2	1	
Totals			15.0	8	3	3	1	15	1	

Source: BaseballReference.com.

1965 MURAKAMI MLB GAME LOG

DATE	AGAINST	RESULT	IP	H	R	ER	BB	SO	HR	DECISIONS
May 9	LAD	W, 6-3	0.1	0	0	0	0	1	0	
May 12	CHC	L, 7-3	0.2	2	1	1	0	0	0	
May 16b	HOU	W, 4-3	1.2	0	0	0	0	2	0	s (1)
May 20	CHC	W, 2-0	2.0	2	0	0	0	3	0	s (2)
May 22b	HOU	L, 3-2	1.1	3	2	2	0	1	1	L (0-1)
May 25	MLN	L, 4-1	3.0	7	6	6	2	1	1	
June 3	MLN	L, 10-3	0.2	1	1	1	1	0	1	
June 11	PIT	L, 5-3	3.0	1	0	0	1	5	0	
June 16	LAD	L, 2-1	1.0	0	0	0	1	0	0	
June 22	PIT	L, 6-0	5.2	5	1	1	1	5	1	
June 26	PHI	W, 6-5	2.0	1	0	0	2	1	0	w (1-1)
June 27	PHI	L, 6-0	1.0	1	0	0	0	1	0	
June 29	LAD	L, 9-3	4.2	2	1	1	1	3	0	
July 3	CHC	L, 4-1	0.1	1	2	2	1	0	0	
July 7	STL	W, 4-2	1.2	0	0	0	0	1	0	w (2-1)
July 9	PHI	L, 10-3	3.1	2	3	3	0	4	1	
July 18	HOU	L, 5-3	2.0	0	0	0	0	2	0	
July 21	CIN	W, 5-4	2.0	0	0	0	0	4	0	w (3-1)
July 22	CIN	L, 5-4	1.0	0	0	0	0	1	0	
July 28	STL	W, 8-5	1.0	0	2	2	2	0	0	H (1)
August 1a	MLN	L, 4-2	2.2	0	0	0	0	2	0	
August 3	CIN	W, 6-3	0.1	0	0	0	0	1	0	H (2)

Date	Opp	Result								
August 5	CIN	W, 18–7	3.0	2	2	2	1	5	1	s (3)
August 6	STL	W, 3–2	0.1	0	0	0	0	1	0	s (4)
August 8	STL	W, 6–4	1.1	1	2	2	2	2	0	H (3)
August 12a	PIT	W, 4–3	0.0	1	0	0	0	0	0	BS (2)
August 15	PHI	W, 15–9	2.1	4	3	3	1	4	0	
August 19	LAD	L, 8–5	0.1	1	0	0	0	1	0	BS (3)
August 21	LAD	L, 6–4	0.2	0	0	0	0	2	0	
August 22	LAD	W, 4–3	0.2	0	0	0	0	1	0	s (5)
August 24	PIT	L, 5–2	1.0	0	0	0	0	2	0	
August 26b	PIT	L, 6–5	3.1	3	0	0	1	3	0	
August 28	NYM	L, 3–0	1.2	0	0	0	1	3	0	
August 29	NYM	W, 8–3	3.0	1	1	1	1	6	1	s (6)
August 31a	PHI	W, 2–1	0.2	1	0	0	1	1	0	
September 3	CHC	L, 5–4	2.0	2	1	1	1	3	0	
September 6	LAD	W, 7–6	2.0	0	0	0	0	2	0	
September 7	LAD	W, 3–1	1.1	0	0	0	0	1	0	s (7)
September 11	CHC	W, 6–4	1.0	4	0	0	0	2	0	H (4)
September 14	HOU	W, 7–5	0.1	1	0	0	1	1	0	H (5)
September 20	CIN	W, 4–0	4.0	1	0	0	0	4	0	s (8)
September 25	MLN	W, 7–5	0.0	1	0	0	0	0	0	
September 26	MLN	L, 3–2	1.0	0	0	0	0	2	0	
September 30	CIN	W, 5–3	2.0	1	1	1	0	1	1	W (4–1)
October 1		L, 17–2	1.0	4	2	2	0	0	1	
Totals			74.1	57	31	31	22	85	9	

Source: Baseball Reference.com

A NOTE ON SOURCES

Masanori Murakami was the most important source for this book. I interviewed Mashi in person in 2003, 2012, and 2013. These interviews were supplemented with numerous telephone calls and emails, as well as his 1985 Japanese-language autobiography, *The Only Major Leaguer*. Although Murakami speaks English reasonably well, these interviews were conducted mostly in Japanese, as he can better express complex ideas in his native language. With the exception of the 2003 interview, which was conducted with simultaneous interpreter Ami Shimizu, Keiko Nishi translated and interpreted the interviews and correspondence with Mashi.

Due to the difficulties of interviewing in a foreign language and having to speak through an interpreter, we often had to revisit the same topic to clarify details or nuances of meaning. As a result, Murakami's quotes based on these interviews are sometimes a combination of statements made on several different occasions. For the reader's ease, I have not attached a source to these quotes. Any quote attributed to Masanori Murakami without a corresponding endnote in this book derives from these interviews. Most of these statements were also made in Japanese, so the quotes are not Murakami's exact words but a translation. Any errors in meaning or fact are my own and not those of Masanori Murakami. Statements made by Murakami outside of these interviews are properly attributed in the endnotes.

Some of the newspaper articles referenced in this book were contained in Masanori Murakami's personal scrapbook. Within the scrapbook, the titles of the newspapers and the article dates are often cut off. When these articles could not be properly identified, they are listed in the endnotes as being from Murakami's Scrapbook, along with the article's author, title, and approximate date when known.

NOTES

CHAPTER 1

1. "Japanese Prisoners of War in the Soviet Union," *Wikipedia, the Free Encyclopedia*, http://en.wikipedia.org/wiki/Japanese_prisoners_of_war_in_the_Soviet_Union.
2. Allinson, *Japan's Postwar History*, 45–51.
3. Salleh, "The World's More Left-Handed Than We Think."
4. Cited in *Los Angeles Herald Examiner*, September 9, 1964.

CHAPTER 2

1. Oh and Falkner, *Sadaharu Oh*, 33.
2. Cited in Whiting, *The Samurai Way of Baseball*, 6.
3. The Ichiko baseball team's approach was also heavily influenced by the philosophy of judo founder Jigoro Kano, who would become the school's headmaster in 1893.
4. Cited in Kiku, "The Japanese Baseball Spirit and Professional Ideology," 41.
5. Reaves, *Taking in a Game*, 52.
6. Whiting, *The Samurai Way of Baseball*, 55.
7. Whiting, *You Gotta Have Wa*, 32.
8. Cited in Whiting, *You Gotta Have Wa*, 37–38.
9. Whiting, *You Gotta Have Wa*, 38.
10. Cited in Kiku, "The Japanese Baseball Spirit and Professional Ideology," 38.
11. Oh and Falkner, *Sadaharu Oh*, 36.
12. Asahi Shimbun, *Fifty Years of National High School Baseball Champions*, 493.
13. Upon marrying an only child, Tsuruoka followed a common Japanese custom of adopting his wife's maiden name of Yamamoto so that the family name would survive. After the birth of Yasushi and the death of his first wife, Tsuruoka reverted to his original family name.
14. Bogin, *Patterns of Human Growth*, 278.
15. Cited in *Hochi Sports*, September 30, 1962, 2; Japan Baseball Hall of Fame Library Scrapbook, September 29, 1962.

CHAPTER 3

1. Cited in Cromartie and Whiting, *Slugging It Out in Japan*, 5.
2. Cited in Whiting, *The Meaning of Ichiro*, 60.
3. Cited in Whiting, *You Gotta Have Wa*, 74.
4. Kawakami, *Japanese Baseball and Zen*.
5. Stanka and Stanka, *Coping with Clouters, Culture, and Crisis*, 82.
6. Stanka and Stanka, *Coping with Clouters, Culture, and Crisis*, 109–10; Kiku, "The Japanese Baseball Spirit and Professional Ideology," 110.
7. Hanta interview, 2003.
8. Hanta interview, 2003.
9. Cited in Fitts, *Remembering Japanese Baseball*, 70–71, 104.
10. Cited in Fitts, *Remembering Japanese Baseball*, 70–71.
11. Cited in Fitts, *Remembering Japanese Baseball*, 70.
12. *Pacific Stars and Stripes*, March 11, 1963, 21.
13. *Baseball Magazine*, March 4, 1963.
14. Japan Baseball Hall of Fame Library Scrapbook, March 1963; *Hochi Sports*, March 3, 1963, 2.
15. *Hochi Sports*, March 12, 1963.

CHAPTER 4

1. Tourist Industry Bureau, *Japan*, 665.
2. Hanta interview, 2013.
3. *Hochi Sports*, May 19, 1963.
4. Cited in *Hochi Sports*, May 19, 1963.
5. *Shukan Baseball*, June 24, 1963, 41.
6. Cited in *Hochi Sports*, June 2, 1963, 2.

CHAPTER 5

1. Asahi Shimbun, *Fifty Years of National High School Baseball Champions*, 502, 504.
2. Cited in Leutzinger, *Lefty O'Doul*, 65.
3. *Santa Maria Times*, March 11, 2010.
4. Walter F. O'Malley to Ford C. Frick, February 17, 1965, unfiled material, National Baseball Hall of Fame Library, Cooperstown NY.
5. *Mainichi Shimbun*, February 22, 1965, 3.
6. Agreement between Giants and Hawks, January 6, 1964, unfiled material, National Baseball Hall of Fame Library, Cooperstown NY.
7. Cited in *Mainichi Shimbun*, February 22, 1965, 3.
8. Cappy Harada to Charles S. Feeney, February 17, 1965, unfiled material, National Baseball Hall of Fame Library, Cooperstown NY.
9. Release form, Murakami from Osaka Hawks, January 13, 1964, unfiled material, National Baseball Hall of Fame Library, Cooperstown NY.

10. Iwase to Stoneham, March 6, 1964, unfiled material, National Baseball Hall of Fame Library, Cooperstown NY.
11. *Sporting News*, March 7, 1964, 11.
12. Cited in *Hokubei Mainichi*, February 25, 1964.
13. *New York Times*, February 23, 1965, S4.
14. *Sporting News*, March 7, 1964, 11.
15. Andy Yamashiro was actually born in Okinawa in 1896 and did not become an American citizen until the 1930s, after his playing career had ended.

CHAPTER 6
1. *Casa Grande Dispatch*, April 8, 1964, 11.
2. Francisco Casa Grande Ballpark History, http://springtrainingonline.com/features/casa-grande.htm.
3. *Sporting News*, March 28, 1964, 13.
4. Cited in *Sporting News*, March 28, 1964, 13.
5. Larry Raines returned to Japan to play for the Hankyu Braves in 1962.
6. *El Paso Herald Post*, March 21, 1964, 10.
7. Cited in *Danville Bee*, April 9, 1964, 12.
8. *Hokubei Mainichi*, April 21, 1964.
9. Cited in *Hokubei Mainichi,* April 21, 1964.
10. For the history of relief pitchers see Vatano, *Late and Close*, and Zimniuch, *Fireman.*
11. The concept of platooning in baseball was not invented by Stengel; it had been practiced extensively in the 1910s, but the Yankee manager became the first skipper to rely on the strategy in the postwar period.
12. Cited in *Hokubei Mainichi*, July 18, 1964.
13. Cited in *Sporting News*, May 2, 1964, 29.
14. Cited in *Danville Bee*, April 9, 1964, 12.
15. Cited in *Hokubei Mainichi*, April 21, 1964.
16. *Fresno Bee Republican*, April 18, 1964, 11.

CHAPTER 7
1. Kiyoto Saiki, interview by Yoshino Hasegawa, August 27, 1980. Special Collections at the Henry Madden Library, California State University, Fresno, http://ecollections.lib.csufresno.edu/specialcollections/item_viewer.php?cisoroot=/SVJAinWWII&cisoptr=719&cisobox=1&rec=18; accessed April 2, 2013.
2. *Fresno Bee Republican*, April 30, 1964, 35.
3. At Masanori Murakami's request this player is purposely not named.
4. *Fresno Bee Republican*, May 15, 1964, 2B; Sievers cited in *Sporting News*, May 16, 1964, 37.
5. *San Francisco Examiner*, May 22, 1964.
6. *Fresno Bee Republican*, May 20, 1964, 2D; *San Francisco Examiner*, May 22, 1964.

7. Despite advertisements stating that all three Japanese would start, Tanaka and Takahashi were not in the lineup and would remain on the bench for the duration.

8. Cited in *Pacific Stars and Stripes*, May 25, 1964, 22.

CHAPTER 8

1. *San Francisco Examiner*, May 22, 1964.

2. *Bakersfield Californian*, June 9, 1964, 16.

3. *Fresno Bee Republican*, May 19, 1964, 1B.

4. *Fresno Bee Republican*, June 20, 1964, 9A.

5. Cited in Turbow and Duca, *The Baseball Codes*, 230.

6. Cited in Turbow and Duca, *The Baseball Codes*, 231.

7. Tom Meehan interview, 2013.

8. As the second game of a doubleheader, this game ended after seven innings.

9. *Fresno Bee Republican*, June 22, 1964, 18.

10. Coverage of the Bakersfield game in the *Fresno Bee Republican* makes no reference to the mound conversation that is discussed below, and Murakami also does not recall such a conversation.

11. *San Francisco News–Call Bulletin,* September 2, 1964.

12. Cited in *San Francisco Examiner*, May 22, 1964.

13. Cited in *Hokubei Mainichi*, August 18, 1964.

14. *San Francisco News–Call Bulletin,* September 2, 1964.

15. *San Francisco News–Call Bulletin,* September 2, 1964.

16. No box score has been located for Murakami's August 1 loss to Stockton, so his statistics for this game are not entered into these totals.

17. *Fresno Bee Republican*, July 29, 1964.

18. *Fresno Bee Republican*, July 18, 1964, 9A.

19. Cited in *Hokubei Mainichi*, August 18, 1964.

20. Cited in *Hokubei Mainichi*, July 18, 1964.

21. *Hokubei Mainichi*, August 18, 1964.

22. *Oakland Tribune*, August 14, 1964, 53E.

23. *Oakland Tribune*, August 14, 1964, 53E.

24. *Hokubei Mainichi*, August 18, 1964.

CHAPTER 9

1. Terrell, "The Sa-fra-seeko Kid."

2. Marichal with Freedman, *Juan Marichal*, 36.

3. Marichal with Freedman, *Juan Marichal*, 34.

4. Cited in Ruck, *Raceball*.

5. Dark and Underwood, *When in Doubt, Fire the Manager*, 17–18.

6. Hirsh, *Willie Mays*, 399.

7. Cited in Bjarkman, *Baseball with Latin Beat*, 228.

8. Cook, *The Summer of '64*, 17–18.

9. Barbee, "Annual Baseball Roundup."
10. Cited in Hirsh, *Willie Mays*, 412–13.
11. Stan Isaacs in *Newsday*, July 23, 1964.
12. Cited in Hirsh, *Willie Mays*, 419. The quotes in the next several paragraphs are from this volume.
13. Cited in *Hokubei Mainichi,* September 2, 1964.
14. Cited in *Hochi Sports,* September 2, 1964, 3.
15. Cited in *Hochi Sports,* September 3, 1964, 3.
16. *San Jose Mercury*, September 1964, article by Jack Hanley in Murakami Scrapbook.
17. Cited in *San Francisco News–Call Bulletin*, September 2, 1964.
18. *San Francisco Chronicle,* September 2, 1964; *San Francisco News–Call Bulletin*, September 2, 1964.
19. *Spokesman Review,* September 3, 1964.
20. *San Jose Mercury*, September 1964, article by Jack Hanley in Murakami Scrapbook.
21. Cited in *Newsday*, September 2, 1964.
22. Cited in *Daily News,* September 2, 1964, 78.

CHAPTER 10
1. Antos, *Shea Stadium*, 25.
2. *Sankei*, September 3, 1964, 12
3. Sato, "The Major Leaguer Murakami."
4. Cited in *San Francisco Chronicle*, September 2, 1964, 49, and *San Francisco News–Call Bulletin*, September 2, 1964.
5. Cited in *New York Post*, September 2, 1964.
6. Krieger, "Ed Kranepool."
7. Cited in *Hokubei Mainichi*, September 5, 1964, and *Newsday*, September 2, 1964.
8. *Pacific Stars and Stripes*, September 4, 1964, 18.
9. *San Jose Mercury News*, September 2, 1964.
10. Cited in *San Francisco News–Call Bulletin*, September 2, 1964.
11. *San Francisco Chronicle*, September 2, 1964, 49.
12. Cited in *Hokubei Mainichi*, September 5, 1964.
13. *Daily News*, September 2, 1964, 78; *San Francisco Examiner*, September 2, 1964, 57.
14. Cited in *Los Angeles Herald Examiner*, September 6, 1964.
15. Cited in *Los Angeles Herald Examiner*, September 6, 1964.
16. *Shukan Baseball*, September 21, 1964.
17. Cited in *Pacific Stars and Stripes*, September 6, 1964, 22.
18. Yoichi Nagata, personal communication, 2013.
19. *Shukan Baseball*, September 21, 1964.
20. *Shukan Baseball*, September 21, 1964. *Ganbare* roughly translates into "Do your best!"
21. Cited in *Sankei*, September 1, 1964, 7.
22. Cited in *San Francisco Chronicle*, November 1964, "Back-Ay-san Is Happy There," by Art Rosenbaum, Murakami Scrapbook.

CHAPTER 11

1. *San Francisco Chronicle*, September 3, 1964, 42.
2. *Oakland Tribune*, September 9, 1964, 23.
3. Cited in *Hokubei Mainichi*, September 5, 1964.
4. Unidentified newspaper article written after September 20, 1964, by Jack McDonald, Murakami Scrapbook.
5. Cited in *Hokubei Mainichi*, September 21, 1964.
6. Garratt, "The Scandal of Candlestick"; Hirsch, *Willie Mays*, 318.
7. Hirsch, *Willie Mays*, 319; Einstein, *Willie's Time*, 121–22.
8. Hirsch, *Willie Mays*, 319.
9. Cited in *Hokubei Mainichi*, September 21, 1964.
10. Cited in *San Francisco Chronicle*, September 10, 1964, 54.
11. *San Francisco Chronicle*, September 17, 1964, 28.
12. "The Trip of My Soul," NHK television documentary, 1998.
13. Cited in *San Francisco Chronicle*, September 17, 1964, 28; "Murakami Would Like to Start," undated newspaper article by Gordon Sakamoto, Murakami Scrapbook.
14. *Hokubei Mainichi*, September 21, 1964.
15. Cited in unidentified newspaper article written after September 20, 1964, by Jack McDonald, Murakami Scrapbook.
16. Cited in unidentified newspaper article written after September 20, 1964, by Jack McDonald, Murakami Scrapbook.
17. Unidentified newspaper article written after September 20, 1964, by Jack McDonald, Murakami Scrapbook.
18. Cited in *Hokubei Mainichi*, September 21, 1964.
19. Cited in *Hokubei Mainichi*, September 21, 1964.
20. Cited in *San Mateo Times*, September 21, 1964.
21. *San Francisco Chronicle*, September 23, 1964, 44.
22. Cited in *San Francisco Chronicle*, September 25, 1964.
23. Cited in *Sporting News*, September 19, 1964, 6.
24. Cited in *San Francisco Chronicle*, September 25, 1964.
25. *San Francisco Chronicle*, September 30, 1964, 136.
26. *San Francisco Chronicle*, October 4, 1964, 33.
27. *San Francisco Chronicle*, October 5, 1964.
28. *San Francisco Chronicle*, October 5, 1964.
29. *San Mateo Times*, October 5, 1964, 13; Dark and Underwood, *When in Doubt, Fire the Manager*, 109.
30. Cited in *Hokubei Mainichi*, September 21, 1964.
31. *Sporting News*, September 26, 1964.

CHAPTER 12

1. Cited in "Murakami Stars in Arizona," unidentified newspaper article from Murakami Scrapbook.

2. Cited in *Hochi Sports*, December 3, 1964, 1; December 17, 1964, and *Pacific Stars and Stripes*, November 24, 1964, 15.

CHAPTER 13

1. *Hochi Sports*, December 16, 1.
2. *Hochi Sports*, December 16, 1.
3. Cappy Harada to Charles Feeney, February 18, 1965, unfiled material, National Baseball Hall of Fame Library, Cooperstown NY.
4. Information and quotes in the next several paragraphs pertaining to December 17, 1964, come from *Hochi Sports*, December 18, 1964, 1.
5. *Hochi Sports*, December 21, 1964, 1.
6. Cappy Harada to Charles Feeney, February 18, 1965, unfiled material, National Baseball Hall of Fame Library, Cooperstown NY.
7. Cappy Harada to Charles Feeney, February 18, 1965, unfiled material, National Baseball Hall of Fame Library, Cooperstown NY.
8. Cited in *Hochi Sports*, December 26, 1964, 1.
9. Murakami, *The Only Major Leaguer*, 42.
10. Cited in *Pacific Stars and Stripes*, January 10, 1965, 19.
11. Murakami, *The Only Major Leaguer*, 162–63.
12. *Hochi Sports*, January 26, 1965.
13. Agreement between the San Francisco Giants Base Ball Club of San Francisco, California, and the Nankai Hawks Base Ball Club and/or Osaka Hawks Base Ball Club of Osaka, Japan, unfiled material, National Baseball Hall of Fame Library, Cooperstown NY.
14. *Hochi Sports*, January 26, 1965.
15. Cited in *San Francisco Chronicle*, January 28, 1965, 43.
16. Benedict, *The Chrysanthemum and the Sword*, 133–44; Davies and Ikeno, *The Japanese Mind*, 95–99.
17. Information and quotes about this practice come from *Hochi Sports*, January 31, 1965, 1.
18. Citations in the next several paragraphs come from *Hochi Sports*, February 1, 1965.
19. Citations in the next several paragraphs come from *Hochi Sports*, February 2, 1965, 1.

CHAPTER 14

1. Ford Frick to Yushi Uchimura, February 2, 1965, unfiled material, National Baseball Hall of Fame Library, Cooperstown NY.
2. Authors unknown but probably Lee Vavuris and Jack Riordan, "Memorandum with Points and Authorities Concerning an Alleged Agreement Dated January 6, 1964, Purportedly by and between the Osaka Hawks Baseball Club and the San Francisco Giants Baseball Club," unfiled material, National Baseball Hall of Fame Library, Cooperstown NY.

3. Agreement between Giants and Hawks, January 6, 1964, unfiled material, National Baseball Hall of Fame Library, Cooperstown NY.

4. Agreement between Giants and Hawks, January 6, 1964, unfiled material, National Baseball Hall of Fame Library, Cooperstown NY.

5. *San Francisco Chronicle*, February 5, 1965, 49.

6. Ford Frick to Yushi Uchimura, April 2, 1965, unfiled material, National Baseball Hall of Fame Library, Cooperstown NY.

7. Cited in *Japan Times*, February 21, 1965.

8. Murakami, *The Only Major Leaguer*, 164.

9. *San Francisco Chronicle*, February 11, 1965, 51.

10. Cited in *San Francisco Chronicle*, February 12, 1965, 49.

11. Cited in *San Francisco Chronicle*, February 12, 1965, 49.

12. Donald Walker, "Questioned Document Examination Concerning the Signature Tsugihiro Iwase," January 29, 1965, unfiled material, National Baseball Hall of Fame Library, Cooperstown NY.

13. Cited in *Salt Lake Tribune*, February 24, 1965, 24.

14. Cited in *Mainichi Shimbun*, February 22, 1965; see also March 1, 1965.

15. Cited in *Pacific Stars and Stripes*, February 26, 1965, 21.

16. *Mainichi Shimbun*, February 22, 1965, March 1, 1965.

17. Ford Frick to Yushi Uchimura, February 17, 1964, unfiled material, National Baseball Hall of Fame Library, Cooperstown NY.

18. Ford Frick to All Clubs, February 16, 1965, unfiled material, National Baseball Hall of Fame Library, Cooperstown NY.

19. Walter O'Malley to Ford Frick, February 17, 1965, unfiled material, National Baseball Hall of Fame Library, Cooperstown NY.

20. Ford Frick to Walter O'Malley, February 23, 1965, unfiled material, National Baseball Hall of Fame Library, Cooperstown NY.

21. *Pacific Stars and Stripes*, February 19, 1965, 19.

22. Cited in *San Francisco Chronicle*, February 18, 1965, 48.

23. Cited in *Mainichi Shimbun*, February 28, 1965.

24. Cited in unidentified newspaper article from Murakami Scrapbook.

25. *San Francisco Examiner*, March 14, 1965, 5C.

26. Yushi Uchimura to Ford Frick, March 17, 1965, unfiled material, National Baseball Hall of Fame Library, Cooperstown NY.

27. *San Francisco Chronicle*, March 17, 1965.

28. Ford Frick to Yushi Uchimura, telegram, March 24, 1965, unfiled material, National Baseball Hall of Fame Library, Cooperstown NY.

29. Cited in *San Mateo Times*, March 25, 1965, 15.

30. Cited in *Reno Evening Gazette*, April 21, 1965, 27.

31. Cited in *San Francisco Chronicle*, April 22, 1965, 49.

32. Yushi Uchimura to Ford Frick, April 21, 1965, unfiled material, National Baseball Hall of Fame Library, Cooperstown NY.

33. Horace Stoneham and Chub Feeney to Yushi Uchimura, telegram, April 26, 1965, unfiled material, National Baseball Hall of Fame Library, Cooperstown NY.

34. Ford Frick to Yushi Uchimura, April 27, 1965, unfiled material, National Baseball Hall of Fame Library, Cooperstown NY.

35. Cited in *San Francisco Chronicle*, April 27, 1965, 45.

36. Cited in *San Jose News*, April 27, 1965, 44.

37. Cited in *Pacific Stars and Stripes*, May 6, 1965, 20.

CHAPTER 15

1. *San Francisco Chronicle*, May 5, 1965, 53.

2. *San Francisco Chronicle*, May 5, 1965, 53.

3. Cited in *Pacific Stars and Stripes*, May 6, 1965, 20.

4. Cited in *San Francisco Chronicle*, May 5, 1965, 53.

5. *San Mateo Times*, May 7, 1965, 23.

6. *San Jose Mercury*, May 2, 1965.

7. *San Mateo Times*, April 30, 1965, 29.

8. Cited in *Los Angeles Times*, May 2, 1965, C1.

9. Cited in *Shukan Baseball*, June 21, 1965.

10. *San Mateo Times*, May 10, 1965, 14.

11. Cited in *Shukan Baseball*, June 21, 1965.

12. *Shukan Baseball*, June 21, 1965.

13. Gaylord Perry interview, August 17, 2013.

14. *San Francisco Chronicle*, May 12, 1965; *Sporting News*, May 15, 1965, 29.

15. *San Francisco Examiner*, July 1, 1965, 5C2H.

16. *San Francisco Examiner*, July 1, 1965, 5C2H; Gaylord Perry interview, August 17, 2013.

17. Ken Henderson interview, January 14, 2013.

18. Cited in *Sporting News*, June 5, 1965, 11.

19. Juli Osaka Tachibana interview, October 2012.

20. Juli Osaka Tachibana interview, October 2012.

21. Walter Osaka interview, December 2012.

22. Walter Osaka interview, December 2012.

CHAPTER 16

1. *Los Angeles Times*, June 15, 1965, B1.

2. Cited in *Hokubei Mainichi*, June 18, 1965; *Sporting News*, July 3, 1965, 8.

3. Cited in *Hokubei Mainichi*, June 18, 1965; *Sporting News*, July 3, 1965, 8.

4. *Oakland Tribune*, June 17, 1965, 40; *Los Angeles Times*, June 17, 1965, B4.

5. *Los Angeles Times*, June 17, 1965, B4.

6. *San Francisco Examiner*, June 18, 1965.

7. *Oakland Tribune*, June 29, 1965, 41.

8. Cited in *Pacific Stars and Stripes*, July 2, 1965, 23.

9. *San Francisco Chronicle*, July 6, 1965.

10. *St. Louis Globe-Democrat*, July 8, 1965.

11. *St. Louis Globe-Democrat*, July 8, 1965.

12. Juli Osaka Tachibana interview, October 2013; Walter Osaka interview, December 2012.

13. Curt Fukuda interview by Ralph Pearce, May 2014.

14. Cited in *Hokubei Mainichi*, August 10, 1965.

15. *Hokubei Mainichi*, August 8, 1965.

16. *Hokubei Mainichi*, July 26, 1965.

CHAPTER 17

1. *Pacific Stars and Stripes*, August 17, 1965, 18.

2. *Nichi Bei Times*, October 13, 1965.

3. Einstein, *Willie's Time*, 216.

4. "U.S. Baseball at Its Best? Ah, So," undated newspaper article by Charles Einstein, Murakami Scrapbook.

5. Cited in *Nichi Bei Times*, October 13, 1965.

6. Rumors that Murakami had a blonde American girlfriend were also unfounded.

7. *Shukan Baseball,* November 29, 1965; *Pacific Stars and Stripes*, October 10, 1965, 23.

8. Cited in *Hokubei Mainichi*, August 5 and 17, 1965.

9. *Hokubei Mainichi*, August 17, 1965.

10. Ken Henderson interview, January 14, 2013.

11. Cited in *Shukan Baseball,* November 29, 1965, and *Baltimore Afro-American*, August 28, 1965.

12. Cited in *Shukan Baseball*, June 21, 1965.

13. Hirsch, *Willie Mays*, 387–88.

14. Cited in *San Francisco Chronicle*, August 16, 1965, 57.

15. Cited in Hirsh, *Willie Mays*, 434.

16. Details that follow from the August 22, 1965, game are drawn from Hirsh, *Willie Mays*, 434–38; Einstein, *Willie's Time*, 242–43; Rosengren, Fight of Their Lives, 107–19; *San Francisco Chronicle*, August 23, 1965; and *Oakland Tribune*, August 23, 1965.

17. *Oakland Tribune*, August 23, 1965, 35.

18. *Oakland Tribune*, August 23, 1965, 37.

19. Cited in *San Francisco Chronicle*, September 13, 1965, 57.

20. Cited in Mann, "They Love Herman and Willie," 24–31.

21. *San Jose Mercury-News,* September 20, 1965.

22. *Oakland Tribune*, September 10, 1965, 50.

23. Cited in *Oakland Tribune*, September 27, 1965, 36.

24. *San Francisco Chronicle*, October 1, 1965, 44.

25. *San Francisco Chronicle*, October 1, 1965, 46.

CHAPTER 18

1. Cited in *Nichi Bei Times*, October 13, 1965.
2. *Nichi Bei Times,* October 15, 1965; *Hokubei Mainichi,* October 18, 1965.
3. *Daily Review*, October 4, 1965, 9; Murakami cited in *San Jose Mercury-News*, October 10, 1965.
4. Unidentified newspaper article, November 5, 1965, Murakami Scrapbook.
5. Cited in *San Francisco Examiner*, September 22, 1965, 48.
6. Cited in *Nichi Bei Times*, October 6, 1965.
7. Cited in *San Jose Mercury-News*, October 10, 1965
8. Cited in *Pacific Stars and Stripes*, November 8, 1965, 19. Sugiura would be lured back and would continue pitching for the Hawks until 1970.
9. Cited in *Pacific Stars and Stripes*, November 8, 1965, 19.
10. Cited in *Pacific Stars and Stripes*, November 9, 1965, 21.
11. *Pacific Stars and Stripes*, November 9, 1965, 21.
12. *Pacific Stars and Stripes*, November 10, 1965, 20; *San Francisco Chronicle*, November 12, 1965.
13. *Pacific Stars and Stripes*, November 22, 1965, 23.
14. Cited in *Pacific Stars and Stripes*, October 26, 1965, 20.
15. Chub Feeney to Kiyoshi Murakami, December 6, 1965, unfiled material, National Baseball Hall of Fame Library, Cooperstown NY.
16. Cited in *Oakland Tribune*, December 14, 1965, 39.
17. Cited in *Oakland Tribune*, December 14, 1965, 39.
18. Horace Stoneham to Masanori Murakami, December 18, 1965, unfiled material, National Baseball Hall of Fame Library, Cooperstown NY.

AFTERWORD

1. *Shukan Baseball,* January 24, 1966, 27.
2. *San Jose Mercury*, ca. 1966, Murakami Scrapbook.
3. *Pacific Stars and Stripes*, February 3, 1966, 21.
4. *Pacific Stars and Stripes*, March 11, 1966, 23.
5. Unidentified newspaper article, May 10, 1966, Murakami Scrapbook.
6. Cited in *Hobs News-Sun*, October 23, 1966, 9.
7. *Pacific Stars and Stripes*, July 23, 1966, 21.
8. *Pacific Stars and Stripes*, August 24, 1968.
9. Cited in *Pacific Stars and Stripes*, June 12, 1966, 22.
10. *Pacific Stars and Stripes*, July 23, 1966, 21.
11. *San Jose Mercury*, July 20, 1966, 3.
12. Cited in *Village Gazette*, July 20, 1966, 19.
13. Cited in *Nevada State Journal*, August 31, 1966, 30.
14. *Pacific Stars and Stripes*, October 12, 1966, 20.
15. Unidentified newspaper article, June 1966, Murakami Scrapbook.
16. Cited in *Oakland Tribune*, November 16, 1966, 57.

17. Cited in *Pacific Stars and Stripes*, November 10, 1966, 20.

18. Cited in *Pacific Stars and Stripes*, November 10, 1966, 20.

19. *Daily Times* (Salisbury MD), December 17, 1965, 15.

20. Cited in *Pacific Stars and Stripes*, August 24, 1968, 18.

21. Cited in *Pacific Stars and Stripes*, August 24, 1968, 18.

22. Cited in *Pacific Stars and Stripes*, August 24, 1968, 18.

23. *Yoshi* is best translated in this case as "all right then!"

24. Cited in *Pacific Stars and Stripes*, August 24, 1968, 18.

25. Cited in *Pacific Stars and Stripes*, August 24, 1968, 18.

26. Cited in *Pacific Stars and Stripes*, August 24, 1968, 18.

27. Cited in *Pacific Stars and Stripes*, August 24, 1968, 18.

28. *Sporting News*, January 17, 1970, 34; *Bridgeport Post*, November 29, 1969, 8.

29. *Monessen Valley Independent*, February 12, 1983, 7.

30. Cited in *Sporting News*, February 28, 1983, 42.

31. Cited in Gallagher, "Masanori Murakami's Historic Return," 39.

32. *Bergen County Record*, May 7, 1995.

33. *Japan Times*, October 10, 2010.

34. Cited in Sloan, "Forget Loyalty, Baseball Is Business, Says Murakami."

BIBLIOGRAPHY

MANUSCRIPT COLLECTIONS

Masanori Murakami, National Baseball Hall of Fame Library Player File Collection. National Baseball Hall of Fame Library, Cooperstown NY.

Masanori Murakami Scrapbook. Private Collection of Masanori Murakami, Tokyo, Japan.

Unfiled Material Relating to Masanori Murakami Affair. National Baseball Hall of Fame Library, Cooperstown NY.

INTERVIEWS

Carlton Hanta, 2003, 2013

Ken Henderson, 2013

Tom Meehan, 2013

Masanori Murakami, 2003, 2012, 2013

Yoshiko Murakami, 2012

Walter Osaka, 2013

Gaylord Perry, 2013

Kiyoto Saiki, interview by Yoshino Hasegawa, August 27, 1980. Special Collections at the Henry Madden Library, California State University, Fresno. http://ecollections .lib.csufresno.edu/specialcollections/item_viewer.php?cisoroot=/SVJAinWWII& cisoptr=719&cisobox=1&rec=18.

Joe Stanka, 2013

Juli Osaka Tachibana, 2013

Taisuke Watanabe, 2013

SECONDARY SOURCES

Allinson, Gary. *Japan's Postwar History*. Ithaca NY: Cornell University, 2004.

Antos, Jason D. *Shea Stadium*. Charleston SC: Arcadia Publishing, 2007.

Asahi Shimbun. *Fifty Years of National High School Baseball Champions* (in Japanese). Tokyo: Asahai Shimbun, 1968.

Azuma, Eiichiro. *Between Two Empires*. New York: Oxford University Press, 2005.

Baldassaro, Lawrence, and Richard A. Johnson. *The American Game: Baseball and Ethnicity*. Carbondale: Southern Illinois University Press, 2002.

Barbee, Bobbie. "Annual Baseball Roundup." *Ebony*, June 1964.

Benedict, Ruth. *The Chrysanthemum and the Sword*. Boston: Houghton Mifflin, 1946.

Bjarkman, Peter. *Baseball with a Latin Beat: A History of the Latin American Game*. Jefferson NC: McFarland, 1994.

Bogin, Barry. *Patterns of Human Growth*. Cambridge: Cambridge University Press, 1999.

Briley, Ron. "The Chinese Wall and Murakami, Too." In *The Cooperstown Symposium on Baseball and American Culture, 2003–2004*, ed. William M. Simons, 123–40. Jefferson NC: McFarland, 2005.

Cook, William. *The Summer of '64*. Jefferson NC: McFarland, 2002.

Cromartie, Warren, and Robert Whiting. *Slugging It Out in Japan*. New York: Kodansha, 1991.

Dark, Alvin, and John Underwood. *When in Doubt, Fire the Manager*. New York: E. P. Dutton, 1980.

Davies, Roger, and Osamu Ikeno. *The Japanese Mind*. Tokyo: Tuttle, 2002.

Dickey, Glenn. *San Francisco Giants 40 Years*. San Francisco: Woodford, 1997.

Einstein, Charles. *Willie's Time*. Carbondale: Southern Illinois University Press, 1992.

Fitts, Robert K. *Banzai Babe Ruth: Baseball, Espionage, and Assassination during the 1934 Tour of Japan*. Lincoln: University of Nebraska Press, 2012.

———. *Remembering Japanese Baseball: An Oral History of the Game*. Carbondale: Southern Illinois University Press, 2005.

Gallagher, Jack. "Masanori Murakami's Historic Return." Unsourced article in the Masanori Murakami National Baseball Hall of Fame Library Player File Collection. National Baseball Hall of Fame Library, Cooperstown NY.

Garratt, Robert F. "The Scandal of Candlestick." Paper presented at SABR 42, Minneapolis, Minnesota, June 2012.

Hirsh, James. *Willie Mays: The Life, The Legend*. New York: Scribner, 2010.

Johanson, Matt, and Wylie Wong. *San Francisco Giants, Where Have You Gone?* Champaign IL: Sports Publishing, 2005.

Kawakami, Tetsuharu. *Japanese Baseball and Zen* (in Japanese). Tokyo: Senga, 2009.

Kiku, Koichi. "The Japanese Baseball Spirit and Professional Ideology." In *Japan, Sport and Society*, ed. Joseph Maguire and Masayoshi Nakayama, 35–54. New York: Routledge, 2006.

Krieger, Tara. "Ed Kranepool." SABR *Baseball Biography Project*. http://sabr.org/bioproj/person/f9491612.

Leutzinger, Richard. *Lefty O'Doul: The Legend That Baseball Nearly Forgot*. Carmel CA: Carmel Bay Publishing Group, 1997.

Mainichi Shimbun. *Fifty Year History of High Schools Participating in the National Baseball Championship* (in Japanese). Tokyo: Mainichi Shimbun, 1978.

Mann, Jack. "They Love Herman and Willie." *Sports Illustrated*, September 27, 1965:24–31.

Marichal, Juan, with Lew Freedman. *Juan Marichal: My Journey from the Dominican Republic to Cooperstown*. Minneapolis: MVP Books, 2011.

Murakami, Masanori. *The Only Major Leaguer* (in Japanese). Tokyo: Koubun, 1985.

Oh, Sadaharu, and David Falkner. *Sadaharu Oh: A Zen Way of Baseball*. New York: Vintage, 1984.

Rafferty-Osaki, Terumi. "Asians and Baseball: The Breaking and Perpetuating of Stereotypes." In *The Cooperstown Symposium on Baseball and American Culture, 2007–2008*, ed. William M. Simons, 131–46. Jefferson NC: McFarland, 2009.

Reaves, Joseph. *Taking in a Game: A History of Baseball in Asia*. Lincoln: University of Nebraska Press, 2004.

Rosengren, John. *The Fight of Their Lives*. Guilford CT: Lyons, 2014.

Ruck, Robert. *Raceball: How the Major Leagues Colonized the Black and Latin Game*. Boston: Beacon Press, 2011. See http://books.google.com/books?id=Ohi8CFRudkMC&pg=PT148&lpg=PT148&dq=cepeda+"We+were+very,+very+close,"&source=bl&ots=uthkUbl-yG&sig=zT4Ez4jZ2eKZaAOFpdxwWoc8KTM&hl=en&sa=X&ei=xasRVMnlFYyzyASskIGgCw&ved=0CCAQ6AEwAA#v=onepage&q=cepeda%20"We%20were%20very%2C%20very%20close%2C"&f=false.

Salleh, Anna. "The World's More Left-Handed Than We Think." *ABC Science*, September 13, 2004, http://www.abc.net.au/science/articles/2004/09/13/1196384.htm.

Sato, Kumio. "The Major Leaguer Murakami, I Saw in Person." *Baseball Magazine*, September 1964.

Sloan, Dan. "Forget Loyalty, Baseball Is Business, Says Murakami." *Thomson Reuters*, September 2, 2009, http://in.reuters.com/article/2009/09/02/us-baseball-murakami-idustre5810no20090902.

Stanka, Jean, and Joe Stanka. *Coping with Clouters, Culture, and Crisis*. Wilmington DE: Dawn Press, 1987.

Terrell, Roy. "The Sa-fra-seeko Kid." *Sports Illustrated*, May 23, 1960.

Tourist Industry Bureau. *Japan: The Official Guide*. Tokyo: Tourist Industry Bureau, 1962.

Turbow, Jason, and Michael Duca. *The Baseball Codes: Beanballs, Sign Stealing, and Bench-Clearing Brawls: The Unwritten Rules of America's Pastime*. New York: Pantheon, 2010.

Vatano, Paul. *Late and Close: A History of Relief Pitching*. Jefferson NC: McFarland, 2002.

Whiting, Robert. *Chrysanthemum and the Bat: Baseball Samurai Style*. New York: Avon, 1983.

———. *The Meaning of Ichiro*. New York: Warner Books, 2004.

———. *The Samurai Way of Baseball*. New York: Warner Books, 2005.

———. *You Gotta Have Wa*. New York: Macmillan, 1989.

Zimniuch, Fran. *Fireman: The Evolution of the Closer in Baseball*. Chicago: Triumph, 2010.

INDEX

Allen, Dick, 101, 158
Alou, Felipe, 80
Alou, Jesus, 80
Alou, Matty, 80, 103, 106, 109, 163
Alston, Walt, 139, 166
Arizona Fall League, 77, 108–11
Averill, Walt, 43, 52–53

Bakersfield Bears, 60, 66–67, 71
Banks, Ernie, 69
baseball brawls, 68–69, 164–65
Bastian, Bob, 97
Belafonte, Harry, 144
Benjamin Franklin Hotel, 102, 137, 142
Berger, Mike, 179
Bolin, Bob, 138, 163–64, 168
Bright, Alex, 72
Brown, Ollie, 57
Burnes, Robert, 153
Bushido, 9–10

California League, 48, 98, 105
Callison, Johnny, 101, 152, 158
Candlestick Park, 35, 100, 106, 137, 144, 154, 156
Cepeda, Orlando, 51, 79–80, 81, 82, 83, 101, 168
Chicago Cubs, 104, 105, 107, 139, 140, 166, 167

Chunichi Dragons, 28, 46
Cincinnati Reds, 83, 104–5, 107, 154, 158, 168–69
Clemens, Gary, 63
Clemente, Roberto, 145–46
Clendenon, Donn, 103, 145
Collins, Dave, 69
Connolly, Will, 62, 65
Corrington, Jim, 64
Crandall, Del, 90
Crawford, Eddie, 74–75
Crawford, Shag, 165
Cromartie, Warren, 19, 186

Daigo, Takeo, 32
Daily News, 87, 93, 97
Daimai Orions, 16, 28, 32
Dark, Alvin, 81–83, 85, 87–88, 91, 93, 98, 100, 101, 102, 103–4, 105, 106, 107, 108, 136
Davis, Tommy, 101
Davis, Willie, 101, 151–52, 153
DiMaggio, Joe, 38, 48, 86, 143–44
Drysdale, Don, 101, 138, 147, 150, 163, 182

Ebony, 82
Eckert, William, 181
Ei, Rokusuke, 89
Einstein, Charles, 152, 157, 159

Enomoto, Kihachi, 32
Estelle, Dick, 102–3

Fairly, Ron, 147–48, 151, 164
Farris, Bruce, 73
Feeney, Chub, 87, 112, 114, 117, 119, 120, 125, 127–28, 133–34, 135, 171, 174–75, 181
Fidalgo, Larry, 63
First Higher School (Ichiko), 9–12, 19, 186
Fox, Charlie, 45, 48, 148, 165
Francisco Casa Grande, 43–45, 47
Franks, Herman, 108, 133, 136, 138–39, 144, 145, 147–48, 149
Fresno Bee Republican, 50, 58, 62, 68, 69, 73, 76, 84
Fresno Giants: anti-Japanese sentiment on, 60–61; background of, 57; brawl with Santa Barbara, 68–69; clinches league title, 71; as ideal team for Murakami, 48; and Japanese American Baseball Night, 59–60, 62–64; players accept Murakami, 59, 72–73
Frick, Ford, 38, 125, 127, 128, 129, 130–31, 132–33, 134
Fujidera Stadium, 18
Fujie, Kiyoshi, 35, 36, 43, 49, 50
Fujimoto, Sadayoshi, 20

Gentleman's Agreement, 55, 142
Gilliam, Jim, 148, 151, 166
Giri, 122, 172, 175–76, 188

Hadley, Kent, 24, 38
Haller, Tom, 99, 141, 153, 163, 185–86
Hankyu Braves, 28, 46
Hanley, Jack, 86, 92, 167
Hanshin Tigers, 20, 25, 28, 95, 178, 185
Hanta, Carlton, 23–24, 30, 33, 127, 130, 178
Harada, Tsuneo "Cappy," 35, 48, 64, 76, 135; arranges Murakami's contract, 39–40, 118; background of, 36–39; brings Nishimura to Fall League, 109–10; character attacked by Hawks, 126, 128–29;

escorts Murakami to United States, 43, 49–50, 54, 113; helps Murakami stay in United States, 49, 73, 77
Harris, Bucky, 51–52
Hart, Jim, 79, 147, 153, 158–59
Hasagawa, Shigeo, 33
Hayashi, Toshihiro, 26, 28–29, 34, 173
Henderson, Ken, 73, 141, 160–61
Henderson, Wallace, 62
Hendley, Bob, 91, 100, 133
Herbel, Ron, 99, 152, 158, 166
Hiatt, Jack, 141, 148
Hirose, Yoshinori, 24
Hiroshima Carp, 27, 28
Hirsch, James, 100
Hochi Sports, 18, 30, 85, 115, 131–32, 179, 180
Hokubei Mainichi, 108, 154, 160, 170
Hoos, Sid, 171
Hope, Bob, 109–10
Horio, Jimmy, 42
Hosei II High School, 6, 7, 8, 10–12, 13, 14, 15
Hosei University, 15, 16, 17
Hoshino, Eikichi, 13–14, 33, 132
Hoshino, Yoshiko, 13–14, 33–34, 94–95, 106, 132, 142, 160, 175, 182–83, 184, 186
Houston Astros, 154, 166–67
Houston Colt 45s, 104, 105, 106, 107
Hruby, Dan, 137, 178, 180
Hubbell, Carl, 45, 46, 77, 137
Hundley, Randy, 150

Ichiko. *See* First Higher School
Isaacs, Stan, 82
Iwase, Tsugihiro, 40–41, 112, 113–15, 116–18, 119, 121, 123, 125, 128

Jackson, Al, 91, 92
Jansen, Larry, 136
Japan Baseball Hall of Fame, 24, 26, 32, 95, 131
Japan Broadcasting Corporation (NHK), 101, 186, 187

Japanese American Baseball Night, 59–60, 62–64

Japanese high school baseball: hazing in, 8, 11–12; history of, 8–10, 12; Koshien, 12–13, 14; players' lifestyle, 11–12; rituals in, 11, 13, team social structure, 8, 11–12; training methods of, 8–11

Japanese professional baseball: African American players in, 46–47; history of, 4, 19–20; minor league organization of, 28; pitching rotations in, 24–25; relief pitchers in, 51; role of coaches in, 22–23; strike zone of, 75; training camps of, 19–23

Japan Series, 13, 25, 33–34, 170, 172–73, 178, 180–81

John Euless Park, 56–57, 59–60, 88

Johnson, Lou, 165

Jones, Bobby, 58

Jupiter, Harry, 86, 153

Kageyama, Kazuo, 26, 173, 174

Kana kuji u chi, 3–4

Kaneda, Masaichi, 18, 35, 177

Kawakami, Tetsuharu, 20–21, 23, 170

Kawasaki City Championship, 15

Keio University, 3

Kiner, Ralph, 92–93

Kintetsu Buffaloes, 16, 28, 32–33, 183, 186–87

Kokutetsu Swallows, 28

Konstanty, Jim, 52

Koshien. *See* National High School Baseball Championship; National High School Baseball Invitational Tournament

Koufax, Sandy, 138, 148, 150–52, 164–65, 182

Koyama, Masaki, 25

Kranepool, Ed, 92

Kure, Japan, 19, 43, 177, 183

Lanier, Hal, 99, 166

Lavagetto, Cookie, 140

Lefebvre, Jim, 139, 148–49, 151

Linzy, Frank, 99, 152, 153

Liu, Robert, 94

Los Angeles Dodgers, 46, 78, 91, 99–101, 130, 137–39, 144, 147–49, 150–52, 163–66, 167–68, 182, 187–88

Marberry, Firpo, 51–52

Marichal, Juan, 44, 80, 84, 98, 101, 138, 144, 147, 150, 163–66, 168

Marquat, William F., 37

Mauch, Gene, 158

Mays, Willie, 41, 46, 79, 82, 83, 89, 107, 137, 138, 139, 140, 144, 145, 153, 159, 161–62, 164, 165, 167

McCovey, Willie, 44, 79, 99, 140, 144, 150, 159

McDonald, Jack, 71, 73, 102–3

McGurn, Tom, 48

Meehan, Tom, 50, 68, 70, 84

Menko, 3

Mickens, Glenn, 24–25

Minagawa, Matsuo, 21, 26, 33, 34

Minidoka Internment Camp, 143

Miura, Kiyohiro, 26, 34

Miyazawa, Toshiyoshi, 174, 181

Modesto Colts, 62, 76

Monroe, Marilyn, 38

Moon, Wally, 148, 166

Morinaka, Chikara, 26, 34

Moriyama, Tsunetaru, 9

Murakami, Kiyoshi, 1–2, 4–6, 7, 73, 107, 111–12, 113–14, 115, 116, 122, 134, 135, 155, 171, 174

Murakami, Maho, 186

Murakami, Masanori: acclimation to America, 49–50, 59, 72, 102, 141, 153; and anti-Japanese incidents, 60–61, 147–48; arm injuries of, 14, 27, 30, 34, 49, 50, 178, 182, 183, 184; as autograph collector, 144, 169; batting ability of, 63, 71, 74, 75, 106, 111, 150–51; becomes reliever, 51–52, 61, 64–65,

Murakami, Masanori (*cont.*)
102; childhood of, 1–7; claims to be
homesick, 126–27; contract disputes,
effect on, 131–32, 133, 170; contract for
1966, 136, 160, 171–72, 174–75; control of pitches, 52–53, 64; curveball of,
30, 51, 58, 62, 75, 139; elevated to *ichi-
gun*, 31–33; elevated to Majors, 77,
84–87; first Major League game of,
88–96, 108; first Major League save of,
104; first Major League win of, 105–6;
and first pro game in Japan, 30–31; and
first pro game in United States, 57–58;
and Giants spring training, 43–53; *giri*
toward Tsuruoka, 121–22, 172, 174–76,
188; and Hawks training camps, 19, 21–
22, 122–23; as high school player, 8–15;
and importance to Japanese, 94–96,
177–78; and importance to Japanese
Americans, 59–60, 62, 149, 154–57;
and Japanese minor leagues, 28–31, 33;
language difficulties of, 59, 73, 75, 86–
87, 92, 102–3, 140–41, 153, 160; Major
League contracts of, 87, 106, 111–12,
171, 175, 181; and Masanori Murakami
Day, 154–59, 188; nicknamed Mashi,
59; pitching style of, 30, 45, 51, 52, 58,
75, 90–91, 105, 139, 167, 177; plays in
Arizona Fall League, 109–11; and popularity in United States, 60, 93–94,
97–98, 99, 102, 137, 139–40, 152–53,
154–57, 171, 180; pranks played on, 59,
99, 141, 157–58; and press conferences,
114–15, 123–24, 136; rejoins Hawks,
122–23, 175; relationship with father,
1–2, 5–6, 73, 107, 111, 115, 121; and rosin
bag incident, 148–49; sense of humor
of, 50, 62, 72, 123, 141, 160–61; shows
emotion, 70–71, 148–49, 179; signs
with Hawks, 16–18, 122, 123–24; and
trouble re-acclimating to Japan, 178–83;
wants to stay in United States, 48–49,
73, 105, 111–12, 171, 176, 179, 184, 185–86

Murakami, Naotsugu, 186
Murakami, Tomiko, 1, 3, 5, 94, 113, 114,
116, 174
Murakami, Yoshiko. *See* Hoshino, Yoshiko
Murayama, Minoru, 25

Nagashima, Shigeo, 25, 35
Nagata, Yoichi, 95
Nakai, Marie, 62
Nakamozu, Japan, 29–30, 122
Nakasawa, Fujio, 116
Nankai Hawks: agreement with San
Francisco Giants, 38–41, 76, 125–26;
contract disputes with San Francisco
Giants, 111–12, 114–35; history of, 16,
23–26; Japan Series appearances of,
170–71, 172–73, 178; minor league
team (*ni-gun*), 28–30; Murakami
returns to, 171–72, 175; pitching staff
of, 24–26, 34; pressure Murakami
to return to Japan, 105, 112, 136; sign
Murakami, 16–18; training methods
of, 21–23
Nara, Japan, 33–34
National High School Baseball Cham-
pionship (Summer Koshien), 12–13,
14, 36
National High School Baseball Invitational Tournament (Spring Koshien),
12–13, 14
Newsday, 82, 93
New York Mets, 83, 84, 88–89, 91–93, 98,
103, 104, 107, 134, 166, 168
New York Times, 41
ni-gun, 26, 28–30, 33
Niiyama, Shigeru, 115, 116–19, 121, 123,
130–31, 135, 181
Nikkan Sports, 89
Nikkei, 59–60, 154–56
Nippon Ham Fighters, 185, 186
Nippon Professional Baseball League
(NPB). *See* Japanese Professional
Baseball

Nisei, 54, 62, 72, 141, 149
Nishimura, Shozo, 109–11, 113
Nishino, Josuke, 116, 119, 176
Nishitetsu Lions, 28, 30, 33, 183
Nomo, Hideo, 186–88
Nomura, Don, 187
Nomura, Katsuya, 18, 22, 24, 32, 44, 122–23, 173
Nushida, Kenso, 42

Oakland Tribune, 76, 97, 150, 167
O'Dell, Billy, 98
O'Doul, Frank "Lefty," 37, 38, 48, 94, 95
Oh, Sadaharu, 12, 13, 173, 177, 180
Okusa, Rokuro. See Sakai, Rokuro
Oliver, Nate, 101
O'Malley, Walter, 38, 130
Onodera, Sho, 86–87, 95
Osaka, Seikichi, 142–43
Osaka, Walter, 142–44, 154, 170, 183
Osaka, Yoshiye, 73, 142, 170, 183
Osaka Stadium, 17–18, 29, 117–18, 123
Otani, Hidehiro, 14
Otani, Kosho, 62
Otsuki, Japan, 2, 8, 16, 36, 77, 94, 116, 119, 131, 174, 177

Pacific League, 18, 23, 24, 31, 116, 180, 182, 184, 186
Pacific Stars and Stripes, 95, 97, 178, 181
Pagan, Jose, 80, 84
Page, Joe, 52
Parker, Wes, 100–101, 147, 166
Pelekoudas, Chris, 157–58
Perry, Gaylord, 98, 104, 107, 138, 140, 141, 150, 160–61, 185
Philadelphia Phillies, 52, 82, 83, 98, 101–2, 103–4, 107, 150, 152, 154, 158–59, 162
Pittsburgh Pirates, 48, 78, 83, 103, 104, 145, 150
Pope, Don, 63–64
Povich, Shirley, 168
Powell, Bob, 58

Pregenser, John, 103
Puyallup Assembly Area, 143

Rawhide, 12, 16, 43, 161
Raymer, John, 70
Reinoso, Pedro, 57, 67, 68–69, 74
Reno Silver Sox, 62–64, 68, 71, 74–75
Reserve Clause, 120, 121, 132, 134, 181, 182
Rigney, Bill, 78
Rikkio University, 25
Riordan, Jack, 126
Robinson, Frank, 168
Robinson, Jackie, 82, 108, 149, 182
Rose, Pete, 146, 168
Roseboro, John, 138–39, 148, 163–66
Rosenblum, Art, 96, 97
Russell, Jack, 131
Ruth, Babe, 4, 19, 86, 131

Saiki, Fumiko, 55–56, 59, 60, 64, 72, 73, 142–43, 170, 183
Saiki, Gregory, 56
Saiki, Howard, 55–56
Saiki, Janis, 56
Saiki, Jereann, 56
Saiki, Kiyoto, 56, 59, 72, 87, 107, 114, 170, 183
Saiki, Mime, 55–56
Saiki, Rokuro 55–56
Saiki, Setsu, 56
Sakamoto, Kyu, 89
Salinas Mets, 57, 67, 68, 74–75
San Francisco Chronicle, 86, 93, 97, 101, 102, 104, 105, 107, 127, 132, 137, 141–42, 148, 168
San Francisco Examiner, 62, 63, 66, 93–94, 131, 149, 174
San Francisco Giants: agreement with Hawks, 38–42, 76, 125–26; assigns Murakami to Fresno, 48; background of, 38–39, 78–83; contract disputes with Hawks, 111–12, 114–35; interested in signing Hideo Nomo, 187; late

San Francisco Giants (*cont.*)
collapses of, 78–79, 167–68; and Masanori Murakami Day, 154–59, 188; offer Murakami Major League contracts, 106–7, 111–12, 171, 174–75; players accept Murakami, 160–61, 162; promote Murakami to Majors, 76–77, 84–87; racial diversity on, 78–79; racial tension on, 78–79, 81–83; spring training of, 43–46; want Murakami to return after 1966, 181, 184–85, 185–86
San Francisco News-Call Bulletin, 71, 73, 86, 93, 153
San Jose Bees, 61, 70–71, 84
San Jose Mercury, 86, 92, 137, 167, 178
Sankei News, 86, 95
Saruhashi, Japan, 2
Saruhashi Middle School baseball team, 5–7
Sato, Kumio, 89, 91
Schofield, Dick, 99
Schroder, Bob, 154, 160
Schumacher, Gary, 111
Schwartz, Jack, 41, 53, 76, 84, 112, 119
Shaw, Bob, 103, 148, 150, 151, 153, 163, 168
Shea Stadium, 85, 88
Shelley, John F., 98, 156–57, 170–71
Shibata, Isao, 12, 14
Shi no renshu, 10
Sievers, Bob, 62
Smith, Charlie, 91, 95
Smith, Reggie, 19
Smoot, Larry, 63, 70
Snyder, Tom, 63
Spahn, Warren, 163, 166–67
Spink, J. G. Taylor, 79
Sporting News, 41, 42, 79, 94, 97, 108, 109, 111, 185
Springfield Giants, 46, 49, 50, 53
Stanka, Joe, 21, 26, 34, 38, 127–28, 129–30, 173
Stargell, Willie, 145, 150
Stengel, Casey, 52, 92

Stevens, Bob, 86, 93, 97, 104, 105, 141–42, 148
Stockton Ports, 58–59, 68, 77
Stoneham, Horace, 38–39, 40, 43, 60, 62, 78, 81, 104, 108, 112, 118, 120, 126–27, 132, 134–35, 174–75, 184
Sugihara, Judy, 157, 159
Sugiura, Tadashi, 25–26, 34, 35, 173
Sukiyaki, vi, 89–90, 137
Sullivan, Prescott, 93–94, 149
Suzuki, Keishi, 186–87
Suzuki, Sotaro, 37, 131

Tachibana, Juli Osaka, 143–44, 154
Tachibana, Makoto, 18, 116, 118
Taiyo Whales, 16, 28
Takahashi, Eiichiro, 32
Takahashi, Hiroshi, 35–36, 39, 41–42, 43, 49–50, 53, 57, 59, 66–67
Tamaru, Hitoshi, 7, 17
Tanaka, Tatsuhiko, 35–36, 39, 41–42, 43, 44, 49–50, 53, 57, 59, 66–67
Taylor, Bobby, 57, 61, 63
Tengu, 179
Thompson, Hank, 46
Thousand Ball Drill, 20–21
Tiede, Tom, 140
Tobita, Suishu, 10, 19, 20, 186
Toei Flyers, 28, 33
Tokyo Orions, 184
Tominaga, Yoshio, 17–18, 40, 111–12, 113–15, 116–18
Tracewski, Dick, 101
Tsuruoka, Kazuto, 30, 49, 64, 112, 114, 116, 124, 129, 176, 183; asks Murakami to stay in Japan, 121; background of, 16; mangerial style of, 21–24, 25–26, 170, 173; meets Murakami, 16; mentors Murakami, 28–29, 122, 123; Murakami's *giri* toward, 121–22, 172, 174–76, 188; negotiates with San Francisco Giants, 118–21, 134; praises Murakami to press, 18, 26–27, 31, 123, 183; promises

to send Murakami to United States, 16; sends Murakami to United States, 34, 36; signs Murakami, 16–18; steps down as Hawks manager, 173–74; use of Murakami in games 26–27, 31–33, 178–84

Uchimura, Yushi, 116, 125, 129–30, 132–33, 134–35, 174

Van Slyke, Andy, 69
Vavuris, S. Lee, 125–26
Vecsey, George, 93
Veeck, Bill, 181
Virgil, Ozzie, 46

Wada, Tsutoru, 59–60, 157
Wakon yosai, 9
Walter, Bucky, 93
Ward, Alan, 97
Waseda University, 10, 13, 20, 186

Watts Riots, 156
Werle, Bill, 48, 49, 50, 51, 52–53, 57, 58, 60, 63, 64, 66, 67, 68, 71, 72, 74, 75–77, 84
Western League, 28, 30, 31, 33
Weyer, Lee, 148–49
Wills, Maury, 101, 148, 151–52, 163, 164, 166
Windhorn, Gordie, 24–25
Working Agreement, 181–82

Yamamoto, Yasushi, 15–16
Yamanashi Prefecture, 34, 122
Yamashiro, Andy, 42
Yamauchi, Kazuhiro, 32, 178
Yomiuri Giants, 12, 19–21, 25, 27, 28, 33, 37–38, 91, 95, 131, 170, 173, 177, 178, 180–81, 182
Yonamine, Wally, 38
Yoshinaga, George, 154
Young, Dick, 87, 93
Yuki, Susumi, 31